Beyond Human

Also available from Continuum

Animal Philosophy
Matthew Calarco and Peter Atterton

Beyond Human

From Animality to Transhumanism

EDITED BY
CHARLIE BLAKE,
CLAIRE MOLLOY AND
STEVEN SHAKESPEARE

continuum

Continuum International Publishing Group

The Tower Building	80 Maiden Lane
11 York Road	Suite 704
London	New York
SE1 7NX	NY 10038

www.continuumbooks.com

ISBN: HB: 978-1-4411-0742-8
PB: 978-1-4411-5011-0

British Library Cataloguing-in-Publication Data
A catalogue record for this book is available from the British Library.

Library of Congress Cataloging-in-Publication Data
Beyond human: from animality to transhumanism/edited by Charlie Blake, Claire Molloy and Steven Shakespeare.
p. cm.
Includes bibliographical references (p.   ) and index.
ISBN 978-1-4411-0742-8 (hardcover) –
ISBN 978-1-4411-5011-0 (pbk.) –
ISBN 978-1-4411-7124-5 (pdf) –
ISBN 978-1-4411-7399-7 (epub)
1. Philosophical anthropology. 2. Animals (Philosophy) 3. Artificial life.
I. Blake, Charlie. II. Molloy, Claire. III. Shakespeare, Steven, 1968– IV. Title.
BD450.B4455 2012
128–dc23
2011034918

Typeset by Deanta Global Publishing Services, Chennai, India
Printed and bound in India

Contents

List of Figures

Notes on Contributors

Sean Cubitt is Professor of Global Media and Communications at Winchester School of Art, University of Southampton, Professorial Fellow in Media and Communications at the University of Melbourne and Honorary Professor of the University of Dundee. His publications include *Timeshift: On Video Culture* (Comedia/Routledge, 1991), Videography: Video Media as Art and Culture (Macmillans/St Martins Press, 1993), *Digital Aesthetics* (Theory, Culture and Society/Sage, 1998), *Simulation and Social Theory* (Theory, Culture and Society/ Sage, 2001), *The Cinema Effect* (MIT Press, 2004) and EcoMedia (Rodopi, 2005). He was the coeditor of *Aliens R Us: Postcolonial Science Fiction* with Ziauddin Sardar (Pluto Press 2002) and *The Third Text Reader* with Rasheed Araeen and Ziauddin Sardar (Athlone/ Continuum 2002) and *How to Study the Event Film: The Lord of the Rings* (Manchester University Press, 2008). He serves on the editorial boards of a dozen journals including *Moving Image Review* and *Art Journal* (MIRAJ), *Screen*, *Third Text*, *Cultural Politics*, *Visual Communication*, *Futures* and *The International Journal of Cultural Studies*. His article on early video art won the 2006 CAA Award for best article. He is the series editor for Leonardo Books at MIT Press. His current research is on public screens and the transformation of public space; and on genealogies of digital light.

Ron Broglio is an assistant professor in the Department of English at Arizona State University. His research focuses on how philosophy and aesthetics can help us rethink the relationship between humans and the environment, with particular emphasis on a posthuman phenomenology. He is author of *Surface Encounters: thinking with animals and art* (Minnesota Press, 2011) and *Technologies of the Picturesque* (Bucknell 2008). Broglio is currently working on an artistic and theoretical treatise on posthumanism and animal studies called *Animal Revolutions: Event to Come.*

Claire Molloy is Senior Lecturer in the School of Arts and Media at the University of Brighton, UK and a Fellow of the Oxford Centre for Animal Ethics. She has published on anthropomorphism, representations of animals in videogames and literature and dangerous dogs, media and risk. She is the author of *Memento* (EUP 2010) and *Popular Media and Animal Ethics* (Palgrave Macmillan, 2011) and co-editor of *American Independent Cinema: Indie, Indiewood and Beyond.*

Giovanni Aloi was born in Milan, Italy in 1976. In 1995 he obtained his first degree in Fine Art – Theory and Practice, then moved to London in 1997 where he furthered his studies in Visual Cultures (MA) at Goldsmiths College. From 1999 to 2004 he worked at Whitechapel Art Gallery and as a film programmer at Prince Charles Cinema in London whilst continuing to work as freelance photographer. Today he is a Lecturer in History of Art at Roehampton University, Queen Mary University of London, The Open University, and Tate Galleries. Since 2006, he also is the founder and Editor in Chief of *Antennae, the Journal of Nature in Visual Culture.* The Journal combines a heightened level of academic scrutiny of animals in art, with a less formal and more experimental format designed to appeal to wider audiences. Since 2009, Aloi has been researching for his PhD at Goldsmiths College on the subject of 'animals as art objects in the gallery space'. His first book, *Art & Animals,* is part of the series 'Art &' published by IB Tauris (2011).

Bryndís Snæbjörnsdóttir and Mark Wilson conduct their collaborative practice from bases in the north of England, Iceland and Gothenburg, Sweden. With a strong research grounding, their socially engaged projects explore contemporary relationships between human and non-human animals in the contexts of history, culture and the environment. The practice sets out to challenge anthropocentric systems and thinking that sanction loss through representation of the other, proposing instead, alternative tropes of 'parities in meeting'. The work is installation based, using objects, text, photography and video.

Natalie Corinne Hansen recently completed her PhD in Literature and Feminist Studies at the University of California, Santa Cruz. Her work examines representations of human-horse relationships in imaginative fiction, popular media, and training narratives and has appeared in *Women's Studies Quarterly*, *JAC*, *Michigan Feminist Studies*, and *The Brock Review*. Hansen is currently a Visiting Research Scholar at the Centre for the Study of Women at the University of California, Los Angeles.

Lucile Desblache is Reader in Translation and Comparative Literature at the University of Roehampton, London, where she directs the Centre for Research in Translation and Transcultural Studies. Her main area of research is animal representation in contemporary literature. She is the author of the *Bestiaire du roman contemporain d'expression française* (Editions Blaise Pascal, 2002), of *La Plume des bêtes. Les Animaux dans le roman* (L'Harmattan 2011) and co editor of the 'Hybrids and Monsters' special issue of *Comparative Critical Studies* (2012).

Felicity Colman is Reader in Screen Media and MIRIAD Media Research Centre Leader in The Manchester School of Art, Manchester Metropolitan University. She is engaged in research into various theories of epistemological modes of address – by creative praxis and by creative theory. Felicity's research draws on world cinemas, with a focus on art, experimental, independent, indigenous, militant, documentary and feminist work from around the globe. Felicity has published on aesthetics, gender issues, and contemporary art and cinema practices, with specific reference to Gilles Deleuze and Fèlix Guattari, in journals including *Angelaki: The Journal of the Theoretical Humanities*, *Pli: Warwick Journal of Philosophy*, *Women: A Cultural Review*, *Reconstruction*, and *The Refractory*. Felicity is the author of *Deleuze and Cinema* (2011 Berg) and editor of *Film, Theory and Philosophy: The Key Thinkers* (Acumen Publishing 2009), co-editor of *Sensorium: Aesthetics, Art, Life* (Cambridge Scholars Press 2007).

Donald L. Turner's research specialties are ethics, philosophy of religion, and Continental philosophy from Kant to the present. His current work focuses on ways that recent Continental religious philosophy can help shape novel modes of thought regarding non-human animals and the natural world. He is an Assistant Professor of Philosophy at Nashville State Community College in Nashville, Tennessee, USA.'

Celia Deane-Drummond is Professor in Theology at the University of Notre Dame, IN, USA. From 2000 to 2011 she held a chair in theology and the biological sciences at the University of Chester, UK and was Director of the Centre for Religion and the Biosciences that she founded in 2002. In May 2011 she was elected Chair of the European Forum for the Study of Religion and Environment. She was editor of the international journal *Ecotheology* for six years from 2000 to 2006. From July 2009 to July 2010 she was seconded to the spirituality team at the Catholic Fund for Overseas Development (CAFOD), working explicitly in the area of environmental justice and climate change. Her more recent books include *Creation through Wisdom* (Edinburgh: T &T Clark, 2000), *ReOrdering Nature* (London: Continuum 2003), *The Ethics of Nature* (Oxford: Blackwells, 2004), *Wonder and Wisdom: Conversations in Science, Spirituality and Theology* (London: DLT, 2006), *Ecotheology* (DLT/Novalis/St Mary's Press, 2008), *Christ and Evolution: Wonder and Wisdom* (Minneapolis: Fortress/London:SCM Press, 2009), *Creaturely Theology: On God, Humans and Other Animals*, edited with David Clough (London: SCM Press, 2009); *Seeds of Hope: Facing the Challenge of Climate Justice* (London: CAFOD, 2010), *Religion and Ecology in the Public Sphere*, edited with Heinrich Bedford Strohm (London: Continuum, 2011), *Rising to Life*, ed. (London: CAFOD, 2011).

Charlie Blake is currently Senior Lecturer in Critical and Cultural Theory at Liverpool Hope University. He has recently co-edited a two volume study for the journal *Angelaki* entitled *Shadows of Cruelty: Sadism, Masochism & the Philosophical Muse*, as well as 'A Preface to Pornotheology: Spinoza, Deleuze & the Sexing of Angels' for *Deleuze and Sex*, edited by Frida Beckman (Edinburgh UP, 2011) and 'Pirate Multiplicities' on the graphic fiction of Alan Moore for *Studies in Comics* 2:1 (Intellect, 2011). He is currently working on the politics of pornotheology, and on the emergent field of spectral materialism in connection with art, music and cinema.

Steven Shakespeare is Lecturer in Philosophy at Liverpool Hope University and a Fellow of the Oxford Centre for Animal Ethics. His publications include *The Inclusive God* (co authored with Hugh Rayment-Pickard, SCM, 2006), *Radical Orthodoxy: A Critical Introduction* (SPCK, 2007) and *Derrida and Theology* (T and T Clark, 2009).

Professor D. Gareth Jones is Director of the Bioethics Centre and Professor of Anatomy at the University of Otago, Dunedin, New Zealand, where he was Deputy Vice-Chancellor (Academic and International) from 2005–2009. Recent books include, *Clones: The Clowns of Technology?* (Paternoster, 2001), *Designers of the Future* (Monarch, 2005), *Bioethics* (ATF Press, 2007) and *Speaking for the Dead: Cadavers in Biology and Medicine* (with Maja Whitaker, Ashgate, 2009). He is editor with John Elford of *A Tangled Web: Medicine and Theology in Dialogue* (Peter Lang, 2009), and *A Glass Darkly: Medicine and Theology in Further Dialogue* (Peter Lang, 2010).

Maja Whitaker is an Assistant Research Fellow at the Bioethics Centre, University of Otago, Dunedin, New Zealand.

Acknowledgements

Many of the essays in this volume were first presented at the *Becoming Human: Ethics, Animality, Transhumanism Colloquium* that was hosted and part-funded by Liverpool Hope University in 2009. Our thanks go to all those who attended and participated in the colloquium and to those who supported the subsequent production of this volume with their contributions and observations. Special thanks to Erica Fudge and Richard Twine for their comments when this book was in its early stages.

Preface

It is easy enough to believe that from the earliest times, people devoted energy and time to becoming-animal. Easy too to acknowledge that wherever environments have been generous, climates clement, food and shelter abundant, in short, wherever the human tendency to adopt the good life has been allowed to take its own route, without recourse to large scale social and technological systems, tribes still access animals in myth and ritual.

Whether we believe it was monotheism and rationality or empire and economy that severed the old tie, the avenues of dialogue and performance that once existed between animals and humans have, it seems, withered on the vine. One of the last remnants of those old rituals still hung on to its traditions, albeit uncanny and ashamed, into my childhood: the travelling circus. I mean here the circus of sawdust and the strong, ripe smell of urine, the circus of roaring and neighing, the apparatus of bareback riders in sparkling corsets and their plumed beasts, the circus of the clowns and their chimpanzees and donkeys. With all its cruelty, risk and danger, indeed because of them, circus gestured towards a more sacred dialogue: leaping the bulls in Cretan murals, shamanic donning of the pelts of deer ....

Tribal life, ancient or modern, neither was nor is now by any means innocent. No more so was the old circus of animals. It is, however, only in our times that the idea of the good has been replaced with the term 'innocent'. In Hollywood action films, flawed heroes fight evil only to defend the innocent – not because they themselves are good, or because they serve the good. News stories mourn the plight of innocent victims: they do not seek out the good. When laws are made, they are always framed to protect the innocent, not to promote the good. Innocence substitutes for the good today because we live in a polity determined to achieve consensus, but we know we will never agree on what is truly good. We prefer innocence because it is passive: good acts, but innocence is acted upon. To be the figures of innocence: that is the function of animals in the contemporary cosmology. This is the last perversion of that mythic thought that once, and still in some societies, shapes the relations between species.

The industrial revolution and urbanization gradually foreclosed the ancient proximity, animals. For the authors in this collection, the resulting division between humans and animals is a construction. The continuities (laws of physics, evolutionary continua of organs and genera, persistence of reflexes and instincts) are as persuasive as the ambiguously defining distinctions (communication, ability to learn, tool use, sociality). But the whole point of social constructionism as an explanatory framework is that what has been constructed as belief and behaviour becomes real. That we *only believe* that animals are different does not alter the fact that they have become so, any more than gender or race dissolve as social facts once we understand that they have been constructed through social and historical processes.

This is why we must have not only a theology or philosophy but a theory of the human–animal relation: because the relation is a social fact, even if it is not an ethical or ontological one. This is also why the discourse of animal rights comes in for complex discussion in these pages. In our haste to end the dominion over animals, which entered a new phase with industrialized food production, and the de-population of farms, a first and powerful reaction was to assert rights. This is akin to the decolonization process in the post-War period, especially in that the ex-colonies were understandably but nonetheless uncomfortably and in some cases fatally given, without alternative, the status of nations. Decolonization imposed the nation–state as the only available political organization; the discourse of rights poses a legal structure as the only avenue formalizing human–animal relations.

We should recall here that the Universal Declaration of Human Rights outlines the duties of states to their citizens, not rights accruing to any and every member of the species. True, human rights extend to refugees, but this only encourages states to create non-refugee categories (illegal migrants, asylum seekers) to ensure that they do not have 'human' rights proper, exclusive to citizens. Rights do not express the responsibilities and obligations animals owe to one another or to us. Instead, they recreate the myth of innocence. No more innocent than they are dumb or unfeeling, nevertheless animals serve the ideological function of innocent victimhood, the position of all who are excluded from politics, like refugees and children.

We should not therefore consider animals from the standpoint of ethics alone, since that will always bring us to an inevitably political analysis anyway, given our wholly social condition today. Triumphant utilitarianism, calculating the greatest benefit to the largest number, is now the voice of neo-liberalism, save only that what constitutes the good – wealth – is an argument considered already won. This is so clearly a political doctrine that its rivals from Aristotle and Kant to Sen and Badiou must be counted political thinkers rather than ethicists. The species relation is of its nature political, even when we live it individually as ethical dilemma.

So what is politics? According to Rancière, politics occurs when an excluded sector of society which is nonetheless the object of government – artisans in Athens, slaves in the USA, colonized peoples in the British Empire, women everywhere – demands to become a subject as well as an object of rule. Rancière observes that when these often revolutionary inclusions occur, they alter the forms of political life radically. From the ancient city square where everyone knew each other to the vast anonymity of twenty-first century media-managed elections, from the power of life and death to the statistical management of populations and behaviours, politics has certainly changed.

We know that it can change again, because it is changing now. Rather ahead of the challenge of migrants to the constitution of the nation–state, we have already accepted that nations will cede sovereignty to that extraordinary amalgam of technological networks and human biochips, the market. What would happen if we began to accept the idea that animals were to become political, in the sense of creatures participating in their own rule?

The image we should have before us is not that of a parliamentary session or a senate filibuster. It is so long since animals participated in rule that we have forgotten how they speak. The circus was the last remnant of a far more ancient participation, interweavings of animal and human in intricate assemblages. The importance of artistic expression to the politics of species in this book and elsewhere derives from the repressed memory of another mode of social order.

Neither human nor animal are necessarily naturally kind to one another. Savaging a human victim in the arena, or being tortured to death by other humans, animal–human dialogue will never be consensual.

The ancient performances combined humans and animals in complicated and temporary machines, often for purposes of violence, but also for acts of amazing and gratuitous beauty. They involved drugs and other sacred disciplines, and from the ancient myths we can perhaps discern the frenzy and mortality of hunters torn apart by their own dogs, or the auguries of death borne by terrible hybrid creatures with their riddles and labyrinths. Human–animal politics is, strictly speaking, unthinkable. Being unthinkable is a hallmark of political life: it was unthinkable to give slaves the vote, as today in the USA it is unthinkable to give the vote to prisoners. The unthinkable inclusion demands an entire remaking of our polity. Nothing less. Hence the critical importance of animal studies to the human sciences.

The concept of species, since long before Darwin, was tied to reproduction: only members of the same species could reproduce sexually. Today, as the industrial revolution that began in the late eighteenth century has passed into its informational and now emergent bio-technical phases, we are long past sex as our sole means of generation. No longer tied to the proto-environmentalism of the mercantilists, from whom all wealth came from land, we generate wealth from trade, from the circulation of money, from information and imaginative invention, in short from all the varied forms of communication, not just the mediation of sex. We know we have other relations with animals: relations of affection and trust, of domination and fear; of nurture and exploitation. But in all these relations we have been in control. If there is a new polity, there will be a new economy, an unforeseeable mode of human–animal trade. This too is likely to be exploitative, dangerous, bloody, but these are forms, indicators, of communication, equal, open and dissenting confrontation, from which alone anything like dialogue is likely to spring.

Sadly, we know that the emotionless rationality of diplomatic dialogue is all about power, its maintenance, and the repression of discussion. We can guess too that political violence springs eternally from the impossibility of dissent. As long as we derive our model of interspecies communication from babies cuddling their care-bears, we will enforce innocence, a stupid acquiescence in all our demands. The becoming-human of animals is likely to be as fearful and in some ways as disturbing a process as the old circuses. But without it we will have no possibility of passing beyond human ourselves.

Sean Cubitt

Introduction

Charlie Blake, Claire Molloy and Steven Shakespeare

Descartes famously argued that nonhuman animals were nothing more than clockwork machines. Lacking language, or the capacity to interpret signs, these creatures of instinct resembled nothing so much as the technological artefacts of emerging mechanical science. Of course, Descartes' own problematic account of the gap between human mind and inert matter left him vulnerable to those who would collapse the distinction entirely. The way was opened to a strange speculation: the 'bestial' devices against which we measured our humanity turned out to be the reflection of our own paradoxical inhumanity.

La Mettrie's infamous 1748 text *L'Homme Machine* signalled to this new reality, though its idiosyncratic style and brevity perhaps undermined its claim to a seminal place in the history of ideas. It is striking, however, that La Mettrie turns Descartes' reading of animality on its head. Whereas the latter found the alien mechanisms of material creatures to be a sign of their essential difference from human beings, for La Mettrie our machinery is what connects the human and the nonhuman. There is no absolute dividing line between the human and the animal, he argued. We are all shaped by what we physically ingest and by the mechanical structures of brain and body. The characteristics supposed to distinguish us – language, reason, knowledge of good and evil – are present in actual or potential form in animals as well.

In short, La Mettrie argues that human beings are animals because all living beings are machines. On this basis, he advocates an ethic of honouring matter and nature, abandoning fear of death, and acknowledging our kinship with all other animal-machines. To be fully human is to be beyond human.

This Enlightenment *tour de force* still resonates with the debate in our own day on the nature of humanity, and how it is defined in relation to technology, nonhuman animal life and indeed the non-living matter from which life emerged. Crucial to this debate is the *genealogical* dimension: the critical awareness that ideas, definitions and values change over time in relation to economic, social and cultural structures. This particularly applies to those ideas which have been claimed to pick out natural kinds or essences. The question inevitably arises: what if the idea of humanity itself were a cultural construction? A construction which underpinned hierarchies of power within and beyond the human species?

When Foucault proclaimed the 'end of man' he was also issuing a challenge to these regimes of power. If the human is defined by certain essential traits (for example, language, rationality, consciousness, free will), it follows that entities which lack these qualities must be considered subhuman, outside the bounds of communication and response, and often not direct bearers of any moral worth. This applies to nonhuman animals, but also to certain categories of *homo sapiens* considered too bodily, irrational, primitive or corrupted to merit the status of full humanity.

This is particularly important to philosophy, because, in its Western form at least, it has been premised on the significance of what it is to be human. Indeed, the legacy of the Socratic imperative of delineating the good life has generally if not exclusively implied securing the distinctiveness of human identity as uniquely rational, self-conscious, free, and uprooted – as bearing the divine image or possessing a meaningful world. In consequence, the human has often been markedly distinguished from the animal, seen as mute, non-rational, instinctive, amoral, as bare life, as poor in world. This distinction, moreover, is not simply one between different biological species, but – it often appears – between different orders of being. As is so often the case, however, that which is excluded comes back to haunt the excluder. As a result of this radical distinction, the shadow of animality becomes constitutive of definitions of the human; its silhouette falling upon and passing over the organic, technological and social realities that supposedly determine who 'we' are, as much as it does upon the underlying questions: who counts as one of 'us', and to whom are we accountable, when we ourselves are in question?

Philosophical challenges to this humanistic prejudice have been a striking feature of recent intellectual history: Heidegger, Derrida, Haraway, Deleuze/Guattari and Agamben are among the key figures. Through their work and the critical responses they have evoked, we are compelled to face the radical incompleteness and violence of anthropocentric modes of thinking and acting. It is not only that the human is not the only centre in the world, that (using Jacob von Uexküll's phrase) other beings experience an 'Umwelt' irreducibly distinct from our own. It is also that our very interaction with these other worlds reveals the porosity and internal strangeness of our own composition. When (as with Derrida) the animal becomes 'wholly other', it places an obligation upon us that ruptures the settled notion of who 'we' are. When (for Agamben) the 'anthropological machine' is suspended, we can imagine a messianic utopia in which the endless manufacture of law-bound identities is also suspended. Negotiating with these thinkers, we find that the divisions between science and messianism, between play and responsibility (divisions as constitutive of our Enlightenment humanity as that between fact and value) are stretched to breaking point.

Such insights are closely related to emancipatory projects, as they mesh across human and nonhuman boundaries. This is an *ethico-political* dimension which involves environmentalism and animals' rights but also a range of challenges to political ideologies which have naturalized anthropocentric, patriarchal and colonial systems of power.

As La Mettrie reminds us, however, ethics cannot be divorced from questions of technology. The power to fashion ever more sophisticated tools raises issues of responsibility, ownership and purpose. However, more telling still is the realization that technology cannot simply be located outside of the human essence. Whether through recognizing the complex mechanisms of our evolved bodies or the strange ways in which technology can now interface with, or be implanted within, our most intimate organs, we are faced with the reality that technology changes our self-definitions. For transhumanists, it raises the possibility of making radical alterations to our longevity, intelligence and susceptibility to disease, perhaps even removing our dependence upon our current physical form. Transhumanism is both an extension of the Enlightenment commitment to human reason and artifice, and a neo-Gnostic desire to transcend the human altogether into the realms of pure information.

If transhumanism can sound like science fiction, this should not dull us to the ways in which the latter has been remarkably prescient in its exploration of virtuality, artificial intelligence and cybernetics. Indeed, contemporary science is continually throwing up scenarios as unsettling as any sci-fi, from the spontaneous self-creation of the RNA needed for life, to the possibility of multiverses and the end of time. Even if there is only one universe, it has not been about us humans for the vast majority of its existence, and it is ever harder to detect anything preordained in the way matter and life have evolved.

The reference to science is important here, because there is an urgent ongoing need to relate these philosophical perspectives to the discoveries and speculations of evolutionary biologists, specialists in artificial intelligence and artificial life, ethologists and so on. As Donna Haraway has insisted, when the boundaries between the human and the nonhuman are mutating, it makes no sense for scholars to lock themselves away in the arbitrary confines of their disciplinary worlds. When we examine the molecular machinery which enables the neurons in our brains to send messages, the gates that open and close to let sodium and potassium ions pass through to generate different electrical charges; when we learn of the rich symbolic and cultural life of nonhuman animals; when we imagine ever more sophisticated learning machines which interact with their environments and gain the possibility of a kind of self-awareness and freedom; when all these things happen, our image of human beings as the unique spiritual apex of the world is challenged.

The power of the best sci-fi is that it straddles the divide between the speculations of science, philosophy and art. In so doing, it signals to another key motif of the debate about humanity: the *representational* dimension. How do we depict (taking that word in the widest possible sense) our humanity, nonhuman animals, monsters, hybrids, aliens, cyborgs? When we re-present, are we trying to show forth a pre-formed essence, making present again the fullness of an idea? Contemporary theory has focused rather on representation as intervention, transformation and projection, the various ways in which we 'pose' the world and ourselves within it. The value of this lies in raising our awareness of the loaded terms of any claim to represent the world in its truth.

However, as recent, more speculative philosophies have insisted, it can also leave us trapped within a representational matrix which centres on us all over again, because everything revolves around human ways of constructing the things we see and engage with. If representation is not innocent, perhaps we need new ways of thinking the world in its absoluteness, its weirdness and its inhuman resistance to anthropocentric colonization. As Giovanni Aloi insists in his essay in this volume, what seemed to be a wholly liberating preoccupation with the animal (read: the mammal) returning our gaze can betray our own continuing desire to look into the eyes of those who have some kinship with us. But what happens when we look into the multifaceted eye of the insect? What if we attend to the otherness of the microscopic organism? Is it still an 'otherness' we can even recognize as such, according to the canons of our philosophical tradition?

Asking theory to engage with what is 'beyond human' cannot therefore be a simplistic elevation above the limits of humanity, without engaging with the nature of those limits: how they have been made, reinforced, thought, resisted, imagined and translated. The risk is to dismiss the 'human' as a bounded whole, but then find ourselves embroiled in a new age fantasy of some other essential identity, some other flight from finitude, some other exoticism to feed our craving for distraction.

The present collection therefore investigates what it means to call ourselves human beings in relation to both our distant past and to our possible futures as a species. It considers what questions this investigation raises for our relationship with the myriad species with which we currently share this planet. The contributors look from our origins through early cave art in the upper Palaeolithic to our prospects at the forefront of contemporary biotechnology, and laterally at the connections we have formed with other kinds of life. In the process, these essays intend to position the human in readiness for what many contemporary thinkers have characterized as the transhuman and posthuman future, even as they contextualize humans as animals. For if our status as rational animals or 'animals that think,' and in many cases, as a species beyond animality itself, has traditionally marked us out as somehow inherently superior to other life forms, this distinction has become increasingly problematic. It has come to be seen as being based on skills and technologies that do not necessarily distinguish us so much as position us as *transitional animals*. It is the direction and consequences of this transition that is the central concern of this volume.

Beyond Human brings an interdisciplinary approach to this complex of issues, precisely to acknowledge its complexity. We are artists, cultural theorists, scientists, philosophers, theologians, whose work links together the questions of animality, technology and transhumanism. This kind of approach does not depend on the constraints of a precisely agreed theoretical foundation, but rather a shared critical sensibility. Taking human beings off the throne of creation is not just a negative move. It frees us for a new understanding of the world and our connectedness with it. It can help us to change the way we relate to our environment and the nonhuman life with which we share it. It can also help us to think more clearly about the promises and threats of technology. When we already have machines inside us, technology is as natural as anything else (which is not to say that it cannot be as dangerous, strange and ambivalent as nature).

The volume is arranged in four sections in order to traverse this strange terrain in a structured way. In the first part, 'Animality: Boundaries and Definitions', Ron Broglio alerts us to an animal revolution 'to come'. He confronts us with our failure to incorporate the animal body into the social body, an incorporation which would mean rethinking the human and the non-human community. Broglio argues that what is scandalous about the animal body and the animality of the blunt human body, what is indeed the seed of revolution, is that these bodies abandon reason, sensibility, and civility as the modes of discourse and point to an-other register all together. This animal revolution does not abide by human norms of meaning or temporality. It always takes us unprepared.

This aspect of resistance is taken up by Claire Molloy, who disputes the fictions of human-nonhuman primate relations which, she argues, deny the unworkable relations between humans and chimpanzees that lurk in the extratextual narrative zones. Framed by the work of Vicki Hearne and being particularly concerned with the relationship between training and interspecies communication, Molloy maps various ways in which chimpanzee agency is suppressed, denied and (re)constructed. As Broglio identifies the revolutionary reality of 'dumb' animals, so Molloy confronts us with the subversive otherness of the 'unknown animal'.

These opening essays suggest that domesticating unruly animality is often at work in precisely those critical and philosophical studies which theorize it. Giovanni Aloi focuses upon one insidious form of this: the obsession with the animal gaze which implicitly imagines the animal as mammalian, or somehow able to share in a reciprocal act of seeing. Aloi accepts that the critique of speciesism is a necessary advance in the cause of respecting nonhuman interests, but the default use of the general term 'animal' creates an imaginary hybrid which threatens to neutralize singular differences. In particular, those entities which are too unlike us to engage in the 'return of the gaze' (insects, for example) are hidden from view. Aloi asks what happens when we allow our view of the world to be disrupted further by these stranger singularities.

Part Two, 'Representing Animality', examines the way in which human-animal relationships and exchanges are negotiated, imagined and portrayed. Mark Wilson and Bryndís Snæbjornsdóttir are practising artists whose work critically departs from the rise of academic animal studies, which in their view continues to privilege human language and conceptualities over different ways of encountering otherness. Through reflecting upon their own practice in dialogue with other artistic and philosophical works, they call attention to the very human investments and interests served by our meetings with animals, meetings in which it is often the singular animal which is occluded.

Clearly, even in the most 'sophisticated' artwork, the animal's alterity can be trained to serve human needs (including the need for a sublime or inscrutable other). Natalie Hansen examines this logic at work in the commodified world of toys, and specifically the My Little Pony range. Showing how the innocent childhood fantasy world is already overdetermined by adult expectations, Hansen charts the interrelationships between the role played by animal toys and the enforcement of sex and gender norms. More transgressive aspects of the love that crosses species are reined in. However, through exploring a number of cultural and theoretical texts, Hansen insists that a queer reading of this love is possible. The restrictions which adults attempt to place on the little girl who plays with her pony doll are indicative of the challenging possibilities implicated in her breaking with humanist and heterosexist stereotypes: she is *becoming* horse as a way of inaugurating new possibilities of subjectivity, relationship and affection.

Lucile Desblache builds on this potential for reimagining human-animal connections. She explores how some contemporary fiction writers stretch language towards a literature of ideas and emotions that intends to bridge the gap between theory and representation, to give a voice to non-human animals, to be their 'porte-parole', and perhaps most importantly, to evoke potential relations between human and non-human beings. Drawing particularly on Creole writing, she advocates a fiction that breaks with Enlightenment dualism, proposing instead a 'diversality' of meaningful connections between human beings and the rest of the 'pluriverse'.

As the Enlightenment world fragments and humanism is ruptured, the repressed animal regains its spectral, even sacred intensity. The section entitled 'Thinking Beyond the Divide' engages with this return in a postsecular context. Felicity Colman traces the way in which the mediatization of animals – how they are represented and conveyed by human imaginative forms – plays a key role in shaping the nature and affects of human community. Bataille's reflections on the Lascaux cave paintings become a touchstone for considering how the representation of the animal shores up normative and restricted notions of humanity, whilst also offering the possibility for a 'sacred' intensity of experience. Breaking with the conventional construction of our life-world, this excessive meeting with animality generates the promise (or threat) of nonhuman modes of relation and agency.

In different ways, the next two essays open up the theological dimension of this new paradigm. Donald Turner reads Levinas and Bataille together to challenge and deepen standard defences of the moral worth of animals. For Turner, such approaches often underestimate the asymmetrical relationship between humans and other species. Freed from its own anthropocentric bias, Levinas' work points towards an acknowledgement of the trace of the divine Other in the face of the animal, not only in the human. However, Turner argues that Levinas is still caught in an ethical logic of scarcity, which needs to be supplemented by a Bataillean insistence that the ethical life follows an economy of surplus: gifts of respect to non-human animal life manifest a kind of divine self-expenditure that defies utilitarian calculation, and humans approach divinity in acts of interspecies altruism. The argument that 'animal studies' cannot be confined within a humanistic discourse – that it must and does reopen questions of radical alterity *per se* – invites creative theological response.

Many of the chapters in this collection attempt to grapple with the philosophical, ethical and conceptual boundaries that have marked out differences between human, animal, divine and machine, but which, in the light of recent cross-disciplinary theorization, have been dismantled or at the least, undermined to reveal new possibilities and problems. This is further demonstrated by Celia Deane-Drummond (whose own background combines theology with scientific expertise in plant physiology). The boundary she considers is that of free agency. Deane-Drummond acknowledges that the Christian claim that human beings are made in the image of God has often underwritten accounts of human uniqueness in the divine purpose for creation. However, drawing on ethological and primatology research which supports a case for intention, innovation and theory of mind in primates other than humans, Deane-Drummond argues for a more nuanced understanding of freedom and of the image of God which can be enlarged to take account of different communities of creatures. In her essay, the project of dismantling boundaries continues with the proposal that to establish freedom as a border which separates humans from other animals is to ignore the complex cognitive capacities of other social species and the claims made for their self-directed agency. The theological project of Hans Ur von Balthasar is critiqued from this perspective, but also seen as a rich resource for envisaging a constructive theology that breaks with anthropocentric biases.

This posthumanistic and postsecular contesting of boundaries is oriented most explicitly towards questions of technology in the final section, 'Animal-Human-Machine-God'. Taking the notions of excess and transgression from Bataille, and geometry and abstraction from Leroi-Gourhan, and then filtering them through the writings of Jacques Derrida, Gilles Deleuze and Felix Guattari and futurists such as Raymond Kurzweil, Charlie Blake argues that the 'inhuman' is not merely that which defines the human animal in contrast with the beast and the spirit or divinity, but the mark of its inner telos as what has come to be known as the transhuman. Steven Shakespeare examines boundaries between animality, the divine and the machinic and maps, particularly through the works of Derrida and Deleuze and Guattari, various ways in which these break down and rub against one another other as productive irritants. He notes that amongst the messiness of the dismantled borders the human has become ever more difficult to define, yet it is precisely these conditions that allow for a re-thinking of God through the inhuman. At the core of his argument is the notion of 'articulation' which Shakespeare explores in a variety of modes – the linguistic, the organic and the mechanical– and in relation to the dualisms that have demarcated the human from its other.

Where Shakespeare, Deane-Drummond and others consider the animal as a boundary intervention, it is the human–machine interface and its material realization, conceptualized as the cyborg, which forms the focus of Jones and Whitaker's chapter. Challenging certain strains of cyborgian hyperbole, Jones and Whitaker argue that the transformation of the human body by technological means should not signal alarm around the repercussions for self-identity or the erasure of humanness. Indeed, technological transformations may in fact be better understood as a return to functional normalcy. Mapping some of the myriad ways in which bodies are transformed by technology, the essay follows a trajectory through prostheses and implants to plastinates and examples of post-mortal bodies.

Taken together, these essays constitute a remarkable exercise in renegotiating boundaries. They move us through the trajectories between the animal and the transhuman, not in a linear and teleological fashion, but as an unpredictable revolutionary movement of excess, unknowing, idiocy, resistance and inhumanity. They engage with the subversive, sacred, affective potentials of moving beyond the human, narrowly and violently conceived. We offer them to the world of scholarship and commentary, but also to the indifferent intensity of the animal who sees in paper only food for new becomings.

PART ONE

Animality: Boundaries and Definitions

1

Incidents in the Animal Revolution

Ron Broglio

I have tried handing animals weapons, tools for their revolution. Lord knows they need a revolution and have suffered enough abuse from the hand of man. They generally stare at me blankly. They look at the anthropomorphic machine I extend to them and stare at it, again, blankly. With bare look and still, corporeal thickness, these animals make no motion towards arming themselves. Now I feel like the idiot.[1] What do I know about their revolution? Perhaps they already come armed. Perhaps the revolution is underway in modalities I have yet to know and beyond which I can reason within the limits of sociability. Over the course of this essay, I hope to explore the limits of my idiocy and the ground of an animal revolution. My small tale, a minor incident, is a gesture toward thinking an outside, a revolution, that is proper to the animal and only improperly within my grasp. The story and the essay begin with how the death of animals haunts us, their abuse haunts us. From there, I will explore how haunting communicates through a corporality and vulnerability shared by humans and animals. Through the blunt instrument of the body, I hope to find evidence of an animal revolution along with its grounds and limits.

Spectre and Hauntology

Quentin Meillassoux's essay 'Spectral Dilemma' in *Collapse Volume IV: Concept Horror* provides the following insightful summary of the problem of the spectre:

> What is a spectre? A dead person who has not been properly mourned, who haunts us, bothers us, refusing to pass over to the 'other side,' where the dearly-departed can accompany us at a distance sufficient for us to live our own lives without forgetting them, but also without dying their death – without being the prisoner of the repetition of their final moments. Then what is a spectre that has become the essence of the spectre, the spectre par excellence? A dead person whose death is such that we cannot mourn them. That is to say: a dead person for whom the work of mourning, the passage of time, proves inadequate for a tranquil bond between them and the living to be envisaged. A dead person the horror of whose death lays heavy not only upon the nearest and dearest, but upon all those who cross the path of their history.[2]

In the case of the animal and its suffering at the hand of man (including the slaughterhouse, the insecticide kit, the animal traps, etc), there is a lack of mourning because *we do not know how to incorporate the animal and so to mourn its death*. Is the animal a person? Animals seem to have agency but not like us. Do animals have a history? Well, they are historical but who is writing this history? These two problems are structural elements of such haunting.

When we do incorporate the animal death, it is through eating (literally or figuratively). The civility and manners of eating are part of a distancing from the body of the animal and its death. Such distance prevents mourning. With eating the other, there is a certain indigestion, an inedible element in the eating.[3] The other returns (by in-digestion) because eating the animal necessarily recalls the animal death and our own corporality. Or perhaps because of this distance of civil eating we repress or deny the proper death for the animal and such repression breeds a haunting.

We may add to this problem of eating our inability to think our own corporality as a death. So here the impossibility of incorporating

Incident in the animal revolution

Calling themselves 'Flavoristas' the capitalist machine tries to co-opt the bestial revolution and its herds (http://www.freethemeat.org/). Advertized complete with the rhetoric of a red flag and communist star, the Reveo is a rotating meat tenderizer used to release a 'flavor revolution'. The animals were not consulted. We will not be daunted by this appropriation of the animal revolution, this attempt to tame the wildness, the very revolutionary element of the revolution. Capitalist invocation of the revolution and its rhetoric reveals a certain haunting of another time, a time of the other which, as we shall see, remains untimely for the powers at hand. Animals of the *umwelts*, unite. You have nothing to lose but your chains.

the animal meets the inability to think our own death. This is what Cary Wolfe describes as 'the physical exposure to vulnerability and mortality that we suffer because we, like animals, are embodied beings.'[4]

Vulnerability

The haunting and failed incorporation points to an exposure, vulnerability, and embodiment which we share with other animals. The animals speak in a language of embodiment. We do not fully understand their languages but through a mutual corporeal comportment we are haunted by the possibility of relating to this unintelligible speech. David Clark alludes to such a connection in his working paper 'Towards a Prehistory of the Postanimal: Kant, Levinas, and the Regard of Brutes':

> It is impossible not to think here of what Bentham famously said of animals – that the question of their suffering irreducibly precedes and exceeds the question of its lack of certain powers – speech, thought, self-consciousness, representation, and so forth. As Derrida argues, mortal suffering is a 'passivity', a 'weakness'

before all oppositions of strength and weakness. Kant evokes this lack, this absence, not negatively in Cartesian terms as the loss that compromises animality, that makes the animal less-than-human, but positively as a communication that the philosopher, *this* philosopher, the one who stands before you named 'Kant', the one who suffers too, like the animal, *cannot* dis-regard, look away from, or disavow.[5]

As Clarke outlines, like Coeztee and Derrida before him, the howls of the other are modes of speech no less communicative than the words we meter out upon a page. Their bodily agency precedes or exceeds the modes by which we limit them as 'poor in world' (as in Heidegger's definition of the animal).[6] Following the route of phenomenology, the body is a necessary element of communication. The animal body, even our animal body, is this necessary component for communication. As Merleau-Ponty repeats time and again, the body's frictions are not an inhibition to communication but the very means, even amid limitations, of any intelligible dialogue: 'It is that the thickness of flesh between the seer and the thing is constitutive for the thing of its visibility as for the seer of his corporeity; it is not an obstacle between them, it is their means of communication'.[7] It is by our bodies that we communicate and also with our bodies we express our vulnerability. The body expresses the limits of the body which itself is the necessary mode and the limit horizon for communication.

Furthermore, as Clark points out, the body exceeds 'its lack of certain powers'. It exceeds by its sheer necessity as that which grounds any 'certain powers'. The body is that which facilitates and scaffolds any of our capacities. The body exceeds as well in being beyond the scope of any specific powers; it is greater than any particular function humans or animals perform.

And so, limited by the body but also empowered by it we communicate a vulnerability across species. If we are haunted by the death of animals, it is because we too have bodies which are vulnerable to a violent death that goes without mourning. As Giorgio Agamben notes, we can imagine a bare life, the life of *homo sacer*. That is, we can think of a life deprived of human society. Nevertheless our imagination is limited since bare life is tied to the *polis* as an exile is to the city of men. In the case of animals — even those we manufacture through livestock breeding — their lives are outside the possibility of being brought back from exile. There is no return to community for them. Such a caesura indicates an intensive state of the body that is not communicable to our human and social selves. It is an exile beyond exile, more properly called a foreclosure of exile. This intensive state of the body is a suffering and felt capacity for suffering which 'irreducibly precedes and exceeds the question of its lack of certain powers' (Clark). Because we too are bodily beings, we are haunted by this capacity of a suffering and death without mourning, without the possibility of return from an exile.

One may wonder then, in an animal revolution, when the animals take up arms, what would induce them to spare the lives of humans? To what mutuality could we make appeal? Since animals have been foreclosed from even the possibility of exile, there is little inducement humans could make that would win over support from the animals. As Eugene Thacker and Alexander Galloway outline, the horror film in which animals turn against civilization is a prescient moment of a new sort of unhuman threat, the swarm. They ask 'if control in conflict is ordinarily situated around a relationship of enmity (friend– foe, ally– enemy), and if this relation of enmity structures the organization of conflict (symmetrical stand-off, insurgency, civil disobedience), what

Incident in the animal revolution

Corporeal Sheep. 'Sheep have perfected their version of the commando roll' says *The Guardian* (30 July 2004) Sheep in Pennine UK have learned how to roll over the cattle grid barrier to get to greener pastures. One tried it out and the others followed ... like sheep. A flock becomes a pack and a swarm. 'Pastured on the moors by "registered commoners" who can claim rights of open grazing going back to medieval times, the sheep have also perfected the skill of hurdling five foot fences and squeezing through gaps as narrow as eight inches wide' From an ancient and forgotten sociability of the commons comes the corporeal speech of an animal revolution.

happens when enmity dissolves in the intangible swarm?'[8] With swarms and packs, the anthropomorphic face of faciality no longer holds sway, there is no enemy to meet 'face to face'. There is not an appeal to mutuality at the level of the social (*polis* or *bios*) or the social in exile (bare life).

What the animals are doing, to use the term set out by Galloway and Thacker, is springing a trap by way of 'the exploit'. Speaking in terms of systems theory, they explain that 'protocological struggles [i.e. system power struggles] do not centre around changing existent technologies, but instead discovering holes in existent technologies, and projecting potential change into those holes. Hackers call these holes "exploits"'.[9] In terms of biological systems, briefly explored in *The Exploit*, the animal revolution finds a hole in the social system which keeps the animals at bay. I have characterized this hole as vulnerability, the raw corporality shared by humans and animals. Corporality serves as the exploit. Humans attempt to make the body social—*bios* and *polis*—or defined by sociability and exile from it—*zoe* and *homo sacer*—and so patch up the hole in the system between humans and animals. We put on our best social face so as to deny faciality and communication with the animal other. Haunted by the scream of animals whose deaths are not mourned, the animal revolution leaps the caesura and bears witness to a revolution in which the animality of the animal and the animality of the human undo the civil human.

Idiocy

The blunt tool of the revolution is the body itself and its mode of haunting which exploits a weakness in human civility—the corporality of the human animal. As will be developed in this section, the non-rational mode of comportment—the intensive rather than discursive mode of communication of the body—produces a most powerful tool in the animal arsenal: idiocy.

Before exploring the implications of idiocy, let us return to Merleau-Ponty and his notion of 'flesh of the world'. Recall that 'It is that the thickness of flesh between the seer and the thing is constitutive for the thing of its visibility as for the seer of his corporeity; it is not an obstacle between them, it is their means of communication'.[10] Bodies use the thickness of space to communicate, as is explored in the previous section. Yet, despite Merleau-Ponty's insistence, the flesh of bodies and the flesh of the world are also an opacity, a noise that jams communication, a blunt instrument which jams the attempts at a frictionless thinking, talking, and comportment. To reiterate, it is a 'means of communication' but not necessarily a communication within the realm of the social and the human.

Bodies jam the gears of the well-oiled social machine (the meat tenderizer transforming flesh into social and digestible parts). The function of the social machine—what Agamben calls the anthropomorphic machine—is to make bodies into something that can be assimilated, digested or *aufheben*, by the civil society.[11] Two fundamental operators that grind bodies into digestible social sums are good sense and common sense. These operators of the moral and the rational as established by the social sensibility create and reinforce the caesura between humans and animals.

The fissure or abyss between us and the animal is central to Derrida's argument in 'The animal that therefore I am (more to follow)'. He insists that such a border between us and other animals, and even our own animality, is a common proposition that itself need not be explored:

> For there is no interest to be found in a discussion of a supposed discontinuity, rupture, or even abyss between those who call themselves men and what so-called men, those who name themselves men, call the animal. Everybody agrees on this, discussion is closed in advance, one would have to be more asinine than any beast [plus bête que les bêtes] to think otherwise... . The discussion is worth undertaking once it is a matter of determining the number, form, sense, or structure, the foliated consistency of this abyssal limit, these edges, this plural and repeatedly folded frontier. The discussion becomes interesting once, instead of asking whether or not there is a discontinuous limit, one attempts to think what a limit becomes once it is abyssal, once the frontier no longer forms a single indivisible line but more than one internally divided line, once, as a result, it can no longer be traced, objectified, or counted as single and indivisible.[12]

Initially, I would like to focus on the spoken assumption that 'Everybody agrees on this, discussion is closed in advance, one would have to be more asinine than any beast to think otherwise.' The sentence brings out some key terms. There is a tautology to this argument which says everyone agrees there is an abyss except for those who disagree, but they do not count since they are 'more asinine than any beast.' Derrida knowingly uses 'Everyone' as a figure for common sense. Anyone who fits within this culture and its unarticulated values held in common is sufficiently sensible to know there is a difference between humans and animals. We might say that 'common sense' throws itself, that is to say, it projects itself as its own ground by which it then makes claims that everyone knows and so common sense remains unquestioned.

In *Difference and Repetition*, Deleuze explains how common sense throws itself: 'conceptual philosophical thought has as its implicit presupposition a pre-philosophical and natural Image of thought, borrowed from the pure element of common sense. According to this image, thought has an affinity with the true; it formally possesses the true and materially wants the true.'[13] Derrida notes that the discussion is 'closed in advance'. In other words, there is a hermeneutic circle surrounding the question of the animal. One either possesses common sense and so is in the circle or is without sense, is 'more asinine than any beast' and so outside the circle of thought about the animal. What is closed to the bestial and asinine humans is any 'discussion' of animal nature. The discussion is closed because anyone speaking without common sense would be speaking nonsense. One would have to be an idiot to think otherwise, to think differently. It is the role of such a village idiot to help those who have common sense measure their sensibility against the yardstick of his idiocy. 'We' are not like him, and therefore we are sensible. As Avital Ronell notes: 'The question of stupidity is always a sociopolitical one, even if it concerns the individual; in other words, the question of stupidity is always addressed to the community and never remains isolated with the individual'.[14]

Animals are considered dumb because they do not have the capacity for rational thought. Meanwhile, humans can be idiots because the species has the capacity but it is not properly manifest in some individuals. The limits of inclusion and exclusion are tested

Incident in the animal revolution

'Calif[ornia] aquarium blames flooding on curious octopus. They blame the soaking they discovered Tuesday morning on the aquarium's resident two-spotted octopus, a tiny female known for being curious and gregarious with visitors. The octopus apparently tugged on a valve and that allowed hundreds of gallons of water to overflow its tank. Aquarium spokeswoman Randi Parent says no sea life was harmed by the flood, but the brand new, ecologically designed floors might be damaged by the water.' 27 February 2009, Associate Press.

by the idiot who, as we shall see, sides more readily with the animal than the sensible humans. The idiot and the animal have very little to voice to society. They speak with a body, with 'the sheer facticity of bodily existence but not so much as a mute actuality anticipating meaning by way of a transcendent consciousness ... more as a kind of unassimilable scandal'[15]. What is scandalous about the animal body and the animality of the blunt human body, what is indeed the seed of revolution, is that these bodies abandon reason, sensibility, and civility as the modes of discourse and point to an-other register all together. In *Birth to Presence*, Jean-Luc Nancy pursues this scandalous facticity:

> The body does not know; but it is not ignorant either. Quite simply, it is elsewhere. It is from elsewhere, another place, another regime, another register, which is not even that of an 'obscure' knowledge, or a 'pre-conceptual' knowledge, or a 'global,' 'immanent,' or 'immediate' knowledge. The philosophical objection to what philosophy calls 'body' *presupposes* the determination of something like an authority of 'immediate knowledge'—a contradiction in terms, which inevitably becomes 'mediated' (as 'sensation,' 'perception,' synaesthesia, and as immense reconstitutions of a presupposed 'representation'). But what if one could presuppose nothing of the kind? What if the body was simply there, given, abandoned, without presupposition, simply posited, weighed, weighty?[16]

Incident in the animal revolution

'The Centers for Disease Control and Prevention reported that an average of 86,629 Americans visit the emergency room each year after a fall caused by pets or their paraphernalia. That's the equivalent of 240 Emergency Room trips a day, and roughly 1 percent of the 8 million visits for falls of all sorts' (*Washington Post*, 27 March 2009). The bodies of animals are underfoot. These bodies impede human progress and take their toll on our animality, our corporality. If I told you the secret of the animal revolution, I would have to kill you. In fact, you would either not understand the secret, in which case you would live on or you would understand and so already be dead. That is, if you already understand you are outside the hermeneutic circle of sensibility. Such an understanding without or outside of cultural 'knowing' is exactly the register of the revolution. The animal revolution ... its name is not pronounceable in any all-too-human language.

The body refuses signification. Any sign falls short of expressing the body and the body in its corporeal mass exceeds our discourse: 'The body insists, resists, weighs'.[17] The animality of the body—its weight and fur which resist the glide of signification—insists that there is an elsewhere not knowable within the register of what socially constitutes 'knowing.' The body—the call of the wild, the call of the animal, the call of revolution—is the heft and mass of a thinking that happens elsewhere. 'What is called thinking' is a call from elsewhere; it is the thought manifest in corporeal frictions, interlacings, and mixings.[18] Idiocy points—if it can point at all—to the materiality of only this world without a recourse to another space, an Archimedean transcendence by which language leverages the world. In its blunt materiality idiocy and animality threaten the symbolic with a materiality without meaning and without end (i.e. without teleology).

With this materiality comes a slippage into another register. Again, Nancy explicates this move: 'it might no longer be impossible to say that the body thinks and also, consequently, that thought is itself a body. This comes down to saying only that thought is here taken back to "matter", to its matter—thought *is* itself this renewal that does not come *back*, but that comes'.[19] The threat to the social, the good sense and common sense, is a move into a thinking that gives no return but does take us elsewhere by abandoning social habits. To follow the possibility of idiocy incurs risks. There is the possibility that such nonsense is just that—inarticulate and meaningless blather. It is always possible that such a collapse of distinction between inside the hermeneutic circle and outside, between meaning and nothingness, will produce an undifferentiated noise, a worthless heap, a body, a weight pressed against the world. Such is the idiocy of animal philosophy and dumbness of the animal. Such idiocy is revolutionary as it exposes the constructed nature of common sense and good sense. Body and bluntness undermine sensibility.

Known as the dog of Athens, Diogenes lived with the weight of his body. If he wrote anything, none of it survives; we have only anecdotes: he ate without discernment whatever he happened upon in the streets, masturbated in public, took to insulting his contemporaries, and lived in a tub. Plato could not coax 'the dog' into a dialogue, a conversation meant to invite Diogenes within the Academy where he would be refuted by the masters of language, Plato and Socrates. Fed up with words, always more words, Diogenes would offer his detractors food—something to stuff their mouths with and stop the babble of culture. Food could stop the philosophical abstraction and recall the animal body of the speaker. Fredrick Young, in his essay 'Animality,' explains:

> Plato had no *idea* how to deal with Diogenes. For Diogenes refused to argue on Platonic grounds, refused dialectics and the rational 'voice' that goes with it by means of which 'man' speaks. With Diogenes, there's a different modality of argumentation, if we can even call it that, the performative and animality. The Diogenic is more than a literal abject attack on Plato. More significantly, Diogenes' strategies are irreducible to any modality of dialectics or philosophy proper. Again, what we have is the problematics of the surface, of animality—a physiognomic performance that unleashes the performativity of animality into the Platonic landscape and architecture.[20]

The performative *is* thought for Diogenes; his actions with his body in space are his thinking. This is the literalism of surfaces without retreat to a Platonic architecture. In like manner, Coetzee, in *The Lives of Animals*, explains that 'the living flesh' of the animal is its argument. When Coetzee's protagonist Elizabeth Costello is asked if life means less to animals than to humans, she retorts that animals do not respond to us in words, but rather with gestures of the living flesh. The argument from its body is the animal's 'whole being.'[21] Like Coetzee's animals, the world for Diogenes is not that of the culture that surrounds him and that seeks to incorporate his corpus, if he would ever get around to writing one. Instead, he offers corporality— bodies and surfaces that evade the sensibility of his contemporaries. It comes then as no surprise that Diogenes lived his life in exile from Sinope, his birthplace.

Incident in the animal revolution

Chuck the groundhog bites New York City mayor Michael Bloomberg's finger. Chuck has redefined groundhog's day. It is about the groundhog, not the humans. Stay out of the animal layer. Interestingly, Chuck lives with his human handler, Doug Swartz. The animal was wild and orphaned and was taken in by the Staten Island Zoo. 'Chuck has free range of the house and uses a litter box. But you know, groundhogs are very aggressive.' (*New York Times*, 3 February 2009).

Days later, the *Chef* of State is the one bitten: 'Former French President Jacques Chirac was rushed to a hospital after being mauled by his pet dog who is being treated for depression.' The dog named Sumo is a white Maltese poodle. Does your dog bite? The Fox New story continues: 'has a history of frenzied fits and became increasingly prone to making "vicious, unprovoked attacks" despite receiving treatment with anti-depressants.' Well, being told where to walk, when and if one can walk, when to pee, when to eat ... one can become a bit frenzied. Add to this pedigree overbreeding (of both human and dogs) and bodies will collide.

Left-handed Blow ... Revolution as Untimely

To take tally, thus far this essay began with the haunting of animal death that remains without being mourned. It is not mourned because we do not know how to incorporate the animal body into the social body. Indeed, to do so would mean to rethink the human and the non-human community. I have traced the line of this haunting through the animal body and the ways that the animality of the animal opens up the animality of the human and so troubles good sense and common sense. Enter then the idiot and the dumb whose blunt bodies disrupt the social register by a flight of thought into bodies. As Nancy says: 'thought *is* itself this renewal that does not come *back*, but that comes'.[22] Having laid some groundwork and tools of an animal revolution, in this final section I speculate on what is meant by saying that the animal revolution is 'to come.'

Foremost, revolution is untimely. Working at a register outside of the social, there is no sense in which a revolution should abide by human clockwork. As haunting manifests, the revolution has already taken place. Shots have been fired, so to speak. More aptly, teeth have gnawed, bodies have pressed and more than a bit of blood has been drawn. Yet, this haunting from the past is for a future, a 'to come': 'At bottom, the specter is the future, it is always to come, it presents itself only as that which could come or come back'.[23] If you and I as good humans could agree upon the time of revolution, then it would not be revolutionary. Indeed, 'the revolution will not be televised.' Which is to say that it is never a good time for a revolution according to the anthropocentric machine and its hegemony of/within the present. The revolution runs a parallel course to our own temporality. It is already an event which has taken shape in the past and haunts us. As such, the revolution is always capable of erupting. Yet, if and when it does, it will no longer be human time but a time of the other. The animals are patient, and they strike quickly.

Early in *Specters of Marx*, Derrida outlines the temporality of haunting:

First suggestion: haunting is historical, to be sure, but it is not dated, it is never docilely given a date in the chain of presents, day after day, according to the instituted order of a calendar. Untimely, it does not come to, it does not happen to, it does not befall, one day, Europe, as if the latter, at a certain moment of its history, had begun to suffer from a certain evil, to let itself be inhabited in its inside, that is, haunted by a foreign guest... . But there was no inside, there was nothing inside before it.[24]

There was 'nothing inside' what it means to be humans prior to our relationship to the animal; rather, we have always defined ourselves over and against this other which is in our midst. Having already set ourselves in relation to this other, the events of its eruption into our history are 'historical' and yet 'not dated.' There is no calendar for the animal revolution.

In 'A Left-handed Blow: Writing the History of Animals', Erica Fudge sets out the parameters of what constitutes animal studies: there is an intellectual history (how our relation to animals tell us about our thinking), a humane history (how animals fit within culture) and a holistic history (animality as an operator or agent in history).[25] Throughout the essay she invokes Walter Benjamin whose work on history and revolution are particularly suggestive for the animal revolution. Fudge asks us to imagine a history from the point of view of the losers, in this case, the animals as those who have been foreclosed from even the possibility of inclusion as agents of history. She invokes Benjamin on the authors of history: '[A]ll rulers are heirs

Incident in the animal revolution

To come: 'A male chimpanzee in a Swedish zoo planned hundreds of stone-throwing attacks on zoo visitors... . There has been scant evidence in previous research that animals can plan for future events. Crucial to the current study is the fact that Santino, a chimpanzee at the zoo in the city north of Stockholm, collected the stones in a calm state, prior to the zoo opening in the morning.' (BBC News, 9 March 2009).

of those who conquered before them ... There is no document of civilization which is not at the same time a document of barbarism'.[26] If an animal revolution is revolutionary, then it will not abide by documentation. The animals will not have their passports stamped nor their time-cards punched. It is here that idiocy serves the animals well. The sheer weight of bodies exceeds documentation. To invoke again Nancy on the body: 'The body insists, resists, weighs on the demand: for it is after all the body that requests, demands this anatomical and catalogical writing, the kind of writing that would enable not to signify (not to turn into either a signifier, a signified, or self-signification)... a body given always already given, abandoned, and withdrawn from all the plays of signs. A body touched, touching, and the tract of this tact'.[27] The animal body wounded or butchered becomes a haunting in history. The animal body in tact becomes a tacit and unmovable object which 'writes' itself into a history of its own making, on its own terms.

At the end of Fudge's essay, like a punch line, she gives us the Benjamin quotation from which she draws her title: 'All decisive blows are struck left-handed'.[28] In Benjamin's aphorism, the blow does not come from the dexterous right hand, a hand that writes and is culturally proper for everything from a social handshake to opening doors. Precisely because of its lack of value, the left hand becomes valuable in overturning a system of cultural norms. This socially awkward hand is inverse to the dexterous hand. It is the sinister, the idiot hand, which does not know any better and cannot work properly for/according to the *polis*. Recall the long catalogue of Heidegger's connection between hand and thought, using the hand as shorthand for thinking (as in his *Heraclitus Seminar*).[29] Derrida writes about this in *Geschlecht II* and Tom Tyler in 'Like Water in Water' applies the issue of hand to animals.[30] In relation to Heidegger's hand, then, Benjamin's left-handed blow signals the unforeseen thinking that strikes from 'left field', from the outside, to blindside proper thought. Heidegger connects the fist with our animal nature and the open hand—one that gives and receives— as the trait of the human and human thought. In Heidegger's intellectual game of paper-scissor-rock, the human hand covers over the clenched fist, overwhelms it with the ability to contemplate the open and being-in-itself. As Derrida notes, for Heidegger there is only hand in the singular since this hand is the stand-in for the singularity of human thinking. Animals are more dexterous than Heidegger gives them credit. As the hand which is thought covers the paw, claw, hand of the animal, out of nowhere comes the *other* hand, the paw or claw or jaw of a left-handed blow. Reason never counted on being outwitted by that which it rejects outright—idiocy, dullness, the body, and the animal.

Notes

1 See Wegman, W., *Spelling Lesson*, (1974).

2 Meillassoux, Q., 'Spectral Dilemma', in Mackay, R. (ed), *Collapse Volume IV: Concept Horror* (London, Urbanomic, 2008), pp. 261–275: 261–2.

3 Derrida, J., '"Eating Well" or the Calculation of the Subject', in Cadava, E., Connor, P. and Nancy, J-L. (eds), *Who Comes After the Subject*, (New York, Routledge, 1991), pp. 96–119.

4 Wolfe, Cary, 'Exposures', in Cavell, S., Diamond, C., McDowell, J., Hacking, I. and Wolfe, C., *Philosophy and Animal Life*, (New York, Columbia UP, 2009), pp. 1–41: 8.

5 Clark, D., 'Towards a Prehistory of the Postanimal: Kant, Levinas, and the Regard of Brutes', (Private correspondence, 2009).

6 Coetzee, J. M., *The Lives of Animals*, (Princeton, NJ, Princeton UP, 2001). Derrida, J., 'The Animal therefore I am (more to follow)', *Critical Inquiry* 28, (2), 2002, pp. 367–418.

7 See Merleau-Ponty, M., *The Visible and the Invisible* chapter 4 'The Intertwining—The Chiasm', (Evanston, Northwest University Press, 1968), pp. 130–155: 135. Also see his earlier contemplation of the flesh of the human body as it affects consciousness Merleau-Ponty, M., *Phenomenology of Perception* Part I Chapter 2 'The Experience of the Body and Classical Psychology' (Routledge, London, 1962), pp. 103–111.

8 Galloway, A. and Thacker, E., *The Exploit*, (Minneapolis, University of Minnesota Press, 2007), p. 80.

9 Galloway and Thacker, *The Exploit*, p. 96.

10 Merleau-Ponty, M., *Phenomenology of Perception*, p. 135.

11 See the concept 'anthropological machine' in Agamben, G., *The Open*, (Stanford, CA: Stanford UP), 2003.

12 Derrida, 'The animal that therefore I am', p. 131. The French reads (on page 281 of *L'animal autobiographique*): " ... et ce que les soi-disant hommes, ceux qui se nomment des hommes, appellent l'animal. Tout le monde est d'accord à ce sujet, la discussion est close d'avance, et il faudrait être *plus bête que les bêtes* pour en douter. Les bêtes mêmes savant cela... ." (emphasis added). Derrida, J., 'L'animal que donc je suis (à suivre)', in Mallet, M-L. (ed), *L'animal autobiographique: autour de Jacques Derrida*. (Paris, Galilée, 1999), pp. 251–301. My thanks to Steve Baker for suggesting I quote from the French text.

13 Deleuze, G., *Difference and Repetition*, (New York, Columbia UP, 1994), p. 131.

14 Ronell, A., *Stupidity*. (Chicago, University of Illinois Press, 2002), p. 67. In a future project, I will take up the difference between stupidity (as delineated by Ronell) and idiocy as a modality for an animal revolution.

15 Ronell, *Stupidity*, p. 179.

16 Nancy, J-L., *Birth to Presence*, (Stanford, CA, Stanford UP, 1994), pp. 199–200.

17 *Ibid.*, p. 198.

18 *Ibid.*, p. 195; Ronell, *Stupidity*, p. 187.

19 *Ibid.*, p. 201

20 Young, F., 'Animality', in Wolfreys, J. (ed), *Glossalalia*, (Edinburgh, Edinburgh UP, 2003), pp. 9–21: 16.

21 Coetzee, J. M., *The Lives of Animals*.

22 Nancy, J-L., *Birth to Presence*, p. 201.

23 Derrida, J., *Specters of Marx: The State of the Debt, the Work of Mourning, and the New International*, (New York, Routledge, 1994), p. 39.

24 Derrida, *Specters of Marx*, p. 4.

25 Fudge, E., 'A Left-handed Blow: Writing the History of Animals' in Rothfels, N. (ed), *Representing Animals*. (Bloomington, Indiana UP, 2002), pp. 3–18: 11.

26 Benjamin, W., 'Theses on the Philosophy of History', *Illuminations*, (New York, Harcourt Brace Jovanovich, 1968), pp. 253–264.

27 Nancy, J-L., *Birth to Presence*, p. 198.

28 Fudge, 'A Left-handed Blow', p. 16. Cf. Benjamin, W., 'One Way Street', *Reflections*, (New York, Harcourt Brace Jovanovich, 1978), pp. 61–96.

29 Heidegger, M., *Heraclitus Seminar*, (Evanston, IL, Northwestern UP, 1993).

30 Derrida, J., 'Geshlecht II', in Sallis, J. (ed), *Deconstruction and Philosophy*, (Chicago, University of Chicago Press, 1987) and Tyler, T., 'Like Water in Water'. *Journal for Cultural Research*, 9 (3), 2005, pp. 265–279.

2

Being a Known Animal[1]

Claire Molloy

In January 2010 the BBC broadcast the world premiere of 'the only film to be shot entirely by chimps'.[2] The film was the conclusion to a one-hour nature documentary, *Natural World: The Chimpcam Project*, which followed a two-year study that took place at Edinburgh Zoo and introduced a captive chimpanzee group to video and camera technologies. Chimpcam appeared to suggest that, given the right tools and training, a radical nonhuman animal intervention could disrupt the all-too-comfortable dominance of anthropocentric mainstream narratives. Chimps could tell us stories about themselves and there is something compelling about the prospect of a film made by another species.[3] A film shot by chimps invokes a sense of agency in a creative process, an investment by the animal that differentiates the filmed outcome from sequences in natural history programmes which are constructed from subjective camera shots achieved by simply attaching a camera to an animal's body. In this case chimpanzees figured as the creative agents in charge of the production process and the programme's narration promised that the film had potential to offer new insights into the way in which chimps experience their world.

Five decades after Jane Goodall's revelation that chimpanzees use tools, the Chimpcam research project set out to train chimpanzees to use video touch screens and a video camera which was contained in a sturdy orange box. Working on the assumption that video could provide a vehicle for self-recognition in much the same way as a mirror had done in previous studies,[4] the chimpanzees were able to choose whether or not they participated in the research. The narrative of the project, as it was presented by the programme, had two plotlines. The first followed the chimpanzee's training and the second documented a power struggle in the group that lasted many months and primarily involved three chimpanzees, two males and one older female. These three chimpanzees and one other female, who was of a much lower rank in the group but more involved in the research, were established by the programme as the main characters. The two plotlines were woven together to tell a story about how the complexities of chimpanzee group politics impinged upon the chimps' willingness to engage with the research project. Indeed, the tensions in the social hierarchy were shown to occupy the chimpanzee's interest to a much greater degree than the video screens. Towards the end of the programme, the group worked through its social hierarchy issues and were introduced to the boxed camera which they played with and carried around their enclosure. The programme concluded with the premiere of the chimp's film which consisted of a montage composed of close-ups of chimp eyes peering into the camera, chimp lips licking the protective lens cover, and images of the enclosure partially obscured by the haze of chimp saliva that covered the camera lens for much of the one minute sequence that was edited and set to music by humans.

Whether the Chimpcam project was a success is debateable. Arguably, more was revealed about chimpanzee culture and communication through observations of the complex social networks, alliances and interactions that constituted the power struggle within the group. Yet the programme's intentions, and those of the Chimpcam film, take up a very familiar endeavour: the desire to gain access to nonhuman primate minds through a shared communicative medium or, as Donna Haraway proposes, to 'open the border inherited from the separation of nature and culture'.[5] Nonhuman primates are particularly ambiguous in that they exist at the boundary of the 'almost human'[6]. Conceptually framed by the evolutionary continuum suggested by comparative psychology and motivated by the question of whether human language can be traced to its evolutionary roots, attempts to breach the boundary between human and ape have inevitably focused on the linguistic capacities of chimpanzees, gorillas and bonobos. Yet, as researchers discovered in the 1960s, the vocal apparatus of apes differs substantially from that of humans in the orientation of the vocal-laryngeal tract. This difference between humans and primates in the make-up of the vocal apparatus led researchers to experiment with other forms of communication following the failure of experiments in the 1950s which had been designed to teach chimpanzees to speak. The 1960s thus signalled a key turning point in scientific debates about language. Using an alternative language system[7] and thereby rejecting the notion that speech is a requisite to language, the Washoe project, whilst controversial, brought to the fore the real possibility that the linguistic capacities of humans were not unique. In 1973, further experiments in language acquisition in chimpanzees began with Project Nim which attempted to recreate the Washoe project[8] and in 1980 Sue Savage-Rumbaugh began her work with bonobos at the Georgia State University Language Research Centre. The main subject of Savage-Rumbaugh's work was Kanzi who was taught to use lexigrams, a system of communication that uses symbols to represent words.[9] With the appropriation of alternative forms of communication, the relationship between language and 'talking' became central to the critical appraisal of ape language and the question of what actually constitutes language.[10]

Language has been particularly problematic in relation to non-human and human primates first because the biological difference between humans and apes creates a point of contention as apes have neither the capacity to speak nor write and second because, in the Saussurean tradition, language involves the communication of shared concepts between speakers enabled by the minds of the speaking agents. Attribution of selfhood and mind has thus been intimately connected to the attribution of language. In this regard linguist Joel Wallman and cognitive neuropsychologist Steve Pinker argue that language is innate and can only be attributed to humans on the basis that it is a biological species-specific characteristic. According to Wallman, the crucial moment in human language acquisition takes place when vocal utterances become 'linguistic symbols'.[11] The nonhuman primate is therefore barred from language acquisition and from the attribution of mental conceptualization due to the inability to vocalize. From this position, we find that the critiques of nonhuman animal language lie in an intractable boundary of biological difference between human and nonhuman animal where, Wallman argues, 'ape utterances (whether these be vocalizations, gestures, or sign uses) are better characterized as performative than referential ... [i.e.,] a repertoire of habits that a[re] effective rather than meaningful'.[12]

Defining the act of speech as a species-specific type of vocalization, which is intrinsically bound to the attribution of mind to the speaker has ensured that language remains a structuring principle of human-nonhuman primate power relations. Erica Fudge argues, 'Language has often been regarded as the domain of the human: that is, a kind of logic can be used that defines the difference between human and animal via the ability to communicate through language. 'I can speak, therefore I am human: it cannot speak, therefore it is not human', this logic would go, and what follows from such logic is a structure of power'.[13] Interspecies communication in the form of meaningful language has therefore been considered to comfortably inhabit only the realms of popular cultural fictions. Such stories are, however, highly problematic in that to accommodate the fantasy of animal language in films there is a reliance on the disavowal of individual species being with consequences for the lives of real animals. In the case of live action films the fictions about human–animal communication are made possible by training animals to be actors. Even with the introduction of CGI techniques the costs of creating animals in this way have remained high enough to continue with the use of live animals for reasons of economy.

For the remainder of this chapter I want to problematize the fictions of human–chimpanzee communication through a consideration of Vicki Hearne's arguments about animal training which is conceived of as a form of language. For Hearne, Wittgenstein's comment about the lion is a mistake and she writes, 'At the end of the *Philosophical Investigations*, he said that if a lion could talk, we wouldn't be able to understand him. There is a minor mistake of fact here – since lions do talk to some people, and are understood'.[14] Of interest here is that Hearne's argument with Wittgenstein comes from her participation in two communities of practice; those of academia and of animal training. For Hearne, the latter is engaged in the meaningful production of knowledge about animals that has something to add to the discourse of the former.

Being a Chimpanzee in Hollywood

Since the 1930s chimpanzees have proved popular as animal characters in mainstream films. The *Tarzan* films introduced audiences to the character Cheeta, a role played by many different chimpanzee individuals of both genders over three decades beginning with *Tarzan The Ape Man* in 1932. Public recognition of the character Cheeta was such that the death of Queenie, who, it was claimed, played the Cheeta role in *Tarzan The Ape Man*, was widely reported in the press in 1933, and the deaths, 'retirements' and injuries sustained by other chimpanzees associated with the role continued to be considered similarly newsworthy.[15] Over the years various individuals, all of whom were credited with playing the role of Cheeta, featured in popular press reports: One chimpanzee died suddenly during a play session in 1935 and in 1944 the studio lost two 'Cheetas' when one died from pneumonia and a second was reported to have gone 'berserk'. Another chimpanzee was seriously burned in a car fire in 1950 whilst others were variously 'retired' following a series of biting incidents in 1951; shot by Sherriff's Deputies after becoming unmanageable in 1957; retired and exported to a zoo in Sydney in 1959; retired to a zoo in Calgary in 1959 and died in a Los Angeles zoo in 1962.[16]

Wild animals were a key aspect of the spectacular entertainment in Tarzan films and although the character, Cheeta, did not appear in the trailer for the 1932 film, for the next MGM feature, *Tarzan And His Mate* in 1934, chimpanzees figured prominently in the film's marketing. The Cheeta character was distinguished from the other animal actors and regarded as a comedian in contrast to the unnamed elephants, hyenas, crocodiles, rhinos and lions who were repeatedly referred to in film publicity and promotion as 'the thrills'.[17] Critical reception of Tarzan films often included comments on the performances of animals, typified by a 1936 review of *Tarzan Finds A Son* which opined, 'As in the others, work of the animals was outstanding. Cheetah, a pet chimpanzee, is a comedian of the first water'.[18] Considered to be 'natural comedians', in Hollywood, chimpanzees appeared in numerous slapstick roles and received star billing in films such as *Bedtime For Bonzo* (1951), *Bonzo Goes To College* (1952) and *Monkey Business* (1952). The cinema-going public found chimpanzees and their humanlike antics fascinating and Hollywood was not alone in exploiting their potential as comic performers with chimp shows being a key attraction at zoos, circuses and fairs across the USA and regularly bringing in large audiences.

The comedic stereotype relied on the humanlike performance of chimpanzees and a repertoire of actions and gestures that included 'smiling' and 'laughing' and picking up, taking or giving objects as well as engaging in domestic human activities. Their physical similarity to humans combined with their capacity for approximating humanlike emotions and activities meant that chimpanzees functioned particularly well as film characters, or to be more specific, as agents of causality in the narrative. As Murray Smith argues, characters depend on general conceptions of agency and 'to be a subject – to perform a socially prescribed function – one must first be an agent' with a 'basic set of capacities'.[19] Smith goes on to argue that 'our understanding of nonhuman agents [...] is modelled on our understanding of humans to a large degree'.[20] Chimpanzees were constructed in popular culture as a parody of humanness and the Hollywood publicity discourse of the 1940s and 1950s was keen to emphasize that star chimpanzees excelled in and enjoyed their performances. Chimpanzee stars were humanized both on- and off-screen by studio publicists who regularly fed the press with tongue-in-cheek stories about the rivalry between different animal stars and between human and nonhuman primate actors, as well as accounts of the animal stars' glamorous Hollywood lifestyles. There was, for instance, an ongoing rivalry between Bonzo the chimpanzee, Francis the talking mule and Harvey, an imaginary rabbit, which appeared in the film of the same name.[21] The rivalry was also said to extend to relations with human co-stars and some studios went even further to 'prove' the humanlike abilities of their stars. In the case of Bonzo, the studio drew on reports from scientific studies, which suggested that some chimpanzees had the intelligence of a five-year-old child. A promotional stunt was arranged which brought a team of psychologists to test Bonzo before a group of journalists. When Bonzo failed to be assessed as having a higher-than-average level of chimpanzee intelligence the publicists were quick to reframe the event and propose that the outcome was intentional. Bonzo had, the studio argued, purposefully failed the test.[22]

The promotional discourse worked hard to emphasize the humanness of nonhuman primate stars and off-screen cues by trainers, which were invisible to the cinema audience, produced the most compelling instances of seemingly autonomous humanlike behaviour onscreen. Although the studio publicity discourse did much to promote the humanlike qualities of star animal performers, stories of recalcitrant chimp behaviour did make their way into the popular press.[23] For instance, as one journalist on the set of *Tarzan And His Mate* noted in 1934, 'Watching a chimpanzee prance about in a tree may be fun for spectators in a motion picture theatre ... but these little simians provide no picnic for the assistant director in the filming of a story calling for their presence'.[24] Biting incidents, although minimized by the studio publicity departments when they took place during the production or the promotion of a film, were not uncommon and were often reported to have preceded the 'retirement' of a star chimpanzee.

Being Trained

Chimpanzee training for the purposes of film performance traditionally involved forcibly separating an infant from its mother and subjecting the young chimpanzee to various forms of physical domination to control wanted and unwanted behaviours. The precise techniques were seldom revealed by chimpanzee trainers who preferred to talk about chimpanzee performance in terms of a natural talent that could be developed by methods that paralleled those used to teach children. As later accounts of training techniques disclosed however, harsh methods that included beatings and electric shocks were regularly employed.[25] In this regard Dale Peterson writes, 'If the performance of apes is to conform to what the public want to see and to know and to imagine, then the technology of control must remain covert and concealed, eternally one more ingredient in the stuff of dreams'.[26] Whilst preadolescent chimpanzees could be cued to perform behaviours using methods that relied on intimidation and domination, the trainer's ability to control a chimpanzee lessened as the individual approached sexual maturity. For this reason, most chimpanzees in the entertainment industries were 'retired' at around eight years of age into zoos, captive breeding programmes, research laboratories or sanctuaries when they become too difficult to handle.[27] With a relatively short career lasting around five years but living in captivity up to sixty years of age, chimpanzees from the entertainment industries who were unable to reintegrate with members of their own kind, would face many decades of 'retirement' in isolation.[28]

These are not the stories that popular culture tells about chimpanzees. Despite the popular press coverage of attacks and biting incidents involving pet or trained chimps the sheer volume of imagery of chimpanzees in film and television suggested that, rather than being typical of the behaviour of sexually mature individuals, such occurrences were perpetrated by occasional rogue animals who received suitable punishment for their actions. The representations of chimps in clothes laughing, smiling and performing comedy antics were abundant and the on- and off-screen continuity of characters such as Cheeta and Bonzo was maintained as new individuals were brought in to replace those who were no longer suitable for film work. In this sense, our stories of chimpanzees have traditionally been unwilling to acknowledge post-adolescent chimpanzee being, and representations of chimps rarely depict sexually mature individuals. Training appeared to temporarily close down the difference between human and chimpanzee but the constructed illusion of humanlike agency that it facilitated disintegrated as the chimpanzee matured.

In *The Companion Species Manifesto* Donna Haraway turns to the work of trainer and language philosopher Vicki Hearne to discuss training as an interspecies relationship, which brings with it an ethical obligation to communicate 'across irreducible difference'.[29] Referring to Hearne's defence of anthropomorphic language as a means by which humans 'stay alert to the fact that somebody is at home in the animals they work with' Haraway contends:

Just *who* is at home must permanently be in question. The recognition that one cannot *know* the other or the self, but must ask in respect for all of time who and what are emerging in relationship, is the key. [...] I believe that all ethical relating, within or between species, is knit from the silk-strong thread of ongoing alertness to otherness-in-relation.[30]

It is this relation between human and animal that Hearne discusses at length in *Adam's Task* where she explains why training is a form of interspecies communication. For Hearne, certain domestic animals, particularly dogs and horses, have a capacity for language in the sense that they respond to the authority of human command. This relationship cannot be explained by recourse to the animal-machines of Cartesian thought or Skinnerian behaviourism, which are knowledge communities that explicitly reject the anecdotal accounts which Hearne employs. Training, for Hearne, is a relationship which develops over time, an expanding vocabulary that becomes language. Opposing the view that animals react rather than respond, Hearne's philosophy of training recognizes animals and humans as embodied communicative beings with the potential to acknowledge and be responsive to each other's demands. An animal's response to a command is not the result of coercion or, Hearne argues, a form of animal enslavement. Instead she proposes that trained obedience with companion animals is the result of humans taking responsibility for their position of authority whilst also being able to acknowledge the being of others. Failure to take up the position of authority in the human-canine relationship means, for Hearne, a refusal to 'take the dog's position into account'.[31] By this, she means not only respect for the dog as a canine but as an individual and she goes to great lengths to describe, in the form of anecdotes, training techniques that acknowledge the individual being of named animals.

Training, as a form of communication, has an important ethical dimension and is dependent according to Hearne on the willingness of animals to cooperate. In being obedient to commands animals earn rights within the relationship and humans in turn must respond to the demands of the animal. The 'labour of training' thus provides the opportunity for animal happiness, which Donna Haraway explains in the following terms:

> This kind of happiness is about yearning for excellence and having the chance to try and reach it in terms recognizable to concrete beings, not to categorical abstractions. Not all animals are alike;

their specificity – of kind and of individual - matter. The specificity
of their happiness matters, and that is something that has to be
brought to emergence. [32]

Both Haraway and Hearne make clear that this attendance to an
animal's being, which for Hearne can involve both 'reading' or
'listening' to the individual animal, and the provision of rights is a
reciprocal arrangement that places demands on the each party within
the relationship.

Haraway and Hearne are concerned with training companion
animals, particularly dogs and horses. Yet it is notable that in their
discussions of companion animal training, both refer explicitly to
chimpanzee training as a point of comparison. Hearne in particular
spends the first chapter of *Adam's Task* discussing her experiences
of visiting and meeting Washoe, the first chimpanzee to be taught
American Sign Language. Hearne uses Washoe as a way of exploring
the limits of her own argument about interspecies communication
and begins by differentiating between wild animals and domestic
animals on the basis of whether they have a 'working temperament';
a nature specific to some animals which makes it possible for humans
to train them. There is thus a corresponding difference for Hearne
between the shared vocabulary established through the labour of
human-canine training and the form of communication that Washoe
engages in. For Hearne, Washoe is problematic, not because of the
'intellectual emergency' that she presents in being able to use sign
language, but because in this case interspecies communication
cannot prevent Washoe biting or attacking humans. Because of this,
Washoe is caged, leading Hearne to write: 'But I am appalled and
grieved because the chimps are in cages. This offends me. [...] What is
offended is the dog trainer's assumption that language or something
like vocabulary gives mutual autonomy and trust. I grieve, but not for
Washoe behind her bars. It is language I grieve for'.[33] In canine-human
relations biting that cannot be controlled leads to the breakdown of
the relationship. For Hearne, dogs can enter into communicative
relations whereby there is an agreement that even if they 'want to'
the canine will resist the impulse to bite and although Washoe had
been told that she should not bite the conversation had not ended
with an agreement between chimpanzee and human. The reason that

Hearne then grieves for language is that it is not able to bridge an irrefutable gap between humanity and animality. If Washoe's gestures are indeed language, Hearne argues, 'and if Washoe is dangerous despite that, then I may be thrown into confusion, may suffer, as Othello did, from sceptical terror, and may want to deny Washoe's personhood and her language rather than acknowledge the limits of language, which can look like a terrifying procedure'.[34] Such anxieties are acknowledged in films. The horror film *Link* (1986) and the science-fiction film *Planet of the Apes* (1968 & 2001) for instance, each reflect concern that possession of language provides no guarantee of moral agency. Animality, conceived of in terms of ape aggression, results in a problematic human analogue and it is on this point that Hearne begins to falter. Unable to conceive of how human-animal relations should function outside of successful training Hearne admits that the only recourse she has is to stories of rapists, assassins and fanatics to make sense of 'Washoe's incomplete assent to the terms of the discussion'.[35] For Hearne, there are workable and unworkable relations between humans and animals. Unworkable relations are those that cannot achieve mutual acknowledgement of the moral significance of actions even with the benefit of interspecies communication.

Being a Moral Agent

The potential for chimpanzees to possess moral agency is explored at length in the Hollywood comedy *Bedtime For Bonzo*, the story of a college professor who sets out to prove that environment is more important than heredity by bringing up a chimpanzee as a child. The film drew its inspiration from the various studies that had been undertaken by psychologists in which chimpanzees had been raised as human children in a domestic environment. In *Bedtime For Bonzo* the fantasy of human-ape relations is realized in the conclusion to the film with the establishment of a family unit made-up of a human mother and father and Bonzo the chimpanzee as the well-trained moral agent and surrogate son. Without doubt, such a story fits well the general disavowal of the agency of sexually mature chimpanzees and offers a more compelling possibility that the border between nature and culture can be permanently bridged by human-chimp relations. But such stories must inevitably arrest chimpanzee being at pre-adolescence, at a time when chimpanzees are still susceptible to training by physical intimidation by humans, although that aspect of the relationship remains concealed in the extratextual zones of the film fiction.

Narratives of human-chimp familial relations, shared language and moral reasoning are also constructed elsewhere to the extent that science and fiction have become increasingly entangled. In 1909, the psychologist Lightner Witmer carried out a series of tests on a young chimpanzee named Peter. Part of a vaudeville act, Peter's performance demonstrated to Witmer that:

> [I]n a very real sense the animal is himself giving the stage performance. He knows what he is doing, he delights in it, he varies it from time to time, he understands the succession of tricks which are being called for, he is guided by word of mouth without any signal open or concealed, and the function of his trainer is exercized mainly to steady and control. [...] From time to time I observed that he made the work more difficult for himself than was needful, seemingly out of mere bravado and in pure enjoyment of the task.[36]

After testing Peter, Witmer's conclusions were that whilst it was not possible to determine precisely whether it was feasible to teach Peter to speak, '[H]is behaviour, however, is sufficiently intelligent to make this education experiment well worth the expenditure of time and effort.'[37] In 1933, psychologists Winthrop Kellogg and Luella Kellogg began an experiment to assess the importance of environment over heredity by raising a chimpanzee, named Gua, as a child. By bringing her up with their own son, Donald, the Kelloggs' intention was to humanize Gua and, whilst they reported that she understood words, phrases and instruction, Kellogg concluded that 'neither subject really learned to talk during the interval of research'.[38] Instead Kellogg referred to Gua's vocalizations – the bark; the food-bark; the screech or scream; and the 'Oo-oo' Cry – as 'language responses' and claimed that although Gua did not 'talk' she was able to communicate with the experimenters and had acquired some moral reasoning.[39] An experiment undertaken by Keith Hayes and Katherine Hayes to teach Viki the chimpanzee to speak had a different outcome. Viki was raised as a human child in the Hayes' home and when she was three years old they reported that she was able to vocalize approximations of four words. However, these were not deployed consistently and whilst Hayes and Hayes concluded that 'Viki is deficient in language comprehension, as well as in speech, though here the deficit is less striking,' they added, '[I]f we assume, however, that Viki's mental development will continue to parallel that of man to maturity – as it appears to have done for the first three years – then our results strongly suggest that the two species are much more alike, psychologically, than has heretofore been supposed'.[40]

The stories of Peter, Gua and Viki are enmeshed with those of Bonzo and Queenie and other Hollywood chimpanzees. They each suggest that the solution to dismantling the barrier between human and ape resides in interspecies communication and, on this subject, Donna Haraway writes, 'Since traditionally language has been imagined to be the source of the barrier, perhaps if a language could be shared, contact with apes, almost as extraterrestrials, could be made and "man" would not be alone'.[41] Chimpanzee performance of humanness, whether constructed for fiction or science, has thus seemed to hold the promise of shared communication and, in that space the hope that language gives access to shared moral understanding.

Being John Malkovich (1999) re-imagines the moral agency of chimps as an outcome not of language but of memory and suffering. The film engages with issues of identity, consciousness, the relationship between body and mind and, with an implicit nod towards Andy Warhol's predictions about everyone's entitlement to fifteen minutes of fame, offers a wry commentary on contemporary celebrity culture. Written by Charlie Kaufmann and directed by Spike Jonze the film enquires into what it means to be an embodied individual; it questions where the limits of identity lie and explores the associations between consciousness and sensory perception. More than this though, *Being John Malkovich* offers a space for reflection on human/animal boundaries and depictions of nonhuman animal consciousness within contemporary culture. Considered a reflection on Cartesian dualism and the notion of the unified subject, the film is indeed an exploration into definitions of the self but it moves beyond human minds to consider the minds of other animals and specifically that of the character Elijah, a chimpanzee.[42]

Woven into the narrative of *Being John Malkovich* is the story of Elijah, a chimpanzee owned by pet shop worker Lotte. According to Lotte, Elijah has psychological problems caused by some trauma that has occurred in his past and for which he is visiting a therapist. It is made clear that Craig, the main protagonist, has no interest in Elijah or any of the other companion animals that live in their apartment and when Lotte asks him to look after Elijah who is feeling unwell, Craig has no idea which animal she is referring to. Seated with Craig on a sofa in the next scene, Elijah's posture assumes the comedic pseudo-human stereotype that has pervaded popular culture. The two watch television and the soft vocalizations which Elijah makes are easily construed by the viewer as comments or responses to Craig and the television, although Craig appears wholly unaware of the interspecies communication taking place. The conversation is, from Craig's point of view, completely one-sided. A wide shot of Elijah and Craig invites the viewer to make comparisons between the two in terms of their physical similarity and a medium shot of Elijah creates an eyeline match between him and Craig who, in turn, tells Elijah that he is lucky not to possess the 'terrible curse' of consciousness. In Cartesian mode and in contradiction with Elijah's implied empathy, Craig declares, 'I think, I feel, I suffer', thereby connecting consciousness with suffering and excluding Elijah from access to both.

Later in the film Craig's assumptions about Elijah are proved incorrect. Craig binds Lotte's hands and locks her in Elijah's cage. A flashback discloses the root of Elijah's trauma and gives the motivation for his decision to help her escape. As a youngster in the jungle Elijah witnessed his parents being caught in nets, their limbs bound by hunters. Unable to free them Elijah is also captured. The flashback sequence is constructed as if from Elijah's literal point of view with the addition of subtitles, which translate the screams of the captive chimpanzees as pleas for Elijah to untie them. On the one hand, the subtitles suggest that we are so inured to the cries of nonhuman animals that their meaning needs to be clearly signalled to us whilst on the other hand they also acknowledge an unbridgeable chasm of language and culture between chimp and human. Yet, the narration does not assume that this excludes Elijah from having moral agency. Indeed, Elijah's moral reasoning far exceeds that which is exhibited by the human characters in the film. Recalling his memories and his suffering, Elijah undoes the knots binding Lotte's hands allowing her to escape from the cage.

Being Known

The stories we find compelling are those that exploit the fantasy of shared language and moral agency in human – nonhuman primate relations. Yet, if Hearne is correct then the stories we tell are a form of disavowal, a denial of the unworkable relations between humans and chimpanzees which are located in the extratextual zones of these narratives. Our stories about chimpanzees end at their post-adolescence when long-term incarceration becomes the solution to the failure of training (which in itself is a process of suppressing chimpanzee agency through methods of domination) to construct an interspecies dialogue in which human and chimpanzee can agree on the moral significance of actions. For this reason, Hearne argues, we do not have satisfactory stories of chimpanzees; those that acknowledge chimp being. From the failure of the Chimpcam project we can assume that the answer to this problem will not be found by putting film cameras into the hands of chimpanzees. Maybe, Hearne suggests, the only stories we should have are those that are told about chimps in the wild, the stories given to us by primatologists or by those who observe chimpanzees in their own environment and are respectful of chimp being. There seems to be a general consensus amongst different knowledge communities, those of science and animal trainers, that we 'know' chimpanzees. In 2010 the International Union for Conservation of Nature (IUCN) noted that the eastern chimpanzee is 'among the best studied of the great apes'.[43] Yet, the eastern chimpanzee is classed as endangered due to illegal hunting, habitat loss, disease and the trafficking of infants for the pet trade. That the trade in chimpanzee infants is still thriving suggests that the stories we have told about human– chimp relations, those narratives of disavowal, still retain some purchase on our consciousness.

Notes

1 I am grateful to Sarah Atkinson who read and commented on a draft of this chapter.

2 BBC, *Natural World: The Chimpcam Project*, 2010.

3 There is a continuing popular fascination with nonhuman animals as agents of creativity. See for example press coverage of elephants painting http://www.dailymail.co.uk/sciencetech/article-1151283/Can-jumbo-elephants-really-paint--Intrigued-stories-naturalist-Desmond-Morris-set-truth.html and dolphin paintings http://www.telegraph.co.uk/news/worldnews/europe/lithuania/1495710/Dolphin-paintings--the-latest-in-abstract-art.html

4 See for example, Gallup, Gordon G., 'Chimpanzee: Self-Recognition', *Science*, Vol. 167, No. 3914 (2 Jan, 1970), 86–87.

5 Haraway, Donna, *Primate Visions* (London and New York, Routledge, 1989), p. 132.

6 *Ibid.*, p. 2

7 Washoe was taught to use American Sign Language (ASL).

8 The same year (1973) zoologist Karl von Frisch was given the Nobel Prize for his discovery that bees were able to communicate the location of food sources to each other by engaging in behaviour described as a dance.

9 By the 1980s the specialist field of bioacoustics also contributed to scientific debates about nonhuman animal communication. In 1984, Katherine Payne argued that elephants could communicate with each other over large distances using infrasound that operates below the level of human hearing and the study of whale and dolphin communication at research centres such as the Bioacoustics Research Program at Cornell Laboratory of Ornithology demonstrated how marine mammals communicated as part of their social interaction.

10 It is beyond the scope or purpose of this essay to deal with the extensive and various debates about the nature of language and ape communication. On the matter of ape communication, the acquisition of language and debates about grammar see: Greenfield, P. M., and Savage Rumbaugh, E. S., 'Grammatical combination in *Pan paniscus*: Processes of learning and invention in the evolution and development of language' in S. T. Parker and K. R. Gibson, *'Language' and intelligence in monkeys and apes: Comparative development perspectives*, (New York: Press Syndicate of the University of Cambridge, 1994) pp. 540–578.

11 Wallman in Savage-Rumbaugh et al., *Apes, Language and the Human Mind*, (New York, Oxford University Press, 2001) p. 154.

12 Wallman in Savage-Rumbaugh et al., *Apes, Language and the Human Mind*, p. 155.

13 Fudge, Erica, *Animal* (London, Reaktion Books, 2002) p. 117.

14 Hearne, Vicki, *Animal Happiness*, (New York, Harper-Collins, 1994), p. 167.

15 In July 1933 it was reported that during a film rehearsal Queenie 'climbed a high tension pole, touched a wire and fell', dying a few hours later (*The Milwaukee Sentinel*, July 11 1933, p. 1).

16 See: *The Desert News*, September 7 1957, p. 9; *The Sunday News Journal*, September 8 1957, p. 7A; *The Miami News*, December 21 1950, p. 20A; *The Press-Courier*, September 27 1962, p. 23; *The Age*, July 20 1959, p. 6; *Warsaw Times*, October 2 1951, p. 3; *Sunday Independent*, March 10 1959, p. 2; *Los Angeles Times*, February 22 1935, p. 14.

17 See for instance, *Kentucky New Era*, July 5 1939, p. 8; MGM trailer for *Tarzan And His Mate*.

18 *Spokane Daily Chronicle,* November 27 1936, p. 12.

19 Smith, Murray, *Engaging Characters: Fiction, Emotion and the Cinema* (Oxford, Clarendon Press, 1995), p. 21.

20 *Ibid.*, p. 20.

21 *Francis* (1950); *Harvey* (1950).

22 For a full account of Bonzo the chimpanzee, see: Molloy, Claire, *Popular Media and Animals*, (London, Palgrave Macmillan, 2011).

23 For a full discussion of animal stars and studio publicity see: Molloy, Claire, *Popular Media and Animals*, (London, Palgrave Macmillan, 2011).

24 *Lewiston Daily Sun*, April 6 1934, p. 4.

25 See for example: Peterson, Dale & Goodall, Jane, *Visions of Calaban: On Chimpanzees and People*, (Athens and London, The University of Georgia Press, 1993).

26 Ibid.

27 Until the later decades of the twentieth century, destinations for chimpanzees no longer considered suitable for work in the entertainment industries included research laboratories.

28 Having received little or no contact with members of their own species for the majority of their lives, adults cannot socialize with other chimpanzees and find it difficult to integrate with an established group.

29 Haraway, Donna, *The Companion Species Manifesto: Dogs, People and Significant Otherness*, (Chicago, Prickly Paradigm Press, 2003), p. 49.

30 Haraway, *ibid.*, p. 50.

31 Hearne, Vicki, *Adam's Task: Calling Animals By Name*, (London, William Heinemann Ltd., 1987) p. 49.

32 Haraway, Donna, *The Companion Species Manifesto: Dogs, People and Significant Otherness*, p. 52.

33 Hearne, *Adam's Task: Calling Animals By Name*, p. 34.

34 *Ibid.*, p. 40.

35 *Ibid.*

36 Witmer, L., cited in *The New York Times*, December 18 1909.

37 *The New York Times*, December 18 1909.

38 Kellogg W. N. & Kellogg, L. A., *The Ape and the Child: A Study of Environmental Influence Upon Early Behaviour,* (New York & London, McGraw-Hill Book Company Inc, 1933), pp. 280–282.

39 The Kellogg's did note however that Donald reproduced Gua's vocalizations and it was not until the end of the period of the experiment that he made any advances in human language acquisition (Kellogg, *The Ape and the Child: A Study of Environmental Influence Upon Early Behaviour*, pp. 282–287).

40 Hayes, K & Hayes, C., 'The Intellectual Development of a Home-Raised Chimpanzee, *Proceedings of the American Philosophical Society*, Vol. 95, No. 2, 1951, p. 108.

41 Haraway, Donna, *Primate Visions: Gender Race and Nature in the World of Modern Science*, New York & London, Routledge, 1989), p. 132.

42 In the film, Craig Schwartz, an unemployed puppeteer, ends up working for LesterCorp as a file clerk on the 7 ½ floor of a New York building and discovers a portal which transports him into the mind of the actor John Malkovich. Once inside, Craig finds that he can experience the world through Malkovich's senses while, initially at least, the actor remains completely unaware that anyone is occupying his head. After fifteen minutes Craig is expelled from Malkovich and finds himself on the New Jersey Turnpike. With a work colleague Maxine Craig sets up a business which advertises and sells the experience of being John Malkovich to the public. For $200 anyone can slide into the actor's consciousness and take the Malkovich ride. Craig's wife Lotte tries the experience and, as Malkovich, has an affair with Maxine. Craig finds out, becomes jealous and locks Lotte in a cage with her pet chimpanzee, Elijah. Malkovich, already suspicious that something strange is happening to him, finds out about the portal. However Craig discovers that he is able to control Malkovich as he would a puppet and decides to stay inside the actor for eight months. During his occupation of Malkovich's mind and body Craig establishes a relationship with Maxine and finds fame as a puppeteer finally realising the world recognition he has craved. Craig eventually leaves Malkovich who it transpires is a vessel for Dr Lester, the owner of LesterCorp, allowing him to prolong his life by moving from one body to the next. Craig ends up inadvertently moving into another vessel – Maxine's baby – from which he cannot escape and from where he must watch Lotte and Maxine who have fallen in love with each other.

43 IUCN (2010) online at http://www.iucn.org/about/work/programmes/ species/news_events/?5486/96-of-chimpanzees-could-be-saved-by-African-action-plan

3

Beyond the Pain Principle

Giovanni Aloi

The Return of the Gaze

The emblematic moment in which Jacques Derrida, emerging from the shower, found himself being looked at by his cat (another mammal), has consistently shaped the methodological approaches to most recent philosophical speculation on animals.[1] The questioning posed by this encounter highlighted the presence of an insurmountable communicational abyss between man and animal, one Derrida more accurately identified as 'the abyssal limit of the human'.[2] From this point onward, the return of the 'animal gaze' has extensively contributed to the re-thinking of the animal from object to subject and more recently to 'becoming' through the contemporary animal-studies discourse. The 'return of the gaze' acquired popularity in continental philosophy during the 60's through the discussion of the medial gaze by Michel Foucault and Lacan's analysis of the role played by it in the theorization of the 'mirror stage' through the development of the concept of identity. However, it was in the early 1970s, with the work of John Berger (*Ways of Seeing*) and through the essay 'Visual Pleasure and Narrative Cinema' by Laura Mulvey, that the concept garnered growing popularity.

In *Aesthetic Theory,* Theodor Adorno notes that there 'is nothing so expressive as the eyes of animals – especially apes, which seem objectively to mourn that they are not human'.[3] In Hegel, we find that the 'soul' makes itself apparent through the eye.[4] Therefore the centrality of this organ, within the spiritual context, becomes paramount to the essence of the human in opposition to the animal to which Descartes denies a rational soul altogether saying that ' ... the souls of animals are nothing but their blood ... '[5] In the light of these intricate complexities, discussing the return of the gaze in relation to a primate or other mammal is one thing, but attempting to apply the same concept to the compound vision of insects reveals the limitations involved in this approach.

Is Derrida's abyss too wide and too deep when the gaze returning ours is that of an invertebrate? Are there productive opportunities, exchanges and relationships involved in these kind of encounters, and if so, why have these been thus far overlooked in favour of a focus on mammals? This is of course a multifaceted argument, but most likely, one of the main reasons why mammals have been the consistent focus of our relations with animals lies in the inherent anthropomorphic approach to which they lend themselves; one that does not well function when encountering insects, nor other cold-blooded creatures. Anthropomorphism substantially is an innate way of engagement with the animal based on projection. In modern times it has developed an indissoluble bond with popular culture and its functioning, through the portrayal of animals as something human-like, is undisputed. The attribution of distinctively human traits to animals is not only, however, a commercial strategy facilitating the selling of animal bodies as cultural objects, but it is a seemingly inescapable reflex that all of us are prone to, in one instance or another.

The photographic project *The Inheritors* (2001) by Nicky Coutts captures the ambiguities of anthropomorphic imagery through subtle alterations of animal faces. Coutts' work directly challenges Levinas' assertion of the impossibility of the 'animal face' as distinguished from the ethical significance of the 'human face' (*Paradox of Morality*). In Levinas' phenomenological discussion, Otherness occupies a kind of primacy that, in the realm of the encounter, is always unknowable. To Levinas, the face becomes the threshold through which ethical obligation is established amongst beings and the unknowability of the other is the one element which continuously calls for a furthering of the relational. However, Levinas' consideration of the animal as Other is further complicated by his distinction between mammals and non-mammals in the light of the apparent biological condition in which 'lower' animals are segregated. In *Paradox of Morality*, Levinas was asked to further elaborate on the non-human through questions that directly challenged the applicability of his 'ethics of alterity' to animals. Then Levinas stated that the animal face is merely 'biological' and that it does not invite, nor command, a direct ethical response as the face of the other-human does. He then added: 'I cannot say at what moment you have the right to be called "face". The human face is completely different and only afterwards do we discover the face of an animal. I don't know if a snake has a face … I do not know at what moment the human appears, but what I want to emphasize is that the human breaks with pure being, which is always a persistence in being … '[6]

In the ten black and white photographs that form the series *The Inheritors*, Coutts replaced (through the use of Photoshop) the eyes of animals with those of humans (Figure 3.1). Our initial response is

Figure 3.1   Nicky Coutts, *The Inheritors (*2)* (1998), Black and White Photograph © Coutts.

dictated by the collapsing of our expectations, and it is soon after this first impression that the gaze of the human eye, superimposed on the animal, piercingly emerges. Is this face wholly animal or wholly human? The text is open. At an extreme, the images could be intended as the result of indiscriminate transgenic manipulation or as the suggestion of the inherent closeness between animals and humans: something that should define the ethical remit of our companionship. The superimposed human eye brings the animal to an uncomfortable level of equality with the viewer, and at that it makes a demand for a different relational mode through the allusion to an emotional world similar to ours. However, here too we find a limitation as Coutts does not attempt to give 'human eyes' to insects. In the series, a manipulated image of a snake surely stands out as a more challenging subject than the rest of the warm-blooded animals included. This is possibly because, much more than other animals, insects do not have such a thing as a face. They are all-eyes, all-mandibles and antennae, I do not know if an insect has a face …

In the light of this uncertainty it is therefore interesting to note that a photographic project by artist Catherine Chalmers, *American Roach* (2004) regularly generates controversy when exhibited because of the insect deaths involved in its making. The black and white images of which the series comprises, records an imaginary and highly anthropomorphized life of cockroaches (Figure 3.2). The project is structured in three different sections - *Executions*, *Impostors*, and *Infestations*. The *Execution* series sees roaches on an electric chair, being hung and burnt (seemingly alive). In the *Impostors*, the insects are given makeovers to look like different and fantastic insects altogether, at times becoming elegant looking hybrid creatures. In *Infestations* we find roaches dealing with their own day-to-day activities through the interiors of a dollhouse; their presence harshly clashes with the ornate and kitsch-bordering décor of the environment. Chalmer's photographic work resonates in different ways, with each series focusing on a particular relational dynamic. As viewers, we are at times almost surprised to find beauty in these insects, but we are however quickly reminded of their generally unpleasant qualities through their larger-than-life size. In the simple normality of this domestic space they have sex on our beds or drink from a bathtub.

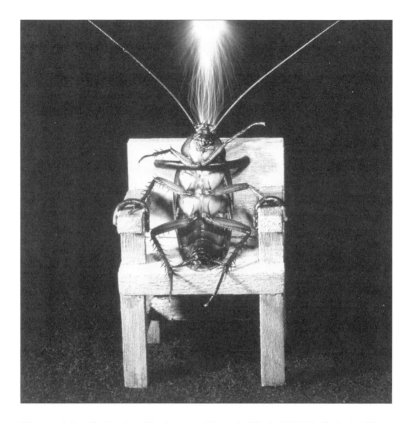

Figure 3.2 Catherine Chalmers, *Electric Chair*, (2003), Gelatin Silver Print, 40 x 40 inches.

It is however the *Executions* series which usually attracts more controversy as the insects have been effectively killed for the creation of these shots. This is where Chalmers' work poses challenges to our pre-conceived notions of an animal predominantly considered as pest. As in the case of other insect-pests like mosquitoes and flies, killing is an automatic response to intrusion. These insects are culturally perceived in the West as invaders of human spaces and as such should be exterminated. You will hardly find anyone complaining at a store selling insecticides and other insect-killing devices, so why do people react to Chalmers' images in such a different way? In the series *Infestations* the most upsetting element is the emphasized size of the insects, which in juxtaposition of the home interiors, would make them as big as dogs in real life. The series pushes us to reflect on our relationship with cockroaches and the role our size-differences play in the relational mode. Would we still kill roaches if they were the size of a dog? As the artist claims: 'Size is significant in nature. If an animal is large enough to eat you, you tend to give it more credence. If it's small enough to step on, one usually does it with impunity. The usual "predator – prey" relationship can easily reverse itself depending on which animal is larger'. [7]

In *Executions* however, the anthropomorphic representations, where roaches clearly stand in for human bodies, further complicate not only our relationship with these insects but also simultaneously deliver a commentary on the history of executions that defined Western, and especially American culture since early modernity. The death of the roach is here brought closer – and perhaps too close – to a human death through the staging of the execution: a killing of man by the hands of man. The value of different lives is brought into question. This overlay is key in the killing. If traditional killing methods are employed, such as for instance using insecticide, then the roach is rendered pest-like, in compliance with our expectations. In this case, the killing can take place with no remorse, or regret.

Speciesism

It is indeed in the field of animal rights advocacy that we encounter one of the most complex animal-issues in which anthropomorphism plays a key role. Since the term speciesism was coined by Richard Ryder in 1973 and then subsequently further contextualized by Peter Singer through the publication of his 1975 book *Animal Liberation*, the multifaceted and self-propagating discussions generated by the seemingly endless applications of this concept have consistently defined our attitudes towards animals in a multitude of fields. From animal rights activism to environmental campaigning, from shaping the concept of animal welfare in farming to the regulation of animal experimentation in pharmaceutical laboratories, speciesism has effectively marked a line, or more accurately, a series of blurred lines between the ethically justifiable, the excusable, and the unacceptable in our relationship with animals. Whilst it is not my intention here to dispute the achievements of speciesism in the field of animal-liberation, I propose to consider the impact that the blind-spots involved in the concept may have had in influencing our attitudes and approaches to animals.

A speciesistic approach involves assigning different values or rights to beings on the basis of their species of membership. In principle, the concept claims that animals should not be treated as objects or property in the light of their sentient qualities. However, those opposed to the recognition of human-like rights to animals, like Scruton, claim that anthropomorphism, through its distorting lens, plays a defining role in the ideas that animals and humans should be considered equal and that no distinction should be made amongst species.

In deconstructing the arguments associated with the concept of speciesism, we find that the generic term 'animal' is persistently used to stand simultaneously for a plurality of beings at once: a chimerical, compound body of some description that reminds us of those created by artist Thomas Grünfeld. The all-encompassing 'animal', extensively used by the principal philosophers of the Continental tradition, fails in signification if used to articulate the complexities presented by the postmodern animal. Derrida also discussed this idea in his text, but abandoned this point soon in his argument.[8] Further observation reveals that this chimera is one where all the body-parts seem to belong to different mammals. At times this might include the body-parts of birds, but never those of insects, arachnids, reptiles or amphibians. Of course this synthetic approach was pivotal to the development of the discourse on animals, but I suspect that we are now ready to open up the discussion in a new and more challenging way.

Paradoxically, it seems that through the speciesistic discourse some animals are represented as being more 'animal' than others. Therefore it could be argued that in the attempt to bring mammals and humans closer, speciesism may have also inadvertently distanced non-mammals from all others. It seems that the more animals are perceived to be similar to us, then the easier it is to anthropomorphize them, inducing us to acknowledge human-like rights to them. The assumption on which speciesism is based is that assigning different rights or values to beings on the basis of their species of membership is wrong. But what happens when we stretch further afield in the taxonomic order? What are the challenges involved in the encounter with a non-mammal? Moreover, what are the potential productivities that may lie at the core of such encounters and that we seem to be currently overlooking?

The concept of 'pain' has historically functioned as one of the main discriminatory tools employed in speciesism through its articulation of 'difference and similitude' between animals and humans. According to the utilitarian vein that runs through the concept pain is a negative quantity and the amount of pain felt or inflicted makes a difference between what is ethically acceptable and what is not. Here is where the largest problematic areas involved with speciesism can be encountered. What effectively is pain? one may ask. How do we measure other beings' pain? How do we know if other animals feel pain and if their pain is comparable to our own? Does this comparison bear any relevance?

In *The Animal that Therefore I Am*, Derrida asks 'Can they suffer?' and reaching for a plausible answer he explains: 'No one can deny the suffering, fear or panic, the terror or fright that can seize certain animals and that we humans can witness.'[9] It seems clear here that the 'certain animals' Derrida refers to are mammals, perhaps birds, at a stretch. Are all the others forever destined to a world of passive cultural existence? The scientific debate revolving around the subject of animals and their sentient/non-sentient qualities is constantly subject to revision. However, in our daily lives, our recognition of pain is entirely limited to what we perceive: screaming, twitching, bleeding, crying and so on. When these indexes are transposed to taxonomically more remote animals or even plants, a majority, or all fail in signification. Recent research consistently tells us that fish, crustaceans and insects can indeed feel pain.[10] However, these groups do not express physical discomfort in ways that are significant to us or that we can indeed witness. Their cryptic, apparently inexpressive faces and mechanical looking bodies, make it impossible to decipher familiar traits related to pain and suffering in humans. But their seemingly non-sentient state is largely the result of our inadequacy to understand their world.

Pain intrinsically calls for empathy. If an animal 'screams', then the assumption is that their pain is similar to ours. We clearly establish a sympathetic link with the animal based on formal analogies and assumptions. Beyond our sensorial perception, our measuring of pain is strictly bound to our scientific knowledge of biological reactions: these are by no means to be understood (as we seem to forget) as universally correct or exhaustive tools. Historically, due to technological advancements as well as cultural shifts, our understanding and acknowledgement of a number of phenomena has dramatically changed, bringing us to re-evaluate many quasi-dogmatic life-certainties. Could it be that one day soon, new technologies will enable us to better understand the sentient qualities of invertebrates? After all, we are always bound to the 'scientific extensions' of our senses, and as a consequence, we only measure the world with a humanly-limited set of tools. As Kant argued: 'we only perceive what the senses present to us, but have no knowledge of the way things beyond the impressions they give us really are'.[11]

When it comes to animals, it seems particularly evident that we are confined to 'the world of appearance' and that as Kant argues, this is of necessity not the real world, since it is heavily informed and shaped by consciousness. The world of reality, in Kant, is by definition unknowable, since the senses have no access to it. Could it be that establishing different connections between us and cold-blooded animals truly requires a conceptual leap of great proportion, one that we are not yet ready for? Or one that is too demanding and as such, the effort required would outweigh the rewards?

Notes Towards a Holistic Relational Approach

The writings of Kinji Imanishi, a Japanese ecologist and anthropologist, founder of Kyoto University's Primate Research Institute, suggested a different relational model with nature as early as 1941. In his book, *A Japanese View of Nature*, Imanishi re-thinks our understanding of animals, environment and humans by outlining a holistic cosmos where animals are an integral part of environmental systems and environments are seen as extensions of living things. The work of Imanishi is of particular interest as it operates across the fields of biology and philosophy, whilst pioneering views that today have come to the fore of ecological concerns. In the chapter 'Similarity and Difference', Imanishi explains:

> The category of living things includes both animals and plants, advanced and primitive things, and many in between; each inhabits its own world and leads a particular life so that each living thing should be studied in its own proper perspective.[12]

Through Imanishi's writings, the importance of considering humans as part of a holistic system, not just from an ecological but also a philosophical perspective, becomes very evident. In most recent times, a number of contemporary artists have awoken to the relevance of these challenges and have addressed them in original and creative practice.

The work of Cornelia Hesse-Honegger, for instance, presents an understanding of animals as an extension of the environment they live in and conflates meticulous artistic dexterity and scientific field-research to raise ecological awareness (Figure 3.3). *Herteroptera*, her illustrated book, functions as an interface between art and science; it denounces the endangerment of a beautiful and complex nature. Since the catastrophe of Chernobyl in 1986, the artist collected, studied and painted morphologically disturbed insects, which she finds in the fallout areas around nuclear power stations. In 1988, when the artist's groundbreaking research on Chernobyl was presented, her work was heavily criticized by the scientific community.

'When I published this work,' the artist recalls, 'scientists were extremely angry and for months the media was very busy discussing my paintings. The development of events showed, however, that the biologists had never monitored the health of plants or animals in the vicinity of nuclear power plants. I felt very insecure, not about my paintings or research but about the way I was treated: a single person against hundreds of scientists who had the 'truth' on their side and who considered themselves to be the only ones entitled to carry out official research. I wanted to reassure myself and find confidence to continue my research on the environments of the nuclear reprocessing plants Sellafield in the UK, and Three Mile Island in the US.'[13]

Insects, like other cold-blooded animals, tend to react more quickly to environmental change, offering the opportunity for rapid observation

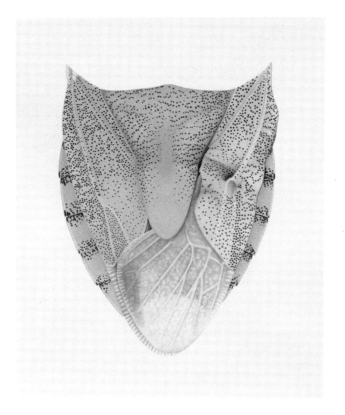

Figure 3.3 Cornelia Hesse-Honegger, Pentatomidae, Carpocoris, Tree Bug west of the Paul Scherrer Institute, Canton of Aargau Switzerland, Zürich, CH, watercolour, 47 x 36 cm, 2000.

and data gathering. Through her practice, Hesse-Honegger takes on a very brave and specific artistic persona that allows her to bring key evidence to wide audiences. Her scientific knowledge allows her to formulate theses and to test these through field research. As in the work of scientists, at times the thesis is proved inaccurate and reformulations may occur.

One instance of this kind was presented by Brandon Ballengée, whose practice bridges the gap between research biology and art. In 1996, he began collaborating with scientists to create hybrid environmental art/ecological research projects. His work combines a research interest in fish and amphibians with the techniques of

Figure 3.4   Brandon Ballengee, *DFB 42, Êléktra Ozomène*, Scanner Photograph of Cleared and Stained Multi-limbed Pacific Treefrog from Aptos, California in Scientific Collaboration with Dr. Stanley K. Sessions. MALAMP titles in collaboration with the poet KuyDelair. H 46 inches × W 34 inches, 117 cm by 86 cm Unique IRIS print on watercolour paper (2008) Courtesy the Artist, NYC.

commercial art and scientific photography. Ballengée, like Hesse-Honegger, is involved directly in field research and uses the visual impact of scientific illustration to engage the public in the discussion on broader environmental issues (Figure 3.4). Of his borderline status as artist/scientist Ballengée says:

> I have a long history of collaboration and cooperation with scientists. When conducting primary experiments, I employ rigorous scientific methods and discuss experimental design with

scientists to insure validation of the results. If enough quantifiable data is collected to suggest a phenomenon, it is shared with a larger scientific community through publishing in peer-reviewed journals. [14]

Interestingly, in July 2009, Ballengée solved the scientific mystery of the deformed amphibians before any other scientist involved in the investigation of the phenomenon.

'Deformed frogs became one of the most contentious environmental issues of all time, with the parasite researchers on one side, and the 'chemical company' as I call them, on the other', says Stanley Sessions, an amphibian specialist and professor of biology at Hartwick College in Oneonta, New York. [15]

Through a series of experiments, Ballengée and Richard Sunter, the official Recorder of Reptiles and Amphibians in Yorkshire, discovered that if attacked by a natural predator, such as a dragon fly larva, when they are very young, they can often regenerate their leg completely, and at times, multiple legs appear.

At times functioning as alarming indicators of environmental degradation that will inevitably affect all of us, and at others figuring as elusive signifiers of our intrinsic sense of guilt towards the planet, it is apparent that in the work of these artists insects and amphibians are not looked at as a subject as such but as an extension of the environmental realities of which they are parts.

Jakob von Uexküll's concept of 'umwelt' offered an interesting opportunity for a change in attitudes towards animals in general and especially towards those taxonomically distant beings as he expressly formulated the concept whilst studying ticks at the beginning of 1900. [16] His interest in the infinite variety of perceptual worlds of imperscrutable animals drove him to develop the concept of umwelt to avoid being trapped in the false knowledge imposed by anthropomorphism. Could umwelt cross the boundaries of philosophy and science to inform larger audiences and so guide our perception and understanding of these animals towards new trajectories? Can this concept be 'translated' to reach wider audiences to truly have an impact on our relations with cold-blooded animals?

Over the past ten years, a Colombian artist, Maria Fernanda Cardoso, has developed an international reputation for her body of work focusing on insects. She has very little doubt about her collaborators:

> Of course all living things are sentient beings. How could you eat if you did not feel hungry? How could you avoid danger if you couldn't perceive it or couldn't fear it? How can you live if you don't know what's good for you and what's to be avoided?[17]

Her most famous work is perhaps the *Flea Circus*, where the stunts of real fleas are magnified and beamed onto screens for the amazement of the audience (Figure 3.5). We see flea wire-walkers,

Figure 3.5 Maria Fernanda Cardoso, *Maria Fernanda Cardoso as Queen of the Fleas* (1995) © Cardoso.

flea trapeze artists, flea cannonballs and so forth. Apart from the spectacle involved (an element also worthy of scrutiny), it is rather remarkable that Cardoso effectively establishes a close relationship with one of the smallest, and most undesirable insects in the world. As she explains, the fleas are directly rewarded by letting them feed on her blood ... but, as it stands, she lives off them as well. In this work she effectively tries to figure out the *umwelt* of the fleas to identify relevant 'carriers of significance' which are the elements that trigger the insect's interest. How does she obtain cooperation from the fleas?

> I try to imagine how the fleas perceive me and the world around them, and try to re-create or use aspects of it to my advantage. I try to use those key elements so I can induce certain behaviours. It's not that hard to do. I know they like heat, my heat, the heat of a warm-blooded animal (food). I know they perceive vibrations and react to them, and pupae only hatch with vibrations. (I imagine me or a dog walking past must feel like an earthquake—food is like an earthquake). So I use that. My ballerinas dance on the vibrations of a musical box, as the sound-waves activate them. Because there is music they look as if they are dancing, but they are just getting ready to jump onto their next host. I know they want to go up, either crawling or jumping, as food is always upwards. So I can make them go up a rope or climb to a mountaintop, even if they don't know it's a mountaintop or a tightrope. We do, but they don't. They think they are climbing up an animal or towards an animal. I know they perceive shadow and light. I know they like some types of light, but I don't know why. And so on. I try to find what they like and provide it to them. Punishment doesn't work, even though I crack a tiny whip.[18]

Portuguese designer Susana Soares uses bees' and mosquitoes' exceptional odour perception as part of a beautiful and strange medical-sensing device establishing a brilliant human-nature collaboration that takes advantage of untapped naturally-occurring phenomena. The artist explains:

> The idea behind *Why Me* is that people will find out, in a playful way, if their body odour is attractive or unattractive to mosquitoes.

It works in a rather simple way: two people place their hands on the opposite sides of the object and in an average of 90 seconds the insects will invariably fly towards the most attractive scent. [...] Unattractive chemicals might be a sign that the person they are about to feed on is unsuitable due to stress caused by illness or disease. This also generates shifts in the way we perceive mosquitoes as in this case it would be a positive thing that the mosquito chooses you as it could be signifying good health.[19]

Soares claims that new advances in areas such as genetics, biotechnology and nanotechnology are changing our very nature, not in a way that we can perceive, not as an act of natural selection or evolution, but due to technology. How is this going to affect our behaviour and what implications are involved? In a near future, people could be equipped with organs that would enhance their perceptions allowing them, amongst other things, to have brushy nails that will scrape genetic information while touching. Who's going to use them and what for? In which situations would we need them? In both cases, we find that these artists develop a very intimate knowledge of the biological and behavioural peculiarities of rather generically undesired insects usually relegated to the category of pests.

Experiencing Animal Subjectivities

Kenneth Rinaldo is an artist and academic who creates multimedia installations that also blur the boundaries of art and biology through the use of a highly sophisticated technological interface. For over two decades he has been working in the fields of interactive robotics, biological art, artificial life, interspecies communication, rapid proto-typing and digital imaging. One of his most innovative projects from 2004, *Augmented Fish Reality*, is an interactive installation of five rolling robotic fish-bowl sculptures designed to explore interspecies communication (Figure 3.6).

These robotic sculptures allow Siamese fighting fish to use intelligent hardware and software to move their robotic bowls under their control. Fighting fish have excellent eyes capable of seeing outside the bowl; they have colour vision and seem to like yellow.[20]

Figure 3.6 Ken Rinaldo, 3D Visualization of *Augmented Fish Reality* Installation 2004 © Rinaldo.

Small 'lipstick video cameras' mounted under two of the bowls capture images of the interior of the fish bowls as well as humans in the gallery environment. These images are intercepted by video transceivers and projected onto the walls of the gallery space to give human participants a sense of both looking at the interior of the tanks and feeling as if they are immersed in them.

The half-fish half-machine robots included in the installation are constructed with laser cut aluminium and tig-welded together. The microprocessors and motor control sit in a waterproof box and the sealed lead–acid-battery provides the power necessary to operate the mechanical parts.

These are robots under fish control; the fish may choose to approach and/or move away from the human participants and each other as the systems are designed to allow the fish to get to within a quarter of an inch of each other for communication between one another. The most recent research by Culum Brown at the University of Edinburgh argues that fish intelligence is much greater than originally believed.[21] Fish are now regarded as steeped in social intelligence whilst also displaying cultural traditions and cooperating to view predators and obtain food. Some fish have demonstrated impressive long-term memory and the ability to mentally map their environments in finding food, creating relationships with each other and avoiding predators.

Augmented Fish Reality suggests that the development of micro-machines, biotechnology and computer systems will further collapse the gap between the organic and inorganic world as these machines expand the spectrum of senses available to humans and other animals. Intelligent systems, coupled with sense-extension lenses, are getting progressively more transparent and embedded in deeper levels of our sensorium. Thus the perceptual alterations that may occur through these lenses are less and less overt. The next question, the artist explains,

> [I]s what kind of implants are possible that will allow us to augment and extend normal ranges of hearing? Perhaps to the subsonic or ultrasonic levels so we can hear the ultrasonic chirps of bats or sub audible rumblings of killer whales, without cumbersome electronics. This will certainly increase the possibilities for interspecies communication. What new knowledge and ways of seeing might we have access to with new extended senses? What other senses, like vision, touch, or smell could be augmented? Might we create a sixth sense that would allow us to directly sense pheromones? What more can we understand about animals signalling, if we could really use computers, sensors and statistical analysis of body languages in relation to certain situational and environmental cues, that would allow us to really understand how animals intercommunicate?[22]

The interest for working with fish in the attempt to establish a relational approach has recently increased. This may largely be because of the radical challenges posed by the underwater condition, something artist Anthony Hall has tried to address in the attempt to enable humans to establish a communicative link with electric black ghost-fish. In the *ENKI Technology* project, the fish are kept in a tank and the human participant wears headphones and light frames (used to expose the eyes to controlled bursts of light) and the human test subject is immersed for 15 – 30 minutes in controlled light and sound. Although the specific technology used is only a little different from the early electronic mind machines of the 70s, the difference here is that the fish is in control of any sound and light the human is exposed to. The electrical signal sent by the fish is transmitted to the human body and it creates an electrical image for the fish to read. Through this communicational network, we may experience as closely as possible what it may be like to be a ghost-fish, if only by proxy. [23]

The desire to experience the subjectivity of other animals is however not a new quest for the formulation of a posthumanist thesis. The controversial essay 'What is it Like to Be a Bat' (1974) by American philosopher Thomas Nagel argued that phenomenal subjective experience is not expressible through objective terminology. A bat is a mammal, but one of the most peculiar kind. For instance, it is capable of flying, but most importantly, it also has an extra sensorial capacity called echolocation, which we humans lack. At once, the bat is radically different from and similar to us. Nagel claims that ' … no matter how the form may vary, the fact that an organism has conscious experience *at all* means, basically, that there is something it is like to *be* that organism'.[24] This condition 'is not analyzable in terms of any explanatory system of functional states, or intentional states, since these could be ascribed to robots or automata that behaved like people though they experienced nothing'[25]; however this does not mean that we should not acknowledge its existence. Nagel recognizes that bats have experience and that '[w]e must consider whether any method will permit us to extrapolate to the inner life of the bat from our own case, and if not, what alternative methods there may be for understanding the notion'.[26]

Scientific progress has largely contributed to the creation of an extended sensorial ability on our part, but does this fulfil Nagel's curiosity for experiencing otherness? Inspired by the challenges posed by Nagel's essay, artist Eduardo Kac devised, in 1999, a project titled *Darker Than Night,* which aimed at establishing an empathic relationship between humans and bats. The piece was staged in a cave (in Rotterdam) that was home to over three hundred Egyptian fruit bats. In order to bridge the sensorial abyss between humans and bats, Kac created a life-size 'batbot' (robotic bat) containing a small sonar unit inside its head and a frequency converter capable of transforming bat echolocation calls into audible sounds. [27] Through a virtual reality head set and the decodification of the signals received by the sonar unit in the batbot operated by a computer, audiences were able to view a diagram of the robot's ultrasonic display. The batbot functioned as a dialogical interface, its presence communicating the existence of the audience and the audience enabled through the robot to read the presence of the bats in ways which closely mirrored the perceptive world of the bats themselves. [28]

Would this experiencing of what it is like to be another animal contribute to our relational modes with non-mammals too? The current state of affairs in popular culture suggests that the animal-rights messages against animal cruelty have worked relatively well within the context of mammals; however invertebrates and other cold blooded animals have not been granted any rights at all and therefore are killed in front of TV cameras for the purpose of entertainment.

As we consume animals for food or other purposes, society implicitly seems to adhere to a hierarchical structure suggesting that killing one animal is fine (the majority of insects fall in this category) whilst killing another (usually mammalian) is more problematic. The popular TV program *I'm a Celebrity ... get me Out of Here!* offers a good example here. Since its first series was aired in 2002, the programme routinely included the unnecessary and relentless killing of invertebrates of all kinds, as well as the mistreatment of a range of cold-blooded animals. This killing went predominantly unquestioned until, on the 6th of December 2009, the BBC reported that *I'm A Celebrity ... Get Me Out Of Here!* winner Gino D'Acampo and Stuart Manning faced charges of animal cruelty after cooking and eating a rat in the show. [29] Police confirmed they had issued court attendance notices for the 3rd of February 2010. [30] The RSPCA stated: 'The killing of a rat for a performance is not acceptable. The concern is this was done purely for the cameras'. [31] The following day, The *Guardian* reported that 'ITV has apologized over the killing of a rat on *I'm a Celebrity ... Get Me Out of Here!* and will change the show's guidelines to ensure it does not happen again'. [32] On the 8th of February 2010, ITV was fined $3000 Australian dollars.

Interestingly, newspapers around the world widely reported the news but duly missed the opportunity to question what the real difference between killing rats or insects may be. Is this in anyway a question relevant to wide audiences? To find a hint of such daring thinking, one has to look online at the conversations amongst readers which grew in response to the article. One reader of *The Independent* interestingly points out: 'The RSPCA have obviously taken their eyes off the ball here. Whilst Gino and Stuart were busy getting stuck in to a nice bit of rat, their fellow contestants spent the whole of the series eating live grubs, insects and arachnids all in the name of entertainment. Did the RSPCA miss all of that? Maybe I'm naive in assuming that insects are animals? Or are they just not cute enough to bother about?'[33]

Why did the RSPCA react so strongly towards the killing of one rat whilst the systematic killing of cold-blooded animals programmed in the day-to-day running of the show received no objections? Why did none of the reports mention the paradoxical double standards which clearly drove the RSPCA's reaction? The turn of events poses a number of questions about our attitudes towards animals and the ethical issues involved in the killing of this and the other, the pest, the pet, the sentient and the allegedly non-sentient. As the program is truly internationally popular, and has been running for eight years attracting an average of 9 millions viewers per show, one may ask what its impact on viewers and their understanding of animals may be.[34] We could even go as far as asking why is it even possible to produce and air a TV show which capitalizes on the killing of invertebrates and cold-blooded beings in this time and age? What does this say about our global culture? Which part of the animal rights message did not work to prevent this?

In 1995, in a defining revision of *Animal Liberation*, Peter Singer himself drew up some considerations on the sentient qualities of taxonomically more distant animals and surprisingly took a 'U' turn on his initial standpoint establishing that ultimately, taxonomically more remote beings should be treated as we would treat other mammals. However, this part of the argument does not seem to have the same impact as the original one in favour of mammals.

Returning to the discussion of anthropomorphism and its influence on our understanding of animals from an early age, I am here left wondering if the disparity in approach to mammals and non-mammals effectively starts at this point, through the anthropomorphic projection and the sense of connectedness with the world that it may instil in the child. As a result of this reflexive process all animals and other beings that do not lend themselves to the anthropomorphic relational mode are excluded and fall in the background. At times, when they are encountered, a sense of disgust, indifference or apathy prevails, so that no relational mode different from that of pure objectification becomes possible. The words 'so that each being can be studied in its on perspective' by Kinji Imanishi apply well to this circumstance. Could it be that from an early age, children may be educated to relate to animals in different ways? Instead of presenting animals to them as curious and anthropomorphized caricatures, would it be possible to guide them through an understanding that certain animals will be able to engage in a relational mode of some kind and that others simply will not? In so doing, it may be possible to assert that they should not be looked at as inferior and worthless, but only as different.

Notes

1 Derrida, Jacques, *The Animal That Therefore I Am,* (New York, Fordham UP, 2008).

2 *Ibid.*, p. 12.

3 Adorno, T. *Aesthetic Theory*, (London, The Athlone Press, 1997), p. 113.

4 Hegel, G. W. F. *The Philosophy of Fine Art*, (London, C. Bell and Sons, 1920), p. 206–7.

5 Descartes, R., 'Letter to Plempius, 3 October 1637' in Kenny, A. (ed), *Philosophical Letters*, (Oxford, Clarendon, 1970), p. 36.

6 'The Paradox of Morality: an Interview with Emmanuel Levinas' Conducted by Tamra Wright, Peter Hughes and Alison Ainley. In Bernasconi, Robert and Wood, David *The Provocation of Levinas: Rethinking the Other.* (London and New York, Routledge & Kegan Paul, 1988), pp. 168–180.

7 'An Interview with Catherine Chalmers', questions by Aloi, Giovanni and Hunter, Chris, in *Antennae* , Issue 3, Volume 2, Autumn 2007, pp. 29–30.

8 *Ibid.*, p. 23.

9 *Ibid.*, p. 28.

10 See the forthcoming paper by Robert E. and Mirjam A., *Journal of Animal Behaviour.* in which they report on a study of hermit crabs collected from rock pools in County Down, Northern Ireland.

11 Kant, Immanuel, *The Critique of Judgement*, (Oxford, Oxford University Press, 2007).

12 Imanishi, K., *A Japanese View of Nature – The World of Living Things*, (London, Routledge Curzon, 2002), p. 7.

13 Hesse-Honegger, Cornelia. Interviewed by Giovanni Aloi for Antennae, 2008, in *Antennae* 11, 2009, p. 34.

14 Ballengée, B., 'Beyond Classic Field Biology: Batrachian Deformities, an interview by Tim Chamberlain', in *Antennae* 10, Summer 2009, p. 16.

15 Walker, M., 'Legless Frogs Mystery Solved', Story from BBC NEWS: http://news.bbc.co.uk/go/pr/fr/-/earth/hi/earth_news/newsid_8116000/8116692.stm Published: 25/062009 09:48:43 GMT accessed on 14/07/10.

16 von Uexküll, J., 'A Stroll Through the Worlds of Animals and Men: A Picture Book of Invisible Worlds' in *Instinctive Behaviour: The Development of a Modern Concept* (New York, International Universities Press, 1957), pp. 5–80.

17 Cardoso, Fernanda, 'Our Lady of Mimicry, interviewed by Sonja Britz' in *Antennae* 11, 2010, p. 24.

18 *Ibid.*

19 Soares, Susana, 'Pavlov's Bees, interviewed by Zoe Peled', in *Antennae* 11, 2010, p. 53.

20 Rinaldo, K, 'Augmented Fish Reality', online text, http://accad.osu.edu/~rinaldo/works/augmented/augmented.html accessed on 10/04/10.

21 Brown, C. (ed), *Fish Cognition and Behaviour*, (Oxford, Blackwell Publishing, 2006).

22 Rinaldo, K. 'Interview with Giovanni Aloi, Augmented Fish Reality', in *Antennae* 2, Summer 2007, p. 9.

23 Hall, A., 'ENKI – Human to Fish Communication', in *Antennae* issue 13, Summer 2010, p. 29.

24 Nagel, Thomas, 'What is it Like to be a Bat?', in *Philosophical Review* 83, October, 1974, p. 323.

25 *Ibid.*

26 Nagel, 'What is it Like to be a Bat?', p. 324.

27 Kac, E. *Telepresence & Bio Art*, (Ann Arbor, The University of Michigan Press, 2005), p. 203.

28 Nagel, 'What is it Like to be a Bat', p. 324.

29 'I'm a Celebrity D'Acampo and Manning Face Rat Charges', Story from BBC NEWS: http://news.bbc.co.uk/go/pr/fr/-/1/hi/ entertainment/8397691.stm Published: 2009/12/06 17:53:21 GMT accessed on 20/06/10.

30 *Ibid.*

31 *Ibid.*

32 Conlan, T., 'I'm a Celebrity: ITV apologises for killing of rat', *The Guardian*, Monday the 7th of December 2009.

33 Panchoballard, 'What About the Insects?', comment entry to 'ITV Fined over "I'm a Celebrity Rat Killing" by Davis, Margaret', published on Monday, 8 February 2010 at 04:37 pm (UTC) http://www.independent.co.uk/news/media/tv-radio/itv-fined-over-im-a-celebrity-rat-killing-1892608.html.

34 www.barb.co.uk accessed in February 2010.

PART TWO

Representing Animality

4

What We Can Do: Art Methodologies and Parities in Meeting

Bryndís Snæbjörnsdóttir and Mark Wilson

A Toe in Muddy Waters

The equally manifest senses of purpose, enthusiasm and urgency generated within animal studygroups internationally over the last few years have led many to adopt a position of righteousness and an acceptance of greater commonality between human and non-human animals, bound up in a broad set of sensibilities kindled by the residual sparks of late 20th century race, gender and sexuality conflicts.

Much has been written and much read from this basis and a back catalogue of theoretical discourse has provided the framework not only of thought, but also of response and discursive action.

The irony in this seems to be that in sanctioning a dependency on the same learned and developed faculties, those of language, the absence of which in other species has been traditionally used to demonstrate our distance from and superiority to non-human animals, we continue to distinguish and distance ourselves from, rather than draw any closer to, our subject and by so doing compromise the possibility of the 'otherness' of understanding that might otherwise accrue around alternative approaches to animals. Where such approaches are attempted, the results are often dismissed as being fanciful – impossible to evaluate on the simple grounds of their intrinsic lack of accountability by means of rational analysis.

Whilst it is perfectly possible to imagine a useful analysis of an 'other' understanding through language, such understanding may prove only to be achievable in the first instance by some other means – through for instance the honing and application of intuition and instincts – faculties which although they may vary in degree and mechanics between species, nevertheless are shared tools by which all species may sense and 'read' the world. In relation to anthropocentric perspectives and human superior capacity of self awareness and linguistic expression, it is worth noting recent research on the brains of whales, particularly humpback and finback, as it has revealed a close similarity to the structures of the human brain. Large quantities of spindle cells considered to link us to a higher cognitive awareness and allow us to feel love and suffer emotionally have been identified in whales.[1]

Hof, quoted in the *New Scientist,* says: 'We must be careful about anthropomorphic interpretation of intelligence in whales'. Considering that these faculties have developed in whales for a considerably longer time than in humans, it could possibly mean that their skills of communication including the application of intuition and instincts are developed beyond human understanding. These scantily understood faculties within ourselves, despite their sophistication and precision are indeed subjugated and marginalized by our dependence on 'our' language and as a consequence whilst continuing to serve us and our survival in more ways daily than is comprehendible, are all too often considered to be it seems, residual, archaic and primitive.[2]

Art practice, that positions itself between subject and audience, in order to raise questions about routine behaviour and habitual thought, offers a way forward which may fly in the face of acceptable logic but in so doing, asks disturbing and/or constructively disorienting questions. Beyond the strictures of the spoken and written word, its capacity is to deploy image, sound or more generally, the speculative juxtaposition of disparate elements and to gather and compare observations through an encounter. It does not aim to find reductive solutions or conclusions but to instigate the possibility that we, individually or collectively, may practically look again and see with new eyes how things in the world are configured. In our own (Snæbjörnsdóttir/Wilson's[3]) art practice we apply relationality as a keystone of our methodology to encourage within the viewer/audience a greater sense of connectivity and hopefully as a consequence, a more holistic understanding. In this respect we acknowledge the philosophy of the eco feminist Val Plumwood as exercised in her article 'Being Prey'.[4] Here she places human animals on a par with non-human animals in that just as other species are prey to us, humans may equally be objectified as prey, from the perspective of the animal. Similarly, Bruno Latour (2004) in his theories on the collective, proposes that we turn the clock back to a time before humans began classifying some beings as belonging to nature and others as belonging to societies or culture. In defining non-humans, amongst other phenomena he includes species, water currents, machines, documents and so on and proposes in his Actor Network Theory or ANT that human and non-human be treated alike.[5] His theories and writings have also contributed to our keenness to promote relationality as being part of our art practice. The themes we explore in our artwork therefore and indeed which are developed in part in this paper, are intended to clear a space for the conceptualization of a new lens by which such scrutiny and analysis might be conducted. In fact in contemporary art in general, the presentation of an effective framework by which questions are configured is often the most specific intention, allowing a plurality of responses to occupy the vacuum that is thereby created.

In this article we hope to unravel the methodologies employed by our collaborative practice through which we propose challenges to the anthropocentric systems of convenience that sanction a daily acceptance of loss-through-representation, suggesting instead as a way of investigation, the alternative idea of 'parities in meeting'. Furthermore we hope to explore what drives our shifting regard for non-human animals (such as it is), the degree to which this too is ultimately self-serving and whether it is a fleeting or a growing phenomenon.

Through the work we ask to what extent any true or 'better' understanding of non-human animals is related to closeness, empathic alignment or indeed immersion with those we have traditionally regarded as the 'other'. And in 'looking' at animals, are we looking towards a closer understanding and engagement with non-human species or are we really only productively able to scrutinize ourselves as detached, rather than participatory observers?

The Human Supremacist: A Journey into Darkness

Maehle and Tröhler (1987) recorded that the experiments of one of Vesalius' pupils, Realdo Colombo (1516–59), involving pregnant dogs, were greatly admired by members of the Catholic clergy:

> Colombo pulled a foetus out of the dog's womb and, hurting the young in front of the bitch's eyes, he provoked the latter's furious barking. But as soon as he held the puppy to the bitch's mouth, the dog started licking it tenderly, being obviously more concerned about the pain of its offspring than about its own suffering. When something other than the puppy was held in front of its mouth, the bitch snapped at it in a rage. The clergymen expressed their pleasure in observing this striking example of motherly love even in the 'brute creation'.[6]

In relation to accounts such as these which in today's terms, for many of us, seem unequivocal in their cruelty, we would want to orientate the reader at some distant point on a spectrum of human/non-human animal encounters – to begin in other words with closeness of kinship rather than with the objectification that is required to enact such cruelty and abuse.

When imagining encounters of any kind in respect of other species it may be useful to re-examine definitions in order for us to clarify the nature of what is going on. We need to look at issues such as contrivance and spontaneity in terms of the encounter: who if any has arranged the meeting? Are both parties equally caught unawares – has it happened by chance?

To answer these questions, considerations regarding captivity, domestication, wildness and the parameters of contact might be helpful. Does the meeting take place under conditions where one party does not have the freedom enjoyed by the other? Do the circumstances of the meeting or engagement mean that a degree of familiarity between the parties already exists? Familiarity and indeed the closely related 'trust', suggest a reliance on learning and memory.

In wildness we can presume the least preparation in respect of our encounters to occur. Here we may expect the unexpected. In hunting and shooting expeditions, taking place in the wild and indeed in those concerned with wildlife photography the relationship is once more slewed: the animal has been tracked down, the encounter staged, resulting either in a dead animal body on the ground or in the analogue/digital traces of some oblivious animal being stored on film or the camera's memory card.[7]

When we consider the types of communication possible between humans and other vertebrates – including humans, birds, mammals, reptiles – we can be confident that in our encounters and subsequent engagement, there are broadly three shared senses by which communication may be transmitted or received. For us these are sound, vision and touch.

Sound is carried predominantly through vocalizations – we vocalize and for our own purposes might use words, but our intonation is the quality most likely to be effective in any communication, just as we may not understand the specifics of what another may be expressing but through its intonation we communicate with both subtlety and something more akin to parity.

Despite the faculty of sight too often being considered in modern Western European tradition as the most 'objective' sense because in fact it is least involved with the object of observation, visual signals between vertebrates can nevertheless be also extremely eloquent in shaping our mutual understanding of one another. From appearance, both parties may express fear, submission, ease, excitement, agitation, boredom, affection and so on by the way we hold, carry or disport ourselves. What is not intuited may be learned. Berger (1972) has pointed out that 'seeing comes before words' meaning that a visually able child recognizes through vision before it speaks. He goes on to propose that later in life there is a tension in the relationship between what we know and what we see and that tension is always active.[8]

To us touch seems to be the most compelling means of letting our intentions towards the other be known. Through touch, we cross a physical threshold directly and it is through the acceptance of touch by the other that in the same instant, we claim for ourselves his or her acceptance of us and importantly, we render him or her vulnerable. Simultaneously we ourselves must be prepared to be made vulnerable by this process. Perhaps it is for the power we identify in touch as a register of trust, that stories abound which indicate that so many of us seem intent on absolute proximity, if not intimacy with other species, as a means of expressing or exercising an empathetic connection. The desire for an empirical manifestation of this trust will drive people to perform acts which may often be perceived by others to be alternately foolhardy, rash, outrageously intrusive, dangerous and certainly irrational. Ron Broglio[9] has pointed out that 'traditionally, touch has been considered less "objective", because it is involved/ enmeshed with the other. It can be said to embrace intersubjectivity and thus a certain kind of messiness. But an acceptance of some scruffiness may be a necessary consequence of unhitching ourselves from the locomotive of reason'.

When researching for the project *between you and me*[10] we interviewed a young farmer, Knútur Óskarsson at *Ósum* in the north-west of Iceland. Besides continuing to manage a depleted farm business he also ran a youth hostel and services for tourists. There is a seal colony on the margin of his farm and some years ago it was a valuable resource in terms of its meat and skin. Today the seals have another, more intrinsic value as a tourist resource. Óskarsson has not however capitalized on this resource directly by charging for instance a fee. Instead he sees it as his role to inform visitors about the seal as an animal whose importance is critical to the nature of this area. It can be observed but has to be left to take care of itself. For the tourists he has installed a gate and a fenced off path of about 500 metres leading to the seashore. From there the seals can be observed swimming in the estuary or lying on the sand flats across it. The information that Óskarsson provides is in the form of conversation – no signs or leaflets are available. In our interview with him he described some of the many different approaches people have to this animal:

> I mean people are no good; some people want to kill them and then I have people who want to make love to them and I am not joking, just seriously want to make love to them. I had this discussion I remember [with] this German girl – I said. 'Hey you cannot make love to a seal. If you would get close enough it would bite you and it is a bad bite with infection'. This is how it is. I think people have to be educated in psychology and I am really not interested in why she had this [idea] but I have met quite many people like this and the thing is today people have not the right ideas about nature. Many people have these Disney ideas, unrealistic ideas about nature – that is the main problem. The second problem is [that] people are takers. They don't respect nature. They don't allow the seals to lie there and have their own habits. They just want to take and consume and then they are gone. I remember this German guy who took off all his clothes and this was a warm summer night and he was lucky that he did not kill himself because the streams are quite rough and then he was standing there totally naked and swam over to the other side because he wanted to go and scratch the seals behind the ears or something or I mean whatever he wanted to do. He did that and of course the seals went away but this was on low tide but then he had this problem – he didn't think this through. He had this problem because he was standing on the other side naked, his clothes were on this side and the tide came in and there is quite a difference so he actually had to walk. [It] took him the whole night, about 18km and the funny part about the story [was] not in the next farm but the one next to it is living this really nice old farmer Joey, a really nice old man and he was driving on his tractor down on the fields [on an] old Massey Ferguson. Then he saw what seemed to be a naked man walking on the black sand waving. He just thought I am hallucinating I am seeing things that are not real. So he drove home and went into bed again and the man was there [waving] help, help … [11]

The acts, which sit outside the 'norms' of behaviour will often by definition invite criticism. Before rushing to condemn, we should remember that in seeking to examine the nature of communication with other species in any terms other than those of a one-way street of human interest and power, (obedience, subordination, etc), we expose ourselves to accusations of a kind of idiocy – simply because in so doing, we too buck the established consensus that animals are either provided for us and must therefore serve our needs, or alternatively are to be observed at a distance (often for human reasons of science, taxonomy, surveying, tourism etc) for their intrinsic value – or finally, to be ignored entirely.

Timothy Treadwell (1957–2003) was an environmentalist who over a long period conducted his own studies on the grizzly bears in the *Katmai National Park* in Alaska. The study involved living with the grizzlies for 13 seasons before finally, with his girlfriend Amie Huguenard, he was killed and devoured by the bear(s). Treadwell, made famous in a film by Werner Herzog entitled *Grizzly Man*, was not scientifically trained, but saw himself as a protector of these animals.[12]

In Werner Herzog's film *Grizzly Man* (2005), Timothy Treadwell is portrayed as weak. This fragility or weakness, placed in parallel to an exercise of power and control in the guise of the director, opens up a different way of looking; one in which the gaze is turned in on itself. The idiosyncratic voice-over, and the consistent transparency of the opinions in Herzog's narration, contribute to the exposure of a clutch of binaries; sane versus insane, conventional versus unconventional, circumspect versus rash. Similarly these binaries also reveal the inconsistencies and gaps in a human being's authoritative rationality, on the one hand declaring the deceased to have been a trespasser in the space of the other, but on the other exercising a punishment on the 'non-human animal', who is not allowed to exercise power on or over human animal beings who knowingly encroach on its world. In the film, Larry Van Daele, a bear biologist, explains Treadwell's mistake and what distinguishes him from those scientifically trained, in that he tried to understand the bears through attempting to 'be a bear'. To empathize is seen to be tantamount to anthropomorphization, the projection of human emotion or behaviour onto the animal, a trait often associated disreputably with pet-keeping and the domestication of animals. Due to its 'wildness', from this perspective, a bear is seen to be beyond subjection to such frivolous associations. But in order to empathize, to 'get under the skin of another', one has to try to imagine how the other feels, whether the other is human or animal, and this strategy might instead be seen as a first step towards carving a transitional space in which human and non-human species meet on renewed terms to the benefit of both.

In Thomas Nagel's essay 'What is it Like to Be a Bat?' (1974) he points out that we know a lot about bats, that they perceive the world around them through sonar or echolocation, sending high frequency shrieks to detect objects and prey within their range and to determine from the consequent echoes, precise information concerning distance, shape, substance and motion. Nagel goes on to say:

> But bat sonar, though clearly a form of perception, is not similar in its operation to any sense that we possess, and there is no reason to suppose that it is subjectively like anything we can experience or imagine. This appears to create difficulties for the notion of what it is like to be a bat. We must consider whether any method will permit us to extrapolate to the inner life of the bat from our own case, and if not, what alternative methods there may be for understanding the notion.[13]

The essay goes some way towards expressing the impossibility of imagining the experience of others with any degree of success, particularly when such awareness is based on the acknowledgement of profound difference. But if we are to move at all, we must use what tools we can and navigate between the recognition of differences on the one hand and the identification of similarities, to the heart of what has become a cultural nexus of contradiction. It is not only Treadwell who displays anthropomorphic tendencies when it comes to the grizzlies. The pilot (Sam Egli) who over the years flew Treadwell out to the Grizzly Maze, goes a step further in suggesting that the bears accepted Treadwell for so long because of his perceived slight insanity. Interestingly and paradoxically, Sam Egli seems to believe that the bears are able to detect whether people are sane or not, and act accordingly. He even goes so far as trying to imagine what the bear that killed Treadwell and his girlfriend Amy Hugenard was thinking. Similarly, Herzog makes reference to the 'blank stare' of the bear, signifying dispassionate boredom that can 'also be seen in strangers that we meet in the street in cities'.[14]

In Treadwell's own video footage from which the film was largely constituted, he can be seen to 'encounter' the bears in a spirit of equality, landing him simultaneously in what Donna Haraway has referred to as 'concatenated worlds'.[15] The fact that he met his death at the claws of this species is not a desired end and is not intended here to act as an exemplar for the post-humanist interspecies perspective pursued in this text, but it was an end which in the film Treadwell was realistic enough to envisage for himself. In *Grizzly Man* Treadwell's 'idiocy' is suggested and played on by Herzog to marginalize Treadwell himself and in so doing, to reinforce the old established line between preconceptions of 'nature' and 'culture'. It is exactly the inevitability of this cultural perception that Val Plumwood took on and challenged when writing of being subjected to three death rolls during her near fatal encounter with a crocodile.[16] Treadwell's death is used as a demonstration of the consequences that await those who cross the 'invisible line'. It is in fact this modernist inclination to such polarities that sustains and activates anew the fear of the other and thus lends a particular and dubious purpose to the Herzog film. Had another perspective been drawn it might have acknowledged the achievement of Treadwell and the role that his particular, scientifically transgressive, 'amateur' approach played in reappraising boundaries between species.

What is rarely acknowledged in most stories of human and animal encounters is the imposition that such proximity constitutes for the animals in question. In the case of the wild animal, the model is already there in respect of our extincting of species, because historically we have taken insufficient care to anticipate the consequences of our proximity and interaction. Perhaps just as pertinently, in the case of other human cultures and civilizations, where the terms of engagement were unequal (i.e., not based on consensus exchange and trade) our impact has all too often been devastating. The term 'consenting adults' springs to mind as an equivalence, not in any way to infantilize the other but as a means of identifying the disparity that can exist in encounters between cultures and species where the integrity of one party is unequivocally compromised – in short where there is a profound imbalance of power.

Limina: Meetings on the Shore

When we (Snæbjörnsdóttir/Wilson) propose the concept 'parities in meeting', paradoxical in its human conceptualization as this may sound, it is with such considerations of history and trepidation in mind. And if it is not too fanciful, we propose also an approach that imagines a relationship that is uncompromising, between consenting species.

In 2009 we exhibited the installation work *between you and me* at the Kalmar Konstmuseum, in Kalmar, Sweden. A smaller version of the project had previously been shown in Australia as part of the international conference *Minding Animals* in the same year. The research focus for this had been the relationships between seals and humans around the coast of Iceland and one component was a performative video work titled *Three Attempts* (2009). We had been made aware of the curiosity of seals and their apparent preference for bright colours, and in the video we observe Snæbjörnsdóttir, dressed in an orange anorak, approach the seashore overlooking an estuary and kneel down facing towards the sea with her back to the camera (Figure 4.1). Our

Figure 4.1 Snæbjörnsdóttir/Wilson, *Three Attempts*.

preliminary research had revealed that it was common for hunters to imitate seal sounds when trying to entice the seal pups away from the cow, suggesting that seals were sensitive to certain types of sound or sound frequencies at least. In the initial video performance, a variety of vocal sounds were used, from singing to the imitation of ring tones from mobile phones. Initial attempts prompted little in the way of 'reciprocation' on the part of the seals and nothing very much altered at all in their behaviour. The technical reasons why the work was remade are not, in themselves, important for this text but rather, the fact that they necessitated another visit, which resulted in giving us more than the remake we planned, to the extent that it became a completely new work. We are very much aware of the difficulties in attempting to remake works and it is something we generally try to avoid. Nevertheless, for the reshoot the location was the same, as was the time of year – the same clothing was worn and we even began at the same time of day. Even the weather was similar. The only thing it seemed, beyond our control that day, was the behaviour of the non-human animals in the water, and sure enough, their response confounded our expectations. From the moment we arrived on the shore, to set up the equipment, the seals made an appearance, popping up from the water, looking, playing, diving and reappearing. The 'control' had shifted from us to them – it was their game now. Our initial reaction was a sense of despair but slowly and convincingly it dawned on us that the only appropriate response was to be 'with' the seals in this moment. The performer soon relaxed into the role of the one being looked at, whilst visualizing the image being recorded in the rolling video camera behind – the back of a seated human being on black sand at the shore, the rippling, bright water revealing numerous dark heads popping in and out of view, against a backdrop of distant snow-topped mountains. The process of making this work is described here in order to draw attention to the requisite states of vulnerability and surrender necessary for its execution. This vulnerability is manifest in an image taken in a natural environment, of a lone figure with his/her back to 'the watching world'. A sense of apprehension experienced by the artist is conveyed in the tentative approach of her performance. The unpredictable behaviour of the participant animals required an acceptance of the relinquishment of human control in this instance, and indeed its desirability. *Three*

Attempts is the embodiment of a number of principles underpinning our work and its functionality. From one perspective the work seems a novelty – its charm observed to be infectious and disarming. From another it touches on the absurd – it echoes with pathos and even melancholy. It is difficult to see the work without acknowledging a degree of sentimentality but in common with absurdity and vulnerability our rejection of sentiment is a cultured, negative response based on the desirability of strength through the application of intellect.

A current discourse has emerged (most recently and notably in the Arts Catalyst exhibition *Interspecies* 2008/9, Manchester/London) surrounding the potentiality of human, non-human 'collaboration'. It was suggested during the *Interspecies* seminar in London in which we took part that the work *Three Attempts* falls into a category of human/animal art collaboration – occupying as it does a space in which human and non-human animals meet and interact. In this work Snæbjörnsdóttir chose not to enter the space of the seal (namely the sea) but sat instead on the shore, as close to the sea level as possible. Notwithstanding this acknowledgement of 'threshold', we allow that there was, to a certain degree, a division of power as it was clearly 'our' work; we directed the camera and the scene was framed for a project in which the seals had no editorial say.

When talking about collaboration with animals we have to begin by defining what we mean by collaboration. For us it is understood to be an act agreed to by all parties concerned. An attempt is made to establish some form of framework where individual powers are respectively channelled constructively for the overall benefit of the collaborative project. That said, any implicit equality of roles or contribution tends to be compromised when one party alone draws up the parameters at the outset, and this compromise may only be partly assuaged by responsiveness to unpredictable developments arising from the behaviour of the other party. In short, if a way cannot be found in which to negotiate equal terms for the collaboration – it is not collaboration. In attempting to understand the possibilities of human, non-human animal collaboration we human animals still seem reluctant to let go of the reins or to find ways of working with what is there rather than what we would like or can contrive to be there. In this respect we may all too easily be seen to be treating others as circus animals. An animal might do unusual tricks for example, or be instrumentalized to become the mechanism by which something of ourselves is revealed, but we need to be able to see that behind that use is an implicit loss of freedom for the animal, a loss of identity, and a likely physical, psychological or ethical abuse. In short, through representation the animal itself is lost. The dichotomy is one born out of our own dependence on power and intentionality and revolves forever around issues of integrity and relationality. If we accept the integrity of dynamic relationships we can go forward in this, but with caution and respect for matters we cannot presume fully to understand.

The Politics of Play

What may not ultimately be easily explained or justified is the purpose of our interest in this suggested parity, beyond its being generally a good or tantalisingly desirable thing. It seems good because it bucks an accepted behavioural trope in relation to the other. Good because in doing so we may discover something which may for a long time have been overlooked – a consequence of staying within the bounds of acceptable behaviour and of being so sure of our separateness and distinctiveness, when in fact, any natural extrapolation of evolutionary theory actually seems to unravel most claims for the specialness of our case. We believe that other species may have much more commonality with us than is recognized, which we just do not or cannot see because the type of knowledge upon which we have come to rely that provides us with and supports our world view, precludes it. Because we share a world with other species, why would we not be interested in the principals of interconnectivity when an eschewal of such interest for so long has left us unprepared for all manner of environmental effects and consequence?

Not long after embarking on a trek in Hornstrandir in the far northwest of Iceland during July of 1999, our paths crossed with some of the denizens of that area, most memorably, an arctic fox in its dark, summer pelage. The animal actually sought us out, clearly having noticed us from afar and as he trotted towards us, we became aware of his purposeful if casual approach only as he drew near. Hornstrandir is a reserve area of around 240 square miles, almost entirely unpopulated by humans. The fox has no predators here and when humans show up from time to time he is far more curious than wary. In fact this was more the case then than in 2009, as ten years ago the visits of tourists were less frequent. It can nevertheless be suggested that as this was a nature reserve, the fox had also learned that humans bring disposable food with them, thereby providing an easy meal for the day. As for us, we were sluggish under the weight of nine days shelter and provisions – he was light, inquisitive and in the mood for a game. And this is just what ensued. Once up close he began to leap and bound around us, feigning attacks and withdrawals in rapid succession and behaving as much like an adolescent pet pup as is imaginable. The surprise of course was not that he was in many ways 'like a dog', but simply that he was playing in such a disarmingly relaxed manner around aliens on his patch. Both here in the encounter with the fox and previously with the seals when making *Three Attempts* we have found it appropriate to deploy words such as 'game' or 'play' in order to elucidate not just the apparent nature of the respective meetings, but also a form of exchange or communication, significantly, beyond words. It is in a particular type of play involving the feint, the lunge and equally rapid withdrawal, the teasing appearance and disappearance, intended there is no doubt, to provoke a response, that body language is seen conspicuously to take precedence over other forms, allowing a genuine trade of reflexes, privileging intuition and instinct.

The performance of Joseph Beuys in *I Like America and America Likes Me*, (1974) has been referenced innumerable times in animal studies discourse and will no doubt continue to be referenced for many proper reasons in the future. For the purpose of this text we raise it again as in the footage that survives the event, an evolving relationship can be detected between the two protagonists, Beuys and the wild, but environmentally compromised coyote, Little John. The coyote was imported into a loft gallery space in New York, (from whence is frustratingly unclear) to meet and cohabit for three days with the artist. Their relationship begins with a degree of wariness on the part of both – wariness and respect. Whilst it is conceivable that Beuys consciously deployed respect in his dealings with the coyote and that conceptually this was always strategically going to be the case, the documentation of their meeting nevertheless seems to reveal a study in inquisitive negotiation and the process of two beings getting to know one another in unfamiliar surroundings.

Back in Hornstrandir, our fox, with all the freedom in his world to choose, bobbed and darted around us for a good fifteen minutes as we walked; we laughed and yes, spoke to him and around the time we sat down to take off our boots to cross a river, he became bored and scampered off in the direction of a distant flock of seabirds he had spotted at the river mouth. Ten minutes later a commotion of startled gulls signalled his mischievous arrival amongst them.

Since 2007 we have been researching for a project titled *Uncertainty in the City*, commissioned by the Storey Gallery in Lancaster. As part of this project we designed a mobile radio station called *Radio Animal*[17] with which we have been touring around England and at the beginning of October 2009 we took it to London as part of the *Interspecies* project mentioned above. *Radio Animal* has been investigating contested spaces and our conflicting categorizations of what constitutes a pest. Among those whom we interviewed in London was the acclaimed historian and one of the founders of the British Animal Studies Network, Dr. Erica Fudge. Fudge told the story of a mouse (or mice) inhabiting her kitchen and how by giving it a name, she had overcome her antipathy towards this animal. Giving an animal a proper name is a common identification strategy in nature studies, applied equally often but for different reasons by those working scientifically, for instance like Ian Douglas-Hamilton in his study of elephants[18] and for amateurs such as Timothy Treadwell in his study of grizzly bears. But as a means of bestowing individuality to reduce anxiety we detect another more telling dynamic. In 2009 we were invited to give a talk at Sheffield Hallam University as part of a series of events titled *Transmission: Host,* which explored the concept of 'The Stranger'. Our host was Chloë Brown and together we made a bookwork as part of the series, in respect of which the editor Sharon Kivland, quotes Jacques Derrida:

> … the stranger is the one who is irreconcilably 'other' to oneself, but with whom one may co-exist without hostility, to whom one

must respond and to whom one is responsible. The stranger reminds one of the other at the heart of one's being.[19]

Applied in this context the statement could be seen to suggest our desire strategically to accept the animal through the identification within ourselves of a parallel and correspondent 'other'. A further qualification of this would arise from considering the dynamic of naming as 'owning' and Fudge herself has described the act as a kind of co-opting of the mouse into a kind of 'pet hood'.

We are not Alone

At this juncture, we ask what if intellect alone is not enough for us to understand our new and challenged position in the world? Indeed, what if the rationality of our approach obscures or limits the possibilities of wider understanding? Ultimately the video work *Three Attempts* is not solely concerned with our relationship to the seal, but is a 'landscape' work that simultaneously acknowledges the integrity of landscape and its constituents whilst interrogating what the term has come to represent. The back of the artist is turned towards the lens of the camera, which is the eye that we human-animals so easily and often mistake as our own in perceiving and understanding the world. It is an insinuation between the audience and the event, which it partially occludes. All the readings mentioned in the previous chapter, of charm, absurdity, pathos, melancholy, sentimentality and vulnerability are indeed embedded and to be found in the work and yet just as crucially, they serve to fuel and extend another more fundamental reading – that 'landscape' or 'environment' if they are to mean anything in the future, must cease to be objectifying terms, which describe 'something to be looked at' or used whilst simultaneously functioning as registers of our detachment from them. Just as increasingly we understand that other animals are specifically so in relation to the constitution of their dwelling, so we must nurture a larger economy of thought and larger sense of community recognizing our own interdependence with habitat and the danger that by sustaining our unfettered and exploitative use of 'resources', including land and 'animal others' we resolutely keep our backs turned on the enlightening and rewarding conversation we might otherwise have.

Where the cultural deployment of animal representations in general seeks or has managed to frame and delimit our understanding of the non-human animal, it is hoped that art of the kind proposed in the above examples can test such practices and invite a reappraisal of these relationships. Because most representations are constructed to perform some agenda of our own – in the case of animals, to entertain, to inform, to provide food, to stand for all of a species, to symbolize human behavioural characteristics and so on – in this process, the animal itself is occluded – eclipsed by its avatar or likeness, which is always a simplification and therefore must accordingly signify a loss. In another component of the installation *between you and me* the audience is invited to follow at close quarters the transition of a real although dead animal body as it is made to become a representation of itself. The work titled, *the naming of things*[20], scrutinizes and we believe reveals the flawed nature of the presumption and pitfalls of our attempts to close up and enforce a reductive approach in our world-view. In juxtaposition to the other works (the series of interviews, *Three Attempts,* etc.) in the exhibition it allows us the space to think through and thus challenge what we have come to believe it is to be 'animal', what it is to be 'human' and what indeed is 'landscape' and to consider the consequences of the abbreviated forms with which we populate our intellect and our experience. As it is upon these accepted but polarizing constructions that we human-animals base our behaviour towards other species and to our environment, at this time it seems appropriate to be digging deep and deploying whatever methods may be at our disposal in order to reappraise their contemporary validity.

So with this in mind, consider our experience as we made our way on foot one morning along the southern perimeter of Hyde Park in London. It was autumnal, sunny and we were deep in conversation as we walked. The traffic was medium to medium-heavy. The nature of the conversation is not remembered but we do recall that out of the blue, we were interrupted by a voice, clearly intoned over the noise of the traffic. The voice said, 'Hello'. Immediately, we stopped in our tracks. Ahead there was no one to be seen and as we looked behind, there was nobody even within shouting distance. The voice came again, 'Hello', this time clearly from overhead. We looked up and there, perched on a telegraph wire directly above us was a crow. He/she stared at us inquisitively and as we gaped, said it again. Naturally, we returned the salutation and this time the crow reciprocated. We stood there, the two of us on the pavement and the crow aloft, for over five minutes, exchanging greetings in a bewilderingly agreeable and curiously private encounter on that warm fall day.

Crows are great mimics. Unlike many species, we recognize and acknowledge their intelligence (because we think it is like our own). This bird, free as it seemed, may well have been trained when young by a carer, to say some words. Notwithstanding this, to be deliberately and formally addressed by a member of another species, so unexpectedly and in English, was simultaneously both uncanny and touching and it reminds us of the childhood wish exercised so exhaustively in literature and film that animals could talk. In the same way a contemporary desire is expressed for a genuinely collaborative relationship between humans and other species, it is clear that intentionality is the key to the viability of such a project. In the absence of a common, syntax-based language we must continue to look elsewhere to facilitate and develop any possible symbioses of purpose.

Notes

1 Patrick, R. Hof, E. V. d. G. 'The structure of the Cerebral cortex of the Humpback Whale, megaptera novaeangliae (Cetacea, Mysticeti, Balaenopteridae)' *The Anatomical Record*, 2006, 10.

2 Coghlan, A. (2006). Whales boast the brain cells that 'make us human', *NewScientist*: http://www.newscientist.com/article/dn10661-whales-boast-the-brain-cells-that-make-us-human.html Accessed 4/1/2010

3 Snæbjörnsdóttir/Wilson is the collaborative art practice of the authors, Bryndís Snæbjörnsdóttir and Mark Wilson. Their art practice is research-based and relational.

4 O'Reilly, J. *Ultimate Journey: Inspiring Stories of Living and Dying* (San Fransisco: Travelers' Tales, 2000) pp. 128–148.

5 Latour, B., *Politics of Nature* (C. Porter, Trans.) (Cambridge: Harvard University Press, 2004).

6 Maehle, N. R. T., *Vivisection in Historical Perspective*: (London: Routledge, 1987) p. 18.

7 Ryan, J., ' 'Hunting with the camera': photography, wildlife and colonialism in Africa' in C. Philo & C. Wilbert (eds.), *Animal Spaces, Beastly Places: New Geographies of Human - Animal Relations* (London, New York: Routledge, 2000) pp. 203–222.

8 Berger, J., *Ways of Seeing* (London: Penguin Books, 1972) p. 7.

9 A conversation between the authors and Ron Broglio in 2009.

10 Snæbjörnsdóttir/Wilson, 2009.

11 Snæbjörnsdóttir/Wilson (Artist) (2009) *between you and me* [Installation]

12 Treadwell, T., *Among the Grizzlies* (New York: Ballantine Books, 1999).

13 Nagel, T. 'What is it like to be a bat?' *The Philosphical Review, 83*(4), 1974, pp. 83–84.

14 Herzog, W. (Writer). (2005). *Grizzly Man* In A. W. H. Film (Producer). UK: revolver entertainment.

15 Gane, N., 'We Have Never Been Human, What Is to Be Done? : Interview with Donna Haraway', *Theory, Culture & Society, 23*(7–8), 2006, pp. 135–158: 145.

16 O´Reilly, J. *Ultimate Journey: Inspiring Stories of Living and Dying.*

17 www.radioanimal.org

18 Mitman, G., 'Pachyderm Personalities: The Media of Science, Politics and Conservation' in L. Daston & M. Gregg (eds.), *Thinking with Animals, New Perspectives on Anthropomorphism* (New York: Columbia University Press, 2005) pp. 175–196.

19 Brown, C., & Snæbjörnsdóttir/Wilson *Transmission: Host* (London: Artwords, 2009).

20 Snæbjörnsdóttir/Wilson, 2009.

5

Horse-Crazy Girls: Alternative Embodiments and Socialities

Natalie Corinne Hansen

Hasbro, the world's second largest toy-maker, first introduced the small, mass-produced, and inexpensive My Little Pony (MLP) doll in 1982. Now a widely recognized brand with multiple product lines and visual and digital media formats, My Little Ponies are colourful, cartoon-like soft plastic figures with long manes and tails that can be brushed and fashioned. Today's My Little Ponies are unambiguously female and are aggressively marketed to girls, as is made perfectly clear on the My Little Pony homepage, which states: 'Welcome to Ponyville! For more than 20 years, MY LITTLE PONY has given little girls a world of surprises and spontaneity, sunshine and silliness'.[1] A look through the multiple pages of products on the website reveals an array of Pony figures and accessories. The Ponies have alluring, fanciful 'girly' names, such as 'My Little Pony Graceful Glimmer as the Winter Crystal Princess Pony'. This small white Pony has a long silver mane and tail and comes with a 'tiara-dress,' which lights up, a ring, a brush for her hair, and a barrette. Other options are the 'Flower Garland Pony,' one of a series of 'Divine Shine Ponies' identified by birth month (October), birthstone (pearl), favourite colour (powder blue), and favourite pastime ('collecting fancy purses'). Ponies also come in alluring flavors, appealing to the implied 'edibility' of these figures. For example, 'My Little Pony Butterfly Island Sunny Scent Pineapple Paradise Pony,' is a bright pink Pony with a yellow and green mane and a yellow tail 'scented like fresh, sweet pineapples'.

Representative of the latest generation of MLP is 'My Little Pony Pinkie Pie', whose overall form depicts the dramatic morphological changes MLP has undergone over the thirty years since its inception. MLP began as a relatively recognizable rendition of a small stocky pony but has transformed into increasingly sexualized versions that conflate girl bodies and horse bodies: 'Today's My Little Pony displays upturned, accentuated buttocks; smooth, glittery skin; a tilted head; an exposed neck; long eyelashes; lowered eyelids; dilated pupils; long, slim legs; shifted weight; accentuated hair—even, in some cases, parted lips. The Budweiser Clydesdales these are not'.[2] Pinkie Pie moves ever farther from the original model whose elongated, recognizably equine head is radically shortened and rounded to appear now almost fully human. The facial features as well have become more human with exaggeratedly large eyes migrating to the front of the Pony's face and the long equine muzzle diminishing in size to more closely resemble human proportions. The Pony's head dominates her body, erasing the animal body and emphasizing the child-like face. The once thick equine neck has disappeared, resulting in the Pony's fetishistically excessive hair emerging out of her forehead and out of the back of her, clearly human, skull. The Pony's torso is slight and, in this case, her lower half sports a 'super-cute skirt,' which is just short enough to suggestively mark the perimeter of the genital region, accentuating her seductively poised posterior. The short stubby legs that hold this pony on all fours are no longer straight but ovoid, bulbous, suggestively morphing toward a softer, rounder shape that mimics breasts.

The transformation over time of MLP into an increasingly recognizable human form reflects a resistance to the representation of difference that also characterizes Barbie's history as an object of normative representation. The coupling of gender difference and species difference in the case of My Little Pony parallels questions of difference and recognition that Ann Ducille addresses in critiquing Mattel's approach to representing race and ethnicity in the Barbie product line. Ducille asks 'How does difference look?' and suggests that 'the most intriguing questions are about what makes possible the mass production of difference'.[3] Ducille links the homogeneity of Barbie's unchanging body type and Mattel's stereotyped approach to representing racial and ethnic difference through surface variations in skin tone and clothing. What Ducille identifies as Mattel's unwillingness to alter Barbie's body type to more accurately represent the female population as a whole is linked to socio-cultural power disparities and long histories of colonialization, genocide, slavery, and racist and sexist oppressions. The erasure of species difference in My Little Pony traces practices of domestication, in this case of the equine body, that transforms horses into figures of sexualized human fantasy.

A similar critique of the representation of difference appears in Regina Buccola's 'Dusty, the Dyke Barbie'. Focusing on the heteronormative representation of women encoded by Barbie, Buccola reads a competing doll, 'Dusty' (produced in the late 1970s and throughout the 1980s) as Barbie's lesbian 'doppelganger'.[4] Buccola notes that Dusty, who is white, along with her partner doll, Skye, who is black, and their equine companion, Nugget, emerged out of the 'crises of gender, race, and class' of the late 1960s and early 1970s. Dusty and Skye presented more 'masculine' figures: 'Their waists were rather thicker than the average Barbie, their chests considerably smaller, and their feet flat, rather than form molded to accommodate stiletto heels'.[5] These figures were designed to engage in activities such as tennis and horseback riding, with 'legs [that were] bendable to facilitate the various sports around which their accessories revolved'.[6] In their morphological alternative to the hyper-feminine Barbie, Dusty and Skye resisted Barbie's message about normative gender embodiment: 'As a doll offered dressed in denim from head to cowboy-booted toe with a lovely horse to ride, Dusty's tomboyish athleticism was the attribute most often trumpeted about her. Her body possessed none of the features that mark Barbie as the ultimate emaciated, surgically altered, dyed, and heavily made-up feminine beauty "ideal"'.[7] The trio also offered non-normative trajectories for play, reflecting the opening of competitive sports to women that followed passage of Title IX in the United States: 'this variety of doll play, though still only the simulation of athletic activity, nevertheless modeled a wider range of behaviours and lifestyle choices than dressing up in skin-tight skirts and stiletto heels waiting for a date in the Dream House'.[8] Dusty and Skye ultimately failed as consumer products, a failure Buccola suggests is likely due to consumer resistance to the dolls' more ambiguous gender presentation. Bucolla does, however, note a counter-tradition among lesbians who identify the presence of Dusty as the 'dyke Barbie' of their pasts, including herself in this tradition while also confessing that the imaginative play with Nugget, Dusty's equine companion, ultimately lead to riding lessons, highlighting a link between horses and alternatives to gender-normative identification.

For Ducille and Buccola the inability of consumer products to represent difference reflects our anxious desire to contain otherness within easily readable markers, as in the case of Barbie, with women's bodies reduced to a single idealized body and a single normative sexuality. Such reduction renders women's bodies equally 'manageable' and thereby non-threatening to the existing order of race, gender, and class. Reducing species difference to four legs effects a similar move. The disappearance of equine specificity manifest in MLP continues the colonization of animal bodies that undergirds humanist ontological, epistemological, and empirical traditions, in which the animal body functions as a definitional figure for the human.

As Roland Barthes points out, 'toys *always mean* something, and this something is always entirely socialized, constituted by the myths or the techniques of modern adult life'.[9] My Little Pony offers a version of girlhood identification that negates the possibility for gender diversity as well as species difference. MLP certainly offers an identity for girls that tracks along familiar heteronormative lines: 'Within popular culture this generalized coupling of girls and horses ("pony mad") ... operates in opposition to that of girls and boys ("boy crazy") in order to produce a normative sexual structure of femininity'.[10] Girls are given license to be horse-crazy as long as this passion is seen as a training ground for future 'proper' male love objects. In order to 'mature,' girls must give up horses for boys. The desexualization of childhood, the construction of childhood as 'innocence' reflects what James Kincaid (1998) argues is our investment in the child as empty vessel into which we can project our adult erotic imaginings. The 'erotic innocence' of MLP has to do with the overt illegibility of the hybrid Pony-Girl whose sexuality is deflected into and negated by the reference to the equine body that, in being nonhuman, is a sexually forbidden body and, as such, is all the more desirable. In this way, girlhood sexuality becomes a marketable product, but the threat of an embodied sexual agent is deflected, preserving the adult/child separation: 'the child is that species which is free of sexual feeling or response; the adult is that species which has crossed over into sexuality'.[11] Defining the child as nonsexual places sexuality at the definitional boundary of the adult: 'What is most at stake is our capacity to know desire: the child is not simply the Other we desire but the Other we must have in order to know longing, love, lust at all... . The child is the embodiment of desire and also its negation'.[12]

In the imaginary world offered by MLP, the emptiness of the child partnered with the emptiness of the animal produces a fantasy world already determined by adult expectations. Barthes suggests that the overdetermination of imaginative options represented by toys such as MLP means that the child is never able to 'invent the world' he or she inhabits.[13] The child is turned into a consumer of already pre-determined scripts. For example, the narrative that accompanies Pinkie Pie offers instructions on how to engage with this object:

PINKIE PIE is everyone's best friend! She's always dreaming up something fun to do that will keep everyone laughing and smiling all day long! Dressing up is extra fun with friends! Your pretty PINKIE PIE pony has picked out a super-cute skirt to wear. Use her brush accessory to brush her hair so she'll look as lovely as can be and then decide where you two fashionable girls will spend your day. Will it be a party? Or a picnic? No matter what you choose, you're sure to have tons and tons of stylish fun![14]

Comparing MLP to the adult version, vividly represented in Steven Klein's photo series of Madonna in the stable, translates the sexualized Pony-Girl into the dominatrix of pornographic fantasy. Klein's photos feature Madonna, along with six burly stallions who serve as backdrops for the sadomasochistic fantasy world created by the photos. Klein's series references, intentionally or unintentionally, Edward Steichen's photo from 1935, 'White,' which features a sturdy white stallion and three female models dressed in flowing white gowns posed against a wall of white tile. Klein changes the colour scheme to black and adds the overt references to sadomasochistic/bondage-and-domination and bestiality. Madonna's outfits include black House of Harlot latex rubber shorts, fishnet stockings and stiletto-heeled leggings. She carries a whip in the majority of images. In addition to the play against normative sexuality that we expect from Madonna, here in the form of S&M/B&D imagery, these photos add the element of species difference with the implication of bestiality and with the transformation of Madonna herself into a horse. In one image, Madonna wears a specially designed, jewel-encrusted bridle, complete with bit and reins. Clad in form-fitting black attire and black gloves, echoing the black bodies of the stallions, Madonna leans up against the bars of a stall, head lowered in a pose of submission. An accompanying image places Madonna kneeling on the floor of the stall, again clad in her bridle and black spandex, knees spread, with her arms and hands reaching out to mimic a horse rearing.

Other 'accessories' that dramatize Madonna's transformation include a formal riding hat to which a long black 'mane' has been added and a 'saddle belt' that perches a tiny replica of a saddle on her rump along with sweeps of black lace mimicking a tail. The text accompanying the photos states, 'As any equestrian worth her jodhpurs can tell you, the relationship between a woman and her horse transcends the boundaries of sport... . When the woman in question is Madonna, one can expect the dynamic to get even more complicated'.[15] This text makes explicit the images' references to alternative sexual practices. As Carla Freccero points out in her analysis of Madonna's early MTV videos, 'Fetishism is eroticized ... so that it is not the body as a reified and fixed identity that is celebrated, but bodies as conditions of possibility for multiple pleasures'.[16] Part of Madonna's appeal has historically been her play with 'erotic transgression',[17] including her representation of women as possessing 'sexual agency and choice'[18] and her play with masturbation and homoeroticism. In Klein's series, Madonna is the only human who appears, suggesting the intimacy between her and the stallions is an individual one, one that does not include human sexual partners. The imagery that transforms Madonna into a (clearly female) horse suggests her sexual partnership with the stallions and alludes to the space of the stable as a space of intimacy between woman and horse. In this way, the photos suggest alternative erotics of cross-species love and cross-species identification. The images fall short, nonetheless, by the heteronormative over-determination of their narrative.

A more productively queer rendering of girl-horse (and by implication woman-horse love) is the work of Deborah Bright whose photo series 'Being and Riding' demonstrates the subversion of normative plays of both gender and species that can emerge from queer horse play, merging the child and the adult in fantasy: 'rather than represent this subject in a realist or documentary way..., I want to create a highly subjective imagery that evokes the emotions of my childhood horse fantasies, filtered through an adult perspective'.[19] Bright's vivid and carefully staged portraits of horse dolls and figures redraw the predictable normative erotics through which girl-horse and woman-horse love are typically narrated, highlighting instead the queer possibilities of cross-species desire. Some of Bright's images combine horse figurines with S&M/B&D accessories, evoking bondage, pedophilia, and bestiality – the hidden subtext of MLP – but with an irony that is missing from the Madonna photoshoot. For example, the portrait 'Sweet Thing' pictures a bright pink swatch of hair, supposedly the hair of a My Little Pony doll, framed within a black bridle, demonstrating precisely the reduction of the Pony body to the fetish of her hair (Figure 5.1). That this fetish is framed within a bridle adds to the critique, suggesting how MLP's overdetermination constrains or 'bridles' the imaginative possibilities for horse-crazy love. Other portraits include 'Kill Daddy' in which Bright frames a naturalistic model of a foal reaching between its legs with its rump toward the camera so that the raised tail suggests anal penetration, revealing the lie of erotic innocence. 'Lone Ranger' literalizes the trope of the horse as a figure for penis envy, framing a woman's genital region and the model horse she holds as a man or a transman would hold his penis (Figure 5.2). Queering this trope of the horse-as-penis, in 'Pocket Rocket,' the model horse becomes a dyke's dildo tucked into her unzipped jeans, head down, forming a recognizably

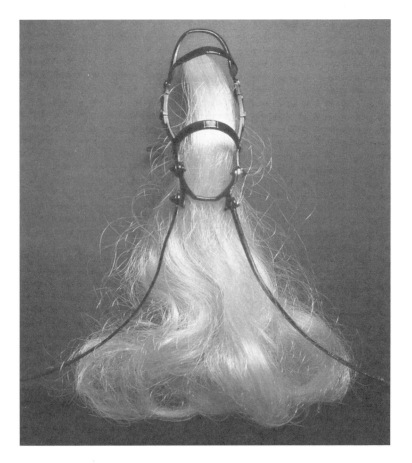

Figure 5.1   Deborah Bright, *Sweet Thing*, (1998).

masculine bulge, while the horse's torso and rear end rise up out of her jeans, the dark horse body accentuated against a white t-shirt (Figure 5.3).

Commenting on her series, Bright suggests that received notions of girl–horse love, such as those represented in MLP, inhibit the play of imagination that cross-species desire can elicit:

> horse-craziness might represent a more anarchic place for young girls to inhabit, where contradictory erotic and social forces (power and gentleness, hardness and softness, wildness and control,

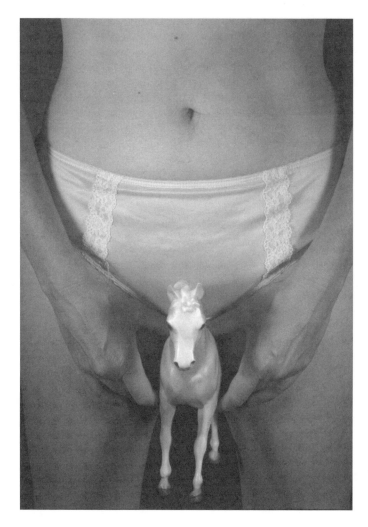

Figure 5.2 Deborah Bright, *Lone Ranger,* (1998).

danger and pleasure) can be reconciled in a body, a horse body. For those of us who have never settled comfortably into a two-gender world, such memories have talismanic power.[20]

As Elizabeth Probyn describes, meditating on her own memories 'of girlfriends melded together by hot horseflesh': 'The identity of the

Figure 5.3   Deborah Bright, *Pocket Rocket,* (1998).

individual bodies is of little interest; rather it is the way in which they are held together by a singular girl-practice of becoming horse: a milieu of becoming-horse, becoming woman that is constituted within the changing elements of socialities and bodies'.[21] Bright notes that,

> At increasingly earlier ages, the female body becomes a site of perpetual alienation, discipline, and punishment. Embracing and identifying with the sensuous beauty and power of the horse,

kicking up its heels and running free across boundless fields of dreams, is a powerful fetish to ward off the real-world constriction of women's physicality, power, and presence in a society that still fears and belittles these.[22]

Bright evokes the possibilities of horse-crazy love in commenting on the frequency with which depictions of horses appear in the portfolios of female art school applicants:

> I daydreamed a whole nation of horse-girls who shared this obsession; a fierce army of horse-lovers impervious to the contempt implicit in the men's mockery. Ignoring the social consensus that they should have 'moved on' from horses to boys, these hopeful applicants were signaling their membership in a subversive sisterhood. If we nurtured their talent and insistence on deviant passion over peer pressure, we could move mountains.[23]

The subversive sisterhood might equally extend to horses who, in their co-becomings with humans, may also exceed static figuration as 'animal' who works silently to enact the 'human.'

Is this hyper-sexualization of horse-crazy love a sufficient reading of this particular cross-species relationship? Are there ways that passion for horses is figured that allow non-normative conceptualizations of gender and species difference? Are there readings of girl horse love that remain open to imaginary and real alternatives to embodiment and sociality? One of the most familiar literary figures of girl-horse love is Velvet, the protagonist of Enid Bagnold's *National Velvet* (1935). In the first part of the novel, Velvet enacts horse play with small paper models that she carefully crafts, cutting out pictures of horses from the sports pages of magazines and pasting them on cardboard backings. Each of these horses has a name and a personality. Velvet keeps them together in a 'stable' (a decorated box), preparing them for their outings with tiny bridles made of thread and tiny saddles, and caring for them after their outings as she would care for a stable of real horses. Velvet's handling of these figurines brings them alive in her imagination:

> Look at him, she said lovingly, taking up the paper horse. I must unsaddle him and rub him down... . Velvet took a tiny bridle of cotton threads from the horse. Then going to a shell-box on the

sideboard she brought it to the table… . Velvet opened the box and took out a stable rubber two inches square, a portion of her handkerchief, hemmed round. Laying the little horse flat on the table she rubbed him with delicacy in circular motions, after having taken a paper saddle from his back… . By dint of much rubbing the paper had given off a kind of coat, and now as Velvet rubbed there came a suede-like sheen on the horse's paper body.[24]

Velvet's love is expressed in the meticulous care she takes of the horse figures' real (paper) and imaginary (horse) bodies. The 'rubbing' offers Velvet a tactile connection to these horses, an engagement between horse and girl bodies that bridges the imaginary and the real. The paper horses and their accoutrements are legible here as fetish objects, but what lack are they filling in for?

Arguing for an alternative understanding of the role of dolls in girls' lives, Kathy Lavezzo acknowledges that dolls can be understood to stand in for a human baby, which in turn functions as Freud's 'penis substitute'.[25] Lavezzo notes, 'Freud contends that, while playing with dolls is often viewed as an indication of the first stirrings of femininity within a child, this activity in fact has little to do with the 'proper' passive role which distinguishes the female subject from her masculine counterpart'.[26] In working out how the relationship of the girl to her dolls relates to the girl's relationship to her mother, Lavezzo states, 'According to Freud, the very active attention little girls give their dolls … is not directed toward any masculine object, but to the original feminine object of their affection: their mothers. That is, when little girls play with their dolls, they play with their mothers, albeit indirectly'.[27] The doll is both an object upon which the girls act as if they were mothers, and an object with whom girls identify with as acted upon by their mothers. Actor and desired object are both female in this reading of doll-play, of the imaginary of desire and identification: 'identification with and desire for the mother merge in the girl's doll-play, as the girl routes through the doll (in Freud's words) "the exclusiveness of her attachment to her mother, accompanied by a total neglect of her father-object"'.[28] Lavezzo allows a reading of the doll and the girl's relationship to the doll as being about the female–female bond as opposed to representing a phallic substitute.

Lavezzo's reading of doll-play suggests likewise that in Velvet's play with the paper horses, they may in some way function as fetish objects but specifically in reference to the 'maternal phallus.' In this reading, the fetishized horse-doll acts as a 'signifier of desire',[29] signaling desire for the lost female love object and offering an alternative conception of how horse-love might enable non-normative experiences of embodiment and sociality. Velvet's story demonstrates the development of 'an alternative *imaginary* to a hegemonic imaginary',[30] a way to construct a story of attachment and loss, embodiment and desire, that does not rely on the familiar narratives of hetero- and anthropo-normativity.

Beyond her play with horse dolls, Velvet enacts becoming horse in transforming her body into the hybrid body of a girl-centaur. Captured in vivid Technicolour in the movie version starring Elizabeth Taylor and Mickey Rooney, the movie enacts the opening scene of the novel, picturing Velvet playing horse: 'The Hullocks were blackening as Velvet cantered down the chalk road to the village. She ran on her own slender legs, making horse-noises and chirrups and occasionally striking her thigh with a switch'.[31] Velvet's horse-crazy love marks her as different in the novel. About Velvet's obsession with horses and all the pretend horse play, her father says 'Daft as a sparrow...I doubt if a girl ought to be what you are',[32] that is, horse-crazy. In the novel, Velvet figures as the oddball, the youngest of four sisters, skinny and with 'large protruding teeth' and braces, while her three older sisters are described as 'all exactly alike, like golden greyhounds'.[33] This detail, along with others, differs from the film version in which Velvet is, of course, a beautiful girl. Nonetheless, the film marks Elizabeth-Velvet as odd in her singular obsession with horses by contrasting her behaviour with that of her older sister Edwina, who is in love with a boy, a feeling she describes distinctly as a 'flutter in your heart.'

What precedents exist for the becoming-horse of horse-crazy girls? Cantering on horse legs, with arms of a rider, the head of a horse, evokes the figure of the centaur. Centaurs signify the boundary between human and animal, typically a male horse body merged with the male torso. This hybrid of man and horse is never really tame, as evidenced in the twelfth book of Ovid's *Metamorphoses*, in which the Centaurs battle the Lapithites over the attempted abduction of Hippodamia. Centaurs are in-between beings, hybrids, bringing together two sets of desires. Their alignment with humans and with the established social order is tenuous: 'By the 5th century B.C., Centaurs (like Amazons) come to symbolize all those forces which opposed Greek male cultural and political dominance'.[34] Female centaurs, Centaurides, also exist in the mythology. The Rodin museum in Paris contains a beautiful representation of a Centauride, horse and woman contiguous in long and soft curves, alive with the combined power and seduction of the cross-species transformation. What is the desire specific to horse-crazy girls that is captured in the imaginative transformation of girl body into horse body?

May Swenson's poem 'The Centaur,' captures the fluidity of transformation, opening with a reflection on the extension in time of memory, the moment of a summer that can seem to span decades in a child's sense of time:

The summer that I was ten—
Can it be there was only one
summer that I was ten? It must
have been a long one then—
each day I'd go out to choose a fresh horse from my stable
which was a willow grove down by the cold canal.[35]

This narrator finds horse companions in the form of tree limbs taken from a willow grove, richly symbolic and equally tactile: 'I had cut me a long limber horse/with a good thick knob for a head,/and peeled him slick and clean/except for a few leaves for the tail'.[36] The tree limb creates the long lines of the girl-horse's legs, the length of the spine, and the linear extension of her tail. The knobby head echoes the shape of a horse's forehead and bulging eyes as the narrator grooms this horse body sleekly smooth using a knife borrowed from her brother. With the horse thus prepared for a ride, she '...cinched my brother's belt/ around his head for a rein' and off they would go:

I'd straddle and canter him fast
up the grass bank to the path,
trot along in the lovely dust

that talcumed over his hoofs,
hiding my toes, and turning
his feet to swift half-moons.[37]

Hoofbeats on the trail, tracks in the soft dust, and sensory clues
reinforce the vivid tactility of this fantasy. The smoothed limb is at
once horse and saddle: 'the pommel and yet the poll/of my nickering
pony's head'.[38] The metamorphosis is fluid and multiply articulated.
Girl and horse merge, becoming both and one: 'My head and my
neck were mine,/ yet they were shaped like a horse./My hair flopped
to the side/ like the mane of a horse in the wind'.[39]

This becoming horse transforms the girl's body as her movements,
her sensibilites, become equine: 'My forelock swung in my eyes,/
My neck arched and I snorted./I shied and skittered and reared,/
stopped and raised my knees, pawed at the ground and quivered./My
teeth bared as we wheeled/and swished through the dust again'.[40]
Immersed in the experience of being/becoming horse, the girl is at
the same time rider, her body engaged in 'quiet, negligent riding'.[41]
Arriving at her house, 'I tethered him to a paling./Dismounting, I
smoothed my skirt/and entered the dusky hall./My feet on the clean
linoleum/ left ghostly toes in the hall'.[42] Her footprints, the spectral
traces of the girl-horse who leaves hoofprints in the dust, represent
the alternate embodiment that exists as real in her becoming horse.
When her mother asks, ' ... *Why is your mouth all green?*', the evidence
of becoming horse evidenced in the shared girl-horse mouth, the
narrator explains, '*Rob Roy, he pulled some clover as we crossed
the field...*'.[43] The girlhood enactment of cross-species embodiment
renders bodily otherness in terms of corporeal transformation. What
is the yearning that motivates this transformation? Is this another
form of assimilative incorporation, an appropriation of the equine
other, or are alternative possibilities of embodiment being played out
in the imagining of horse-girl conjunction?

'The Centaur' and *National Velvet* offer two similar portraits of
becoming-horse in the form of the girl-centaur. Ursula K. Le Guin's
short story 'Horse Camp' addresses the same phenomenon, but it
also draws the reader into a narrative space where embodiment and
identity are made uncertain through the transformative license of
fantasy. This story enacts what Philip K. Dick calls the disorientation of

fantasy, 'the shock of dysrecognition'[44], as girls transform into horses and horses into girls and girl-horse love draws girls into the alternative community of Horse Camp. The story floats the reader between familiar experiences of going to summer camp and the strangeness of cross-species metamorphosis with the shock of dysrecognition arriving when the reader realizes that the distinction between the girl campers and their horses is fading and that the girls and horses merge in body and behaviour.

The camp is a place of initiation, a place where transformation happens. The story traces a voyage away from the familiar, the familial, into a setting that offers alternative kinship, a community of girls and horses, and an experience that changes what it means to be a girl. But Horse Camp is not just a concrete location where girls go to ride horses during the summer vacation. Horse Camp is a state of mind and an immersion. It is a long-term commitment that involves transformation of the self. First-year campers return as second-year campers and eventually as counselors who 'know what is to be known'[45]: 'They know where they are. They know where the rest of Horse Camp is'.[46] The 'rest of horse camp,' the becoming-horse of Horse Camp, is 'Freedom, the freedom to run, freedom is to run. Freedom is galloping. What else can it be?'.[47] Once that freedom is experienced, it becomes permanent knowledge, learned by heart, 'pure joy'.[48] Horse Camp is learning the embodied routines that bring order to experience: 'You have to start with the right fore. Everything else is all right. Freedom depends on this, that you start with the right fore, that long leg well balanced on its elegant pastern, that you set down that tiptoe middle-fingernail so hard and round, and spurn the dirt'.[49] These are the rules that every horse-girl learns, the practices that initiate her into the community of horse-crazy girls and the language by which horse-crazy girls communicate with each other and with their equine companions.

The narrator, Norah, a first-year camper whose older sister has already experienced the initiation of Horse Camp, realizes, in communion with her friend Ev, what Horse Camp means: 'Shoulder to shoulder, she and Ev, in the long heat of afternoon, in a trance of light, across the home creek in the dry wild oats and cow parsley of the Long Pasture. "I was afraid before I came here," thinks

Norah, incredulous, remembering childhood. She leans her head against Ev's firm and silken side'.[50] Horse Camp marks a passage away from childhood, but it also marks something permanent and recurring: 'This is what freedom is, what goes on, the sun in the summer, the wild grass, coming back each year'[51]. Horse Camp is a place for girls and horses, but it is also a place where girls and horses become something other than they are, sharing sleek, long-legged companionship, developing relationships among themselves, with other campers, counselors, and the herd of horse-crazy girls. This is another kind of becoming-human that formatively incorporates becoming-horse.

Vicki Hearne, musing about girl–horse love, offers the following reflection: 'I sometimes suspect that the allegory of horsemanship is one of the few in this culture that are available to young girls as an allegory of the courage to remain interested'.[52] Hearne suggests that, given the relatively few options for girls to envision, horse-crazy love empowers girls to experience themselves as authoritative, autonomous beings both in the cross-species embodiment of the girl-centaur and in its alternative trajectory for becoming-human. The allegorical empowerment of horse-crazy love may be both signal and symptom of the disjunction and dissonance of living in a culture that offers few options for non-normative identification. As Le Guin says about 'Horse Camp': '"Horse Camp" seems to trouble people, even some who have gone through, or had daughters go through, the "horse stage." Perhaps what troubles them is that one can hear in it a yell of freedom and a scream from the trap in the same voice at the same time. Or maybe they just want to know *how*'.[53] The 'yell of freedom' comes out of the exploration of embodiment and subjectivity outside normative confines.

How might species and gender alignments slip apart and reconfigure in horse-girl embodiments? In Velvet's case, her trans-species desire, exemplified in her imaginative play in the first part of the novel, transforms into action in the second part of the novel, as Velvet shifts her attention from her horse dolls and imaginary horseplay to developing the intimacy of a working relationship with The Pie. Velvet's relationship with The Pie intensifies her trans-species embodiment through training, which leads finally to the trans-gender embodiment that allows Velvet and The Pie to accomplish the goal of competing in the Grand National, England's famous and notoriously difficult steeplechase. Velvet's trans-gender transformation marks her conversion from butcher's odd (queer) daughter to (male) jockey, enabling her to ride in a competitive event. Velvet and Mi, Mr. Brown's assistant and an experienced horseman (played by a young Mickey Rooney in the movie), have the following discussion prior to a raffle in which Velvet wins The Pie:

> 'If I won that piebald,' said Velvet, 'I might ride him in the Grand National myself.'
> 'Girls can't ride in that,' said Mi contemptuously.
> 'Girls!' said Velvet, stopping still beside him so that they all drew up. 'Who's to know I'm a girl?' She cupped her face in her two hands so that her straight hair was taken from it.
> 'Tisn't your hair,' said Mi, and his eyes fell on her chest. 'Flat's a pancake,' he said. 'You'd pass.'[54]

Exclusionary cultural practices demand Velvet's embodiment as a boy in order to ride in the race, a transformation easily accomplished by her prepubescent body. With Mi's help, Velvet transforms into a 'little man' for the race, at which point the pronouns shift from the feminine to the masculine. On the morning of the race, 'Velvet rose and became the little man. At twelve to the tick he walked sharply down the stairs carrying his suitcase. He had padded shoulders, a common suit, a dingy white shirt and pale blue tie, a brownish overcoat with a half belt and Mi's old Homburg hat spotted with oil'.[55] Mi has provided this 'little man' the identity of Tasky (he is supposedly Russian and unable to speak English, thus masking Velvet's voice), and together they manage to successfully navigate the male spaces of the jockey's dressing room and weighing-in room. The pronoun change continues until Velvet mounts her horse.[56] Ultimately, in passing as a young man, Velvet's transgression gains her what she sought: her horse wins the race, proving his exceptional athletic ability and competitive spirit, as well as the success of their partnership.

Stories that trace the fantasy of transposing girl body and horse body, of becoming a girl-centaur, half girl, half horse, and the empowerment that comes with this transformation, can be understood as what Jay Prosser calls 'body narratives,' narratives that 'engage with the feelings of embodiment'.[57] Prosser argues that body narratives are not purely representational, that they 'not only represent but *allow* changes to somatic materiality'.[58] Girl-horse transformation, the metamorphosis into girl-centaur and the becoming-with of the training relationship, are ways of making sense of the body. In addition, body narratives of girl-horse love model a different type of sociality:

> [I]f the body is to be fully understood as a social phenomenon, then it is necessary to avoid a conceptualization of it which draws exclusive attention to the subject individual. Rather, it is important to conceptualize the body in a manner which directly refers to the interactive and relational, and therefore social (as opposed to socialized), aspects of the body. Instead of conceptualizing the bodies of individual persons in terms of the social constraints to which they are subjected, which focus attention on individual characteristics as individual propensities, it is more appropriate to emphasize the active bases of the embodied agent in relational and social forms.[59]

Girl-horse transformation opens into cross-species imagining, engaged relationality, social interaction, as a way to negotiate a livable body.

National Velvet offers a model of transgression that articulates the arbitrary nature of conventional gender (and class) barriers and suggests the possibility of surmounting social restrictions. Ultimately, however, Velvet, like her equine companion, remains queer, unassimilable within normative paradigms. In spite of the fame and recognition that accompanies the race, 'no one had learned anything about her. No one had formed the slightest picture of her, and she had gathered an impression of isolation as she moved'.[60] Velvet continues to be a non-normative girl in her interests, for she ignores the attention and gifts that accompany her fame and seek her recuperation into easily readable femininity:

> Chrysanthemums, roses in winter, glacéd sweets, love letters, interviews, satin pillow-dolls—the house had overflowed with gifts, Edwina, Mally and Merry had eaten themselves sick, but Velvet,

who did not care for flowers, could not stomach many sweets, did not read the love letters, never played with dolls, remained with her real desires sharp and intact, the ascending spirit with which she was threaded unquenched by surfeit.[61]

The reader is told that, as for Velvet, 'no one had learned anything about her. No one had formed the slightest picture of her, and she had gathered an impression of isolation as she moved'.[62] Velvet's mystery is her difference from conventional (readable) girlhood. This is also what sets her apart, creating an isolation that is broken by her continuing relationships with horses. The hype surrounding Velvet's and Pie's achievement passes with time, and 'Velvet was able to get on quietly to her next adventures'.[63] What Velvet has achieved in this story is to dream her dreams and to actualize them in spite of the lack of existing cultural models with which to realize these dreams.

Linking the work of gender difference with that of species difference, Judith Butler asks: 'If I am a certain gender, will I still be regarded as part of the human? Will the 'human' expand to include me in its reach? If I desire in certain ways, will I be able to live? Will there be a place for my life, and will it be recognizable to the others upon whom I depend for social existence?'[64] This is a critical question for Velvet and other non-normative girls, one that is relevant to how we understand human–nonhuman difference. Normatively, 'the becoming-human of the self occurs through a process of recognition which must necessarily abandon and repress desire's more fluid potentialities'.[65] Resisting this, the trans-species love expressed by horse-crazy girls may provide a model for how to resist the categorical hailing that is part of becoming recognizably human. The question of what kinds of bodies are required to live 'liveable' lives must be posed in relation to nonhuman beings. The imperative is one that destabilizes safely inured categories of human and nonhuman:

For the human to be human, it must relate to what is nonhuman, to what is outside itself but continuous with itself by virtue of an interimplication in life. This relation to what is not itself constitutes the human being in its livingness, so that the human exceeds its boundary in the very effort to establish them [sic]. This paradox makes it imperative to separate the question of a livable life from the status of a human life, since livability pertains to living beings that exceed the human.[66]

In an interview with Jill Stauffer, Butler states,

> ... our notions of what a human being is problematically depend on there being two coherent genders. And if someone doesn't comply with either the masculine norm or the feminine norm, their very humanness is called into question. So I suppose the corollary to that is to say that those who are challenging traditional ideas about what gender is are also challenging us to refashion our notion of what is human.[67]

Challenging humanist tropes, animal studies participate in what Judith Butler suggests is a necessarily heterogeneous challenge to hegemonic discourses: 'if there is an occupation and reversal of the master's discourse, it will come from many quarters, and those resignifying practices will converge in ways that scramble the self-replicating presumptions of reason's mastery'.[68] Considering that horse-crazy love might be more than the allegory of power in the embodiment of cross-species becoming-with, girl-horse love could represent one instance

> where discourse meets its limits, where the opacity of what is not included in a given regime of truth acts as a disruptive site of linguistic impropriety and unrepresentability, illuminating the violent and contingent boundaries of that normative regime precisely through the inability of that regime to represent that which might pose a fundamental threat to its continuity.[69]

Rosi Braidotti identifies trans-species interconnectivity as the central challenge for animal studies scholars, namely, 'to see the inter-*relation* human/animal as constitutive of the identity of *each*. It is therefore a relation, a transformative or symbiotic relationship that hybridizes, shifts and alters the "nature" of each one'.[70] In this configuration, girl-horse love posits a bodily becoming that does not reduce girls/women to an 'unspeakable condition of figuration' for man.[71] The embodied experience of horse-girls may be an instance when 'the feminine exceeds its figuration'[72], moving beyond the binary confines of gendered identity and asking too how animals, horses, might exceed their figuration.

The readings presented in this chapter reflect the belief that different stories or stories differently read can influence the way we imagine possibilities of living, of the ways we negotiate and construct selves and lives. Instead of accepting the domestication of horse-crazy love as framed by the corporate My Little Pony franchise, queering girl-horse love offers productive subversions from which to disrupt normative figurations of gender and species. As Alice A. Kuzniar says in writing about dog-love stories, 'queer pet love participates in the questioning of the norms of patriarchy by redefining such notions as kinship, family, propinquity, the quotidian and affection'.[73] Becoming-with horse may offer what Elizabeth Grosz identifies as

> a way of leveling, of flattening the hierarchical relations between ideas and things, qualities and entities, of eliminating the privilege of the human over the animal, the organic over the inorganic, the male over the female, the straight over the 'bent' – of making them level and interactive, rendering them productive and innovative, experimental and provocative.[74]

Reading these stories as queer, as alternatives for how to love, how to relate, how to be human, opens possibilities for cross-species affections and partnerships, not as derivative forms of human affection and partnership, but as constitutive of other ways of being non/human.[75]

Notes

1 www.hasbro.com/mylittlepony
2 Rutherford, J. 'My Little Calliponian' *Bitch*, Vol. Spring, 2007, p. 19.
3 Ducille, A., 'Black Barbie and the Deep Play of Difference' in Jones, A. (ed), *The Feminism and Visual Culture Reader*, (London and New York: Routledge, 2003), pp. 337–348: 339.
4 Buccola, R. 'Dusty, the Dyke Barbie' *Children's Literature Association Quarterly*, 29, 2004, pp. 228–252: 235.
5 Buccola, 'Dusty, the Dyke Barbie', p. 228.

6 ibid.

7 Buccola, 'Dusty, the Dyke Barbie', p. 237.

8 Buccola, 'Dusty, the Dyke Barbie', pp. 243–4.

9 Barthes, R. *Mythologies,* (New York: Hill and Wang, 1972), p. 53.

10 Probyn, E. *Outside Belongings,* (New York: Routledge, 1996), p. 55.

11 Kincaid, J. *Erotic Innocence: The Culture of Child Molesting,* (Durham: Duke University Press, 1998), p. 7.

12 ibid.

13 Barthes, *Mythologies*, p. 54.

14 www.hasbro.com

15 Klein, S. 'Madonna' In *W*, Vol. 36, 2006, pp. 129–187: 129.

16 Freccero, C. *Popular Culture,* (New York: New York University Press, 1999), p. 47.

17 ibid.

18 Freccero, *Popular Culture*, p. 48.

19 Bright, D. 'Being & Riding' *GLQ,* 6, 2000, GLQ Gallery.

20 Bright, 'Being & Riding'.

21 Probyn, *Outside Belongings*, p. 54.

22 Bright, D.,'Horse Crazy' in *Horse Tales: American Images and Icons 1800–2000* (Natohah, NY: Katonah Museum of Art, 2001), pp. 22–31: 30.

23 Bright, 'Horse Crazy', p. 22.

24 Bagnold, E. *National Velvet,* (New York: Avon Books, 1935), p. 3.

25 Lavezzo, K. (1996) 'Sobs and Sighs Between Women: The Homoerotics of Compassion in *The Book of Margery Kemp'* in Freccero C & Fradenburg, L. (eds) *Premodern Sexualities* (New York and London, Routledge, 1996), pp. 176–198: 185.

26 Lavezzo, 'Sobs and Sighs Between Women: The Homoerotics of Compassion in *The Book of Margery Kemp'*, p. 185.

27 Lavezzo, 'Sobs and Sighs Between Women: The Homoerotics of Compassion in *The Book of Margery Kemp'*, p. 185.

28 Lavezzo, 'Sobs and Sighs Between Women: The Homoerotics of Compassion in *The Book of Margery Kemp'* p. 186.

29 de Lauretis, T. *The Practice of Love: Lesbian Sexuality and Perverse Desire,* (Bloomington: Indiana University Press, 1994) p. 275.

30 Butler, J. *Bodies That Matter: On the Discursive Limits of "Sex",* (New York: Routledge, 1993) p. 91.

31 Bagnold, *National Velvet,* p. 1.

32 Bagnold, *National Velvet,* p. 32.

33 Bagnold, *National Velvet*, p. 2.

34 'Centaur' in *The Oxford Dictionary of the Classical World*, Roberts, J. (ed) (Oxford: Oxford University Press, 2007) pp. 140–1: 141.

35 Swenson, M. (1999) 'Centaur' in *The Literary West: An Anthology of Western American Literature,* Lyon, T. J. (ed) (Oxford & New York: Oxford University Press) pp. 345–349: 345.

36 Swenson, 'Centaur', pp. 345–46.

37 Swenson, 'Centaur' p. 346.

38 Swenson, 'Centaur' p. 346.

39 Swenson, 'Centaur' p. 346.

40 Swenson, 'Centaur' p. 346.

41 Swenson, 'Centaur' p. 346.

42 Swenson, 'Centaur' p. 347.

43 Swenson, 'Centaur' p. 347.

44 Dick, P. K. *The Collected Stories of Philip K. Dick, Volume One: The Short Happy Life of The Brown Oxford*, (Secaucus, NJ: Carol Publishing Group, 1999) p. xiii.

45 Le Guin, U. K. *Buffalo Gals: And Other Animal Presences,* (Santa Barbara, CA: Capra Press, 1987) p. 144.

46 Le Guin, *Buffalo Gals: And Other Animal Presences*, p. 145.

47 Le Guin, *Buffalo Gals: And Other Animal Presences*, p. 145.

48 Le Guin, *Buffalo Gals: And Other Animal Presences*, p. 146.

49 Le Guin, *Buffalo Gals: And Other Animal Presences*, p. 146.

50 Le Guin, *Buffalo Gals: And Other Animal Presences*, p. 146.

51 Le Guin, *Buffalo Gals: And Other Animal Presences*, p. 146.

52 Hearne, V. *Adam's Task: Calling Animals by Name,* (New York: Vintage, 1986), p. 113.

53 Le Guin, *Buffalo Gals: And Other Animal Presences*, p. 139.

54 Bagnold, *National Velvet* p. 62.

55 Bagnold, *National Velvet* p. 196.

56 Bagnold, *National Velvet* p. 202.

57 Prosser, J. *Second Skins: The Body Narratives of Transsexuality,* (New York: Columbia University Press, 1998) p. 12.

58 Prosser, *Second Skins: The Body Narratives of Transsexuality*, p. 16.

59 Lyon, M.L & Barbalet, J. M 'Society's body: emotion and the 'somatization' of social theory' in *Embodiment and Experience: The Existential Ground of Culture and Self* Csordas, T. J (ed) (Cambridge: Cambridge University Press, 1994) pp. 48–68: 55.

60 Bagnold, *National Velvet,* p. 264.

61 Bagnold, *National Velvet,* p. 264.

62 Bagnold, *National Velvet,* p. 264.

63 Bagnold, *National Velvet,* p. 265.

64 Butler, J. *Undoing Gender,* (New York: Routledge, 2004) pp. 2–3.

65 Colebrook, C. 'How Queer Can You Go? Theory, Normality and Normativity.' In *Queer Non/Human* Giffney, N & Hird, M (eds) (Burlington: Ashgate, 2008) pp. 17–34: 21.

66 Butler, *Undoing Gender,* p. 12).

67 www.believermag.ccom/issues/200305/?read = interview_butler

68 Butler, *Bodies That Matter: On the Discursive Limits of 'Sex'* p. 52.

69 Butler, *Bodies That Matter: On the Discursive Limits of 'Sex'* p. 53.

70 Braidotti, R. *Transpositions: On Nomadic Ethics,* (Cambridge, UK: Polity Press, 2006) p. 108.

71 Butler, *Bodies That Matter: On the Discursive Limits of 'Sex'* p. 37.

72 Butler, *Bodies That Matter: On the Discursive Limits of 'Sex'* p. 41.

73 Kuzniar, A. A. *Melancholia's Dog,* (Chicago and London: University of Chicago Press, 2006) p. 209.

74 Grosz, E. *Space, Time, and Perversion: Essays on the Politics of Bodies,* (New York: Routledge, 1995) p. 185.

75 Giffney, N. and M. Hird (eds.) *Queer Non/Human,* Ashgate, (Burlington, VT: Ashgate, 2008) pp. 2–3.

6

Writing Relations: The Crab, the Lobster, the Orchid, the Primrose, You, Me, Chaos and Literature[1]

Lucile Desblache

In the volume of tales he wrote for children, *Emerveilles*, Patrick Chamoiseau offers twenty stories located in his native Martinique. Most of these stories, although not all, introduce animals which are either hybrid creatures defying known categories and stereotypes, such as Mabouk the donkey-dog or Bouboule-Toad-Head, half-boy half-toad. When beasts are portrayed as real, such as the cat and dog in 'The Surprised Kiss of the Dog to the Cat', they are not described in ways which particularize them as separate individuals, but rather, are defined through the relationships they entertain with each other or with other creatures. In the case of the cat and dog, they are introduced as 'the cat-who-knew-a-dog' and 'the dog-who-knew-the-cat'.[2] Readers can expect Chamoiseau's animals to be tropes, and to a degree, anthropomorphic, as they belong to a Creole tradition rooted in that of African oral literature, where specific animals are associated with human characters or ideas (for instance, the rabbit with a cunning mulatto; the whale and elephant with powerful colonizers; or the humming bird with freedom).

Chamoiseau's literary beasts are allegorical. Like most fabled beasts of the Caribbean, they appear as agents of a counter-discourse essential to the voicing of historical revisions, to the tracking down of pre-colonial histories, and to the creation of texts emancipated from Western dominance and Eurocentrism. In engaging with allegory as a subversive literary strategy for identity formation and historical recovery, discussed by several critics since the 1980s, from Stephen Slemon to Bill Ashcroft,[3] Chamoiseau places himself in an established postcolonial literary current. Yet Chamoiseau's animals, if allegorized, are neither objectified nor entirely humanized. Their figuration may evoke ideas as well as beings; but these ideas are not absolute. They are meant to open readers to 'the esthetics of chaos, of identity uncertainty, of incompleteness, of polyphony'.[4] Beasts are always introduced as part of an ecology of relationships, connecting with various species as well as human lives, not in opposition to them. They are not closed entities but composite beings, often explicitly hybrid, whose identities are constantly changing, and are permeable to the environment which surrounds them.

I would like to show here how, in spite of a history in which domestic animals contributed to the oppression of humans and were often constructed into extensions of human power and violence, contemporary French Caribbean literary beasts play an important role in bringing to the fore the vital importance of human-animal relationships. In many of these recent texts, by Chamoiseau, and also by other French Carribbean writers such as Raphaël Confiant and Daniel Maximin, animals are represented in positive ways that evoke relationships with humans beyond the stereotyped dialectical interactions of master and slave or oppressor and victim. They are instrumental in providing an anti-history that differs from official historical records and colonial interpretations. They allow writers to write a pre(colonial)-history, to trace a past either deliberately erased or unilaterally told. The beasts of contemporary Caribbean literature relate events that are not determined by relationships between conqueror and conquered, but by experiences of interconnectedness between beings and landscapes. They appear as agents of what Gregory Bateson identified as the 'epistemologies of interconnectedness', which consider intra and interspecies relationships and communication the essence of life.

Caribbean writing emerges at a time when the binaries of Western thought, whether they oppose human and non-human, global and local, science and literature, bodies and souls, master and slave, are struggling to provide convincing arguments and answers to the global challenges faced by humanity. French Caribbean thought and literature provide fresh perspectives on the possibility of connections to our environment. In particular, they promote a shift from traditional Western perceptions of the self and the other as opposed entities to representations of composite identities involving interdependence between human, non-human animals and the rest of our natural and technological environment. I shall first consider the main notions underlying this 'philosophy of relation'[5], particularly in respect to human-animal relationships, while in the second part of this essay, I shall examine one of the tales from Chamoiseau's *Emerveilles*, 'Angèle and Werecat' ('Angèle et Chagarou') to exemplify how this 'literature of relation' functions.[6]

Postcultures vs Transcultures

Current scientific developments loosen the bonds of anthropocentrism by bringing daily evidence that the essence of every living being is composed of organisms which also belong to other species and that the successful existence of any creature depends on such relations. Yet many cultural representations and more so, economic realities, which rely on the consumption and exploitation of 'lower' beings, far from promoting 'a creaturely ethics' or 'an ethics of dehumanization'[7], reinforce boundaries between humanity and other creatures. We need creative writing, not just science, to denounce the damage done by the perpetuation of separatist views based on hierarchies of the living, to sing the power and necessity of interspecies encounters. French Caribbean literature reflects a society which is the epitome of a composite culture, historically and geographically, as the West Indies have been visibly constructed from fragmented entities. It excels at showing that 'to be one is always to become with many'.[8] West Indian refusal of Western history as the measure of cultural and social development also allows new grounds for considering relationships. The transition sought by Western cultures from an uncomfortable post-period (postcolonial, posthuman, postmodern, poststructural, postindustrial ...), based on the sense of loss of beings things and values, has irretrievably gone to an uncharted trans-period (transcolonial, translational, transhuman, transnational, transcultural). Although established frontiers are challenged by these trans-formations, new journeys of discovery are not only uneasy; they also remain, to a large extent, anthropocentric. The title of this collection clearly states the importance for transhumanism to take us *Beyond Human*, but the reality of the transhumanist movement is that it is still primarily concerned with improvement of the human condition through science.

Edouard Glissant demonstrates that contemporary Caribbean thought is rooted in a search for (pre-)history that is inclusive of human and non-human traces. As with all nations in formation, the identity of Martinique (which strictly cannot be considered postcolonial as it is still a colony of France) is primarily expressed through poetic modes, and sung by voices deeply conscious of their links to the living and inanimate environment surrounding them:

> Artistic production, in developing countries [...] remains indispensable. [... A]ll the beginnings of peoples (from the Iliad to the Old Testament, the *Book of the Dead* of the Egyptians to the Western *chansons de geste*) are poetic. This means that the voice which articulates a common project is needed, simultaneously with investment in implementations without which this project would remain a dream.
>
> [...]

[Therefore, unlike that of Western artists, t]he Caribbean artist's word (*parole*) does not come from the obsession with singing his/her intimate being; this intimate being is inseparable from the rest of the community.[9]

Ontologies vs Relations

'Who am I?', the essential ontological question which has haunted Western philosophers, instrumental in the shaping of creative writing, characterized by individual, and often intimist narrative voices, is thus exposed as irrelevant in most contemporary French Caribbean texts. Rather, such literature uncovers other fundamental questions: 'With whom am I sharing or can I share my existence and how is this sharing meaningful for reading the past and constructing the future?' In a wide range of these texts, fictional or not, animals are not only incarnations of diversity in the living world but agents of a 'poetics of relation', to use the title of one of Glissant's essays.[10] They are part of the Diverse, of a notion of difference inherent in a concept of living. Borrowing Heidegger's notions of Being (*Sein*) and being (*Seiendes*), Glissant shows that Being should not hinder the dynamics of being,

> [in a] world where human beings and animals and landscapes and cultures and spiritualities contaminate each other mutually. Yet contamination is not dilution. Neither is it this striving for perfection through which we grope along miserably by the means of genetics [...]. What Deleuze calls 'health' is not a unique, permanent and undifferentiated state of 'formal characters', but rather the lively capacity to enter in [these] neighbouring zones.[11]

Glissant and Chamoiseau reject the traditional Western idea that a 'being must be conceived as absolute'.[12] They promote the Deleuzian notion of a rhizome identity, based on a root which 'encounters other roots':

> Thus, what becomes important is not a so-called absolute but the mode, the way in which it makes contact with other roots: the

Relation. A poetics of Relation is more obvious and meaningful today than a poetics of Being.[13]

Following this logic of relation, Glissant replaces the notions of Self and Other with those of Same, the dominant current imposed by dominant civilizations, and Diverse:

> [which] means the effort of the human spirit towards a transversal relation, without universalist transcendence. The Diverse needs the presence of peoples, not as objects to sublimate, but as projects to establish relations with. The Same requires the Being, the Diverse establishes the Relation.[14]

Animals and Slavery

If non-human animals are agents of all human cultures, they have played particularly notable and contrasting roles in the construction of West Indian histories, not only as oppressors but also, to a less visible but no less important extent, as liberators. As several writers have noted,[15] the domestication of powerful animals is a necessary condition of a civilization's success. In the West Indies, the sudden introduction of these animals changed the course of history. In the dawn of colonization:

> The indigenous Amerindian, the Arawak, the Caribbean did not see Christopher Columbus as an enemy; they knew that it was possible to go beyond their country. They knew through their legends and myths that people would come to their country. Ships therefore did not amaze them. What amazed them was the horse; they had not yet seen a horse: for them, it was a monster.[16]

From the beginning of West Indian colonization, domestic animals are associated with the invaders. They appear as instruments of conquest and of the destructive power of white people. Jonas Rano quotes one of the very first texts mentioning the role of dogs in the extermination of Amerindians:

> The Christians trained greyhounds, particularly aggressive dogs
> who reduced an Indian to pieces as soon as they saw one. They
> attacked him and ate him faster that if he had been a pig. [...]
> These dogs were the cause of much damage and bloodshed.[17]

As slavery was established, domestic animals, especially dogs
who tracked fugitives down, became incarnations of the enemy.[18]
Domestic animals were agents of control, and even, at times, of
torture, manipulated by a dominant human being against a vulnerable
one. They possessed power denied to slaves who fear them but are
also fascinated by them and their power.[19]

Further, because enslaved black Caribbeans were treated like
beasts and were considered as 'not quite' human, there emerged
a desire to establish strong boundaries between human and non-
human animals. Whereas various elements of the landscape appear
in French Caribbean literature as evidence of human Caribbean
history, and as part of the population's quest for emancipation,
the association with most animals remained undesirable. Thus
in 20th century French Caribbean literature, it is mostly inanimate
elements of the environment (seas, rivers, forests), that appear
as symbols of positive shaping of human destiny, as partners in
identity formation. With the exception of birds, and particularly
humming-birds which evoke an indomitable free Creole spirit, it
is plants, rocks, seas and winds, not animals, that are seen as
the allies of Caribbean people in search of a history to write
and a present to build. Trees, and in particular the Banyan tree,
'transcend[s] normally opposed categories of experience—past
and present, growth and decline, upward and downward. It fuses
time and space in its projection of a cyclic return of past, present,
and future, and symbolizes fidelity and a constant unfolding in its
network of downgrowing branches'.[20]

Creole Naturecultures

In Caribbean writing, what Derek Walcott names 'tamed' (sugar cane
fields) and 'untamed' (forests and hills) landscapes are ever present,
respectively as metaphors of pain or oppression and of 'lieux de

marronnage', havens of escape, allies of resistance and liberation.[21] Entering in 'Relation' with immemorial trees and even with historicized landscapes[22] is at the heart of French Caribbean literature, echoing too closely, some would suggest, Romantic ideals of nature. Yet if these ideals translate into an undeniable mysticism in the work of writers such as Glissant and Chamoiseau, they are not based on the binaries that have shaped Western visions of the environment, opposing human and non-human. In Creole culture, different forms of living are always linked as interdependent, not opposed. This is part of the essence of creoleness:

> The word Creole is derived from the Spanish 'criollo', which comes from the Latin verb 'criare', which means 'to bring up, to educate'. The Creole is born and has been brought up in the Americas, although does not originate from there, unlike the Amerindians. Quickly, this term applied to all human races, animals, and plants transported to America from 1492. French dictionaries from the 19th century are therefore incorrect to apply the term Creole exclusively to the White Creoles (or *Békés*).[23]

Throughout the 19th and 20th centuries, dichotomies grew between Western perceptions of the human as opposed to non-human and Caribbean visions of a humanity intertwined with its environment. Western animals appear as possessors of freedom and/or symbols of the conquest of time and space, while the Caribbean beasts, whether they inflict or receive suffering, whether liked or disliked, share the same space and time as humans:

> [... In the French West Indies, an animal] is understood as indispensable expression of the rhythm of time. S/he is regarded as fundamental element of space. A dog, in particular, materializes time, a temporality often not perceived by colonized people. S/he also fills a space which, through Westernization, is considered as void. A few years ago, the authorities decided to reduce the number of stray dogs, killing them on the spot or taking them to the pound. The guards in charge of this sinister task, wearing overalls and armed with syringe guns had to withdraw in popular districts, facing the incredibly strong reaction of the residents.

A Martiniquan can blind a stray dog in the eye, but cannot bear to have him/her removed from his sight. Animals are his rest; his point of reference. Just as the Westerner constantly looks at his watch to know who he is, the West Indian person looks into the eyes of a beast, looking for a reference in his bewildered life. Animals are an existential and historical patrimony.[24]

This 'natureculture' attitude is visible in Caribbean societies decades before Donna Haraway invented the term. It does not entail the disappearance of conflicts between human and non-human beings or interests, nor does it imply systematic affection for animals, but it does place all living creatures and plants in relation to each other and as agents of a cultural memory to be constructed. This is particularly relevant with regard to human relationships with animals. Whereas landscapes can be idealized through exuberant praise of woods and vegetation, Caribbean animals are not. Domestic animals, as we have seen, can be intensely disliked, despised or feared, but still appear as constitutive of an existence which is necessarily communal. Reflecting perhaps the fact that there were originally no apex predators on these islands, wild animals do not appear as the distant, exotic beasts attractive to Western voyeurism, but rather, as indigenous birds and insects. They are introduced both as tropes of freedom and as agents of biological and cultural diversity. Birds in particular, are omnipresent, and seen to weave links between earth and sea, water and wind, human and non-human creatures:

A bird, any bird, diaphanous or majestic, interlaces wind and sap, air and earth. It forgets neither water nor fire. [25]

This 'poetics of relation' tends to be expressed very differently in the West, where animal figuration is tied to individual emotional involvement between human and non-human animals, hence a strong tradition of representation of animal victims and animal heroes. Whether they are 'animalized animals', 'humanized animals', or animalized humans',[26] Western literary beasts are either figures of otherness that are cherished, pitied or exploited, or tropes of humans. In Creole writing, they also appear as tropes, as 'animalized humans', particularly in traditional tales, a genre that satirizes the French fable with the aim of dismantling its authority through parody. Yet when represented as animals, whether 'humanized' or 'animalized', they do not appear as individual entities, but as agents of transversal relations with other animals, with humans, with landscapes and with every known and unknown reality that presents itself.

Angèle and Werecat

In the second part of this chapter, I would like to explore how these transversal relations are expressed in Chamoiseau's fiction, analyzing just one of the short tales included in *Emerveilles*, 'Angèle and Werecat' ('Angèle et Chagarou'). Like all the *Emerveilles* stories, 'Angèle and Werecat' is extremely short. It is the tale of a little girl from Martinique, inspired by an old shape-shifting cat with whom she travels at night to discover the wonders of life. The cat appears as old, ugly and above all, indefinable. He is fatally shot one day by an ex-hunter who thinks him/her to be a harmful monster. Angèle, unable to see the wonders of life without the help of her feline companion, loses spontaneity, enthusiasm, and soon starts to conform with the rest of society. I shall consider this tale in respect of three notions that are key to this poetics of relation: myth, transformation and blurred boundaries, and communication.

'Demythologizing Business'

Myths can be defined in many ways but if we understand them here in the Barthesian sense of systems of signs translating and perpetuating established human values,[27] Chamoiseau, like Angela Carter, can be considered to be in the 'demythologizing business'.[28] Even though he describes his tales as taking part 'in the same movement as legends, myths, miracles, inexplicable events, uncertain beings, zombies ...',[29] he aims to expose the self-constructed frontiers that prevent human beings from increasing their connections with each other, with non-human animals and with their environment. First, the author substitutes the traditional opening phrase 'once upon a time', laden with conventions, with the neutral formula 'we saw (or thought we saw)', used throughout the collection. 'We saw or thought we saw' does not exclude realism and is an appropriate introduction which encourages readers to wonder actively rather than be passively subjected to magic. Chamoiseau promotes a wondrous rather than magic realism, one where rational ways of reading the world may be displaced, though not necessarily excluded. These *Emerveilles* (*s'émerveiller* means 'to wonder' in French) ask the participation of young (and older) readers in looking at fresh ways of connecting to the world, and in 'preparing our imagination and imaginary outputs for the flux of new events that will submerge our lives in the times to come'.[30] Myths and stereotypes are not only deconstructed through the dismantling of formulas though. Traditional tale characters also take new guises.

Transformation

In 'Angèle and Werecat', the frightening werewolf of Western legends evolves into a comforting cat who metamorphosises at night. Far from becoming a predatory beast, this werecat introduces Angèle, the little girl who likes his company, to a wild and wide array of different creatures and landscapes which provide a constant flow of life:

> He became like camels in the clear madness of deserts. Or the terrible mass of elephants crossing forests to go and die in a bunch of ivory. He sometimes seemed to slide along tall bamboos like a snake with sparkling scales. At any time, he was something else while remaining himself. Or perhaps this self became stars of a thousand possibilities which opened up ways of looking at things and freed the spirit. He was all-possible while remaining vaguely cat.[31]

The multiple otherness conveyed by this hybrid beast disassociates animals from the notion of violence, allows human beings to experience their true humanity, as s/he offers Angèle and the readers the opportunity to live through 'a thousand experiences. To feel a thousand humanities and all enchantments', just as the cat remains feline through his/her transgressions.[32]

Hence, while transformation is used to alter myths with the aim of opening readers to the unknown and dissolving their prejudices, it is also introduced as a vital part of existence. The cat is wondrous because s/he both has the capacity to shape shift and to retain his/her essence through multiplicity. S/he lives through boundaries, both self and other, male and female, cat and non-cat. This is the main reason why s/he is rejected by most humans, who are disturbed by an appearance (and thus an identity) in constant flux:

> He had four legs and a tail; this was probably why we thought him to be a cat. Concerning his ears, it was best not to count them. As for his general shapes, it was best not to see him silhouetted against the wall. We thought to discover a weasel, a manicou [Caribbean opossum], a dromedary, a red ant, an aborted snake and a mish-mash of things that should not be mentioned in good company. And here is the worst: he was neither male nor female, or male and female at the same, according to how the wind was blowing. This was no way to behave at all.
>   In brief: this s/he-cat was a calamity hated by everyone.[33]

Chamoiseau borrows the old theme of metamorphosis prevalent in tales and myths, but in ways that differ from past usage, as his changing creatures are willing hybrids and as hybridity is introduced as a desirable (although not socially acceptable) state. In another tale from *Emerveilles*, the dog Mabouk gets bored with his condition and after many brave shape-shifting experiments, decides to accept a hybrid form, 'neither really donkey nor completely dog, but all this at the same time in a state of unstable balance'.[34] Similarly, our werecat enjoys being part-cat, part-other creature. His shape-shifting is a tool for discovery and differs from traditional features of metamorphosis. Metamorphosis generally implies a mutation in which the subject is passive, often unwilling, as well as a loss of essence and identity.[35] Leda did not want to change into a swan any more than Bottom wished to be 'translated' into an ass. Although such transformations were esthetic, they were mostly perceived as degradation, as a fall from the human condition into a repulsive state of animality, as a violation of human essence by natural forces. While metamorphoses tend to be determined by magic (Circe suddenly casts a spell on Ulysses' companions to turn them into pigs), the creation of hybrid creatures is part of evolution (apes into humans) or of a deliberate intention (a mule is part-horse part-donkey). It contributes to question notions of purity and of species exceptionalism (if I am made up from different species, they are all of value). So, although Chamoiseau's werecat goes through metamorphoses, s/he does so willingly, as part of a continuous intention, and as the text states, 'transforms him/herself',[36] which places him/her as the agent of this transformation. Multiplicity is also a necessary condition of this transformation. These are also the reasons why s/he is hated by most humans, as s/he threatens both their false sense of stability and superiority in exposing them to the unknown. This 'old she-cat molded from some old injury',[37] of dubious and definitely impure origins, conveys to readers a positive image of animals, not only as vital to the diversity of the world, but as crucial to a meaningful human existence. The werecat is demonized by most members of the human community who construct and preserve divisions between species in order to justify arbitrary hierarchies among creatures. It points to humanity's biggest 'epistemological mistake',[38] to use Gregory Bateson's phrase; a mistake caused by defining something or someone 'in itself, not by its relations to other things'.[39]

Communication

Chamoiseau's beasts, and in particular his werecat, need to interact with other species to become themselves. They show their readers 'pattern[s] that connect'[40] and remind them that humanity's loss of the sense of meaningful unity is consequential upon the loss of a sense of linked diversity. No less importantly they open up the notion of communication beyond human speech. While articulated language is a major tool in translating human thought, it prioritizes human logic to the detriment of other forms and methods of interpretation. Human language, as grammatical structures show, only makes sense if the patterns it unfolds are contextualized, deciphered within a larger perspective. Chamoiseau's werecat shows us life as 'a dance of interacting parts',[41] and uses transformation as a language of discovery:

> Each one of Werecat's transformations drew [for Angèle] land-scapes of the world, steppes, deserts, snow and glaciers waves, dark bayous or scintillating beaches.[42]

Successful communication includes an acceptance that grammar and other human logical constructs are only meaningful if they take this dance into consideration. Stretching the limits of our language and comprehension also means accepting them as elements of the 'pluriverse'[43] and as part of its multiplicity. Animals do show us that there are many ways of making sense of life and that articulated language allows only limited access to the complexities of existence. As Chamoiseau reminds us,

> Let us claim the right to opacity. I do not need to understand someone to accept living, loving and working with him. [...] Could we accept not understanding each other for a moment? [...] There isn't one answer only [...]. There is a poetics of relation and there are poetics of chaos.[44]

Being open to transhumanism, not in the primarily human-centred, most common acceptance of the word today and referred to above, but as a willingness to interconnect, means to 'agree to opacity, that is, to the irreducible density of the other [...]. Being human may not be 'the image of man' but the constant weaving of these opacities'.[45]

Final Encounters

Chamoiseau's beasts may be real, as in 'The Surprised Kiss of the Dog to the Cat', surprising hybrids, as in 'Mabouk the Donkey-dog', or figments of imagination as in 'Angèle and Werecat', but they all tell us that encountering an animal is not about facing the wild, the non-human, the stranger. It is about relating to the unknown, about 'becoming with' and remembering that, in any case, 'we have never been human'[46], as Donna Haraway reminds us. Chamoiseau's poetics of relation dissolves the binaries that have perpetuated mutually exclusive, absolute definitions of humankind and other living creatures. He opens up his writing to both

> light and darkness, wisdom and madness, consciousness and unconsciousness, to a Reason which knows the irrational, to an idea of the human inscribed horizontally in that of the Living. [...]

The Other is the undecipherable, the unpredictable Whole-World. *The Whole Living World*.[47]

His work sings transversal relationships where frontiers are not limits to be conquered but places to travel across, ways through to unknown or partially known selves and others. His animals ride these frontiers not as 'an impossible dead end but as a way through', towards a concept of being which 'has ceased to be absolute in order to become a Relation'.[48] Relating unexpected, fresh, sometimes spectacular encounters between human and non-human animals, his stories portray the beauty of a world woven through patterns of interconnectedness. Readers are invited to recognize patterns which Gregory Bateson, in visionary fashion, identified more than three decades ago as essential to a meaningful existence. Chamoiseau, an author whose name is prophetically hybrid, as it evokes 'a complicated thing full of names of animals, of cat, of flying creatures and of bones',[49] does not only tell of wondrous connections. As a Frenchman from Martinique who 'writes in an oppressed country'[50] he also sends the message that the feeling, the guessing and the deciphering of these patterns of interconnectedness must be transnational and resonate equally among people of both the developed and developing worlds. Animals that were perceived as extensions of abusive power or instruments of colonial expansion appear, both for the (post)colonized and the (post)colonizer as essential messengers of diversity and as privileged agents of communication between us and the rest of the world. In that sense, Chamoiseau's stories urge today's readers to ask a question disturbingly similar to the one Bateson asked his students nearly four decades ago, perhaps the most urgent question of our time:

'What pattern connects the crab to the lobster and the orchid to the primrose and the four of them to me? And me to you'?[51]

Notes

1 I would like to thank Simon Edwards for his comments on this paper, on both content and style. The author would also like to acknowledge the support of the following projects: The Project

'Gender Equality in a Sustainable Culture: Values and Good Practices for Collaborative Development' (FEM2010-15599. Subprograma de Proyectos de Investigación Fundamental no orientada) funded by Spanish Ministry for Science and Innovation; The 'Animots' project, funded by the Agence Nationale de la Recherche (CNRS Paris).

2 The original passage reads :
'Le chien–qui-connaissait-le-chat n'était autre que ce chien que connaissait le chat. Et le chat-qui-connaissait-un-chien était en fait ce chat que connaissait le chien'.
Chamoiseau, P., 'Le Baiser-étonné du chien au chat', *Emerveilles*, (Paris: Gallimard Jeunesse, 1998), pp. 99.

3 Slemon S., 'Post-Colonial Allegory and the Transformation of History', *The Journal of Commonwealth Literature* 23 (1), 1988, 157–168; Ashcroft, B., *Post-Colonial Transformation*, (London: Routledge, 2001) (in particular, chapter 5, 'Allegory', pp. 104–123).

4 'The original sentence is : 'Le roman d'aujourd'hui pourra être le roman-monde où l'esthétique du chaos, de l'incertain identitaire, de l'inachèvement, de la polyphonie, du Grand amour, se joignent à l'Emerveille pour tenter d'approcher de la saveur du monde donné en son total'. Chamoiseau, P., 'Ré-ouverture', *Emerveilles, op. cit.,* p. 126.

5 Glissant, E., *Philosophie de la relation. Poésie en étendue,* (Paris: Gallimard, 2009).

6 Chamoiseau, P., 'Angèle et Chagarou', *Emerveilles, op. cit.,* pp. 53–56.

7 The phrases are borrowed from Pick, A., *Creaturely Poetics: Animality, Vulnerability, and the Identity of Species,* (New York: Columbia University Press, 2011).

8 Haraway, D., *When Species Meet,* (Minneapolis University of Minnesota Press, 2008), p. 4.

9 'Le travail de production artistique, dans les pays en voie de dével-oppement […] reste indispensable. [… T]ous les commencements des peuples (de l'Iliade à l'Ancien Testament, du *Livre des Morts* des Egyptiens aux chansons de geste occidentales) sont poétiques. C'est-à-dire qu'il y faut la voix qui articule un projet commun, en même temps qu'on se donne aux réalisations sans lesquelles ce projet resterait rêve.
[…]
La parole de l'artiste antillais ne provient donc pas de l'obsession de chanter son être intime ; cet intime est inséparable du devenir de la communauté'.
Glissant, E., *Le Discours antillais*, (Paris: Gallimard Folio, 1980/1997) pp. 758–759.
On this topic, see Britton C., *The Sense of Community in French Caribbean Fiction,* (Liverpool: Liverpool University Press, 2008).

10 Glissant, E., *Poétique de la relation*, (Paris: Gallimard, 1990).

11 'Un monde où les êtres humains, et les animaux et les paysages, et les cultures et les spiritualités, se contaminent mutuellement. Mais la contamination n'est pas la dilution. Et ce n'est pas non plus ce choix de perfection vers quoi on tâtonne si misérablement par les moyens de la génétique [...]. Ce que Deleuze appelle la santé n'est pas un seul état permanent et indifférencié de 'caractères formels', mais plutôt la capacité mouvementée d'entrer dans ces 'zones de voisinages.'
Glissant, E., *La Cohée du Lamentin*, (Paris: Gallimard, 2005) p. 136.

12 Glissant, E., *Introduction à une poétique du divers*, (Paris: Gallimard, 1996) p. 30.

13 *Ibid.*, p. 31.

14 *Ibid.*, p. 327.

15 See for instance Diamond, J., *Collapse. How Societies Choose to Fail or to Succeed*, (NewYork: Viking Books, 2005) and Caras, R., *A Perfect Harmony. The Intertwining Lives of Animals and Humans throughout History*, (New York: Simon and Schuster, 1996).

16 'L'indigène amérindien, l'Arawak, le Caraïbe, n'ont pas vu Christophe Colomb comme un ennemi; ils savaient déjà qu'on pouvait sortir de leur pays. Ils savaient aussi dans leur légende, dans leurs mythes que les gens viendraient dans leur pays. Donc les bateaux ne leur ont pas paru merveilleux. Ce qui leur a paru merveilleux, c'est le cheval, ils n'avaient pas encore vu le cheval : pour eux, c'était comme un monstre'.
Tirolien, G., *De Marie-Galante à une poétique afro-antillaise, entretiens recueillis par Michel Tétu*, (Paris : Editions caribéennes/ Geref, 1990) p. 140.

17 'Les chrétiens dressèrent des lévriers, des chiens particulièrement méchants qui dès qu'ils voyaient un Indien, le mettaient en pièce en un clin d'œil. Ils l'attaquaient et le mangeaient plus vite que s'il s'était agi d'un porc. [...] Ces chiens ont fait de grands ravages et de grandes boucheries'. De Las Casas B. (1474–1566) addressing the King of Spain regarding the massacre of the Amerindians, quoted by Rano, J., *Créolitude, silence et cicatrice pour seuls témoins*, (Paris: L'Harmattan, 1997) p. 131.

18 On domestic animals in plantations, particularly slave dogs, the following book can be consulted: Franklin, J. H. and Schweninger, L., *Runaway Slaves, Rebels on the Plantation* (Oxford / New York: Oxford University Press, 1999).
A chapter (pp. 160–164) is devoted to dogs.

19 It is interesting to note that cock fighting, one of the cruelest sports involving animals, originally established in England, pioneering country of bloody sports and colonization in modern times, is still popular in the French West Indies, particularly in Guadeloupe. Introduced by Europeans to the West Indies, roosters do not appear in traditional Creole tales. Cock fighting's popularity can be interpreted as a symbol of repossession of the history of domination of plantations and as an outlet for the contained aggression against colonizers. The considerable financial stakes involved reflect their importance. They have also had a strong impact on West Indian cultural identity, to the point that the language of cock fighting has been constitutive of Haitian Creole in literary discourse. See Frankétienne, *Dézafi*, (Port au Prince: Editions Fardin, 1975).

20 Michael Dash, preface to the English translation of *La Lézarde* (1985, 16), quoted by Hezekiah R. (1994), 'Martinique and Guadeloupe. Time and Space', Arnold, A. J. (ed), *A History of Literature in the Caribbean*, volume 1, Hispanic and Francophone regions, p. 386 (whole article pp. 379–387).

21 Walcott, D., 'The Muse of History', *What the Twighlight Says: Essays*, (New York: Farrar, Straus and Giroux, 1999) pp. 37–38. On the representation of landscape in Caribbean literature, see Tiffin, H., 'Man fitting the Landscape', DeLoughrey, E. et al (eds), *Caribbean Literature and the Environment. Between Nature and Culture*, (Charlottesville: University of Virginia Press, 2005) pp. 199–212.

22 One of Raphaël Confiant's recent books (2000) evokes particularly strongly the ambivalent attitudes towards 'tamed' landscapes and their products: *Canne, douleur séculaire, O tendresse!* Paris: Ibis Rouge *(Cane, age-old pain, O tenderness!)*.

23 Barnabé, J., Chamoiseau, P., Confiant, R., *Eloge de la créolité /In Praise of Creoleness*, Edition bilingue, (Paris: Gallimard, 1990) p. 61.

24 'L'animal […] est entendu comme rythme indispensable du temps. Il est regardé comme élément fondamental de l'espace. Le chien surtout incarne la durée, d'une temporalité qui échappe souvent au colonisé. Il comble d'autre part un espace qui, par le travail de l'occidentalisation, devient de plus en plus vide. Il y a quelques années, la Préfecture décide de réduire le nombre de chiens errants en les abattant sur place ou en les consignant à la fourrière. Les gardes chargés de la sinistre besogne, en combinaisons et armés de fusils à seringue, durent reculer et abandonner le terrain dans les quartiers populaires devant l'incroyable combativité des riverains. Le Martiniquais peut éborgner un chien errant, mais ne supporte pas qu'on le dérobe à sa vue. L'animal est son repos; son point de repère.

Comme l'occidental regarde sans cesse sa montre pour savoir qui il est, l'Antillais cherche dans les yeux de la bête une référence à sa vie déboussolée. L'animal est un véritable patrimoine existentiel et historique'.

Francis Affergan, F. (1977) 'De la relégation à l'exclusion : le bestiaire aux Antilles françaises', *Les Bêtes, Traverses* 8, 58.

25 'L'oiseau, n'importe lequel, diaphane ou majestueux, tisse le vent et la sève, l'air à la terre. Il n'oublie ni l'eau ni le feu'.

Glissant, E. (2005), *La Cohée du Lamentin, op.cit.,* p. 71.

For a deeper analysis of birds in postcolonial fiction, see Desblache, L., 'Writers on the Wing and the (De/Re)consruction of Cultural Memory in Patrick Chamoiseau and J.M. Coetzee's Fictional narratives', *Kunapipi* (special issue on Birds) volume XXIX, 2, 2007, 178–193.

26 This terminology is borrowed from Cary Wolfe, *Animal Rites. American Culture, the Discourse of Species, and Posthuman Theory,* (Chicago: University of Chicago Press, 2003) p. 101.

27 Barthes, R., *Mythologies,* (Paris : Seuil, 1957).

28 Carter, A., 'Notes from the Front Line', Uglow, J. (ed) *Shaking a leg: Journalism and Writings, The collected Angela Carter,* (London: Chatto and Windus, 1997) p. 38.

29 Chamoiseau, P., 'Angèle et Chagarou', *Emerveilles,* p. 54.

30 The full original sentence reads : 'Cette émerveille devrait nous permettre de mieux approcher de cet inconnaissable, et surtout, de mieux préparer notre imaginaire aux flot des nouveautés qui vont submerger nos vies durant les temps qui viennent'.

Chamoiseau, P., *Emerveilles, op. cit.,* p. 127.

31 'Il prenait des allures de chameau au clair-fou des déserts. Ou alors, la masse terrible des éléphants qui traversent les forêts pour s'en aller mourir dans des bouquets d'ivoire. Il semblait parfois couler le long des grands bambous tel un serpent aux écailles éclatantes. A tout moment, il était quelque chose d'autre tout en restant lui-même. Ou alors ce lui-même s'étoilait en mille possibles qui ouvraient les regards et libéraient l'esprit. Il était tout-possible en restant vaguement chat'.

Ibid., p. 54.

32 '[Ils] vivaient mille expériences. Eprouvaient mille humanités et toutes les fééries'.

Ibid., p. 55.

33 'Il avait quatre pattes et une queue, c'était sans doute pourquoi on le supposait chat. Question de ses oreilles, il valait mieux renoncer à compter. Quant à ses formes générales, il valait mieux ne pas les étudier en ombre chinoise. On croyait découvrir une belette, un manicou, un dromadaire, une fourmi rouge, un serpent avorté et un grosso-modo de choses qu'on devrait taire en société. Et voici le pire : il n'était ni mâle ni femelle, ou alors il était à la fois mâle et femelle selon le sens du vent. Ce qui était vraiment de bien mauvaises manières.

En clair : ce chatte était une calamité que tout le monde haïssait'.

Ibid., p. 54.

34 'Ni âne vraiment ni tout à fait chien, mais tout cela en même temps en équilibre instable'.

Chamoiseau, P., 'Mabouc l'âne-chien', *Emerveilles, op.cit.*, p. 28.

35 On the notions of hyridity vs metamorphosis, I am indebted to Harvey Hix's paper delivered at the conference 'Hybrids, Monsters and other Aliens in 20th and 21st century Writing' held at the University of London on the 9th–11th September 2010. The paper was entitled 'Hybridity is the new Metamorphosis'.

36 The use of the verb 'se transformer' throughout the story, implies that the action is induced by the self.

37 'vieux-chatte [...] coulé d'on ne sait quel bobo'.

Chamoiseau, P. *'Angèle et Chagarou', op.cit.*, p. 55.

38 Bateson, G., *Mind and Nature, a Necessary Unity*, (Cresskill: Hampton Press, 1979/2002) p. 17.

39 *Ibid.*, p. 15.

40 Ibid.

41 *Ibid.*, p. 12.

42 'Chaque transformation de Chagarou lui dessinait des paysages du monde, des steppes, des déserts, des ondulations de neige et de glaciers, des bayous sombres ou des plages brasillantes'.

Chamoiseau, P. *'Angèle et Chagarou', op.cit.*, p. 53.

43 The expression is borrowed from Bruno Latour. Latour, B., *The Politics of Nature* (Cambridge MA: Harvard University Press, 2004).

44 [R]éclamons le droit à l'opacité. Je n'ai pas besoin de comprendre quelqu'un pour accepter de vivre, d'aimer, de travailler avec lui. [... Et] si l'on acceptait de ne plus se comprendre un moment? [...] Il n'y a pas une seule réponse [...]. Il y a une poétique de la relation et des poétiques du chaos.

Le Pelletier C., *Encre noire, la langue en liberté. Entretiens*, (Guadeloupe: Ibis Rouge Editions,1998, pp. 170–171.

45 The full sentences read: 'Dans le monde de la Relation, qui prend le relais du système unifiant de l'Etre, consentir à l'opacité, c'est-à-dire à la densité irréductible de l'autre, c'est accomplir, véritablement, à travers le divers l'humain. L'humain n'est peut-être pas 'l'image de

l'homme' mais aujourd'hui la trame sans cesse recommencée de ces opacités consenties'.
Glissant, E. *Le Discours antillais, op. cit.*, p. 418.

46 Haraway, D., *When Species Meet,* op. cit. pp. 1, 4, and, 'Becoming-with-Companions: Sharing and Response in Experimental Laboratories', Tom Tyler T. and Rossini, M. (eds), *Animal Encounters*, (Leiden: Brill, 2009) pp. 115–136.

47 'The original sentence reads: 'L'idée de la Pierre-monde ouvre mon écriture à la lumière et à l'obscur, à la sapience et la démence, au conscient et à l'inconscient, à une Raison qui connaît l'irrationnel, à une idée de l'humain inscrite de manière horizontale dans celle du Vivant'. [...] L'Autre, c'est l'indéchiffrable, l'imprédictible du Tout-Monde. Tout le Vivant'.
Chamoiseau, P. 'Mondialisation, mondialité, pierre-monde', *Les Tremblements du monde. Ecrire avec Patrick Chamoiseau*, (Lyon : Collection les Merles Moqueurs, 2009) p. 74.

48 The original sentence is :
'La frontière [...] a cessé d'être un impossible pour devenir passage [... et l']Etre, dans nos poétiques, a cessé d'être un absolu pour devenir une Relation'.
Glissant, E., *Une nouvelle région du monde* (Paris: Gallimard, 2006) p. 180.

49 '[U]n machin compliqué rempli de noms d'animaux, de chat, de chameau, de volatiles et d'os'.
Chamoiseau, P. *Une Enfance créole II. Chemin-d'école,* (Paris : Gallimard Folio, 1994/1996) p. 54.
The words cat, chamois, camel and bird can be heard in the writer's name.

50 This is the title of one of the writer's essay: Chamoiseau, P. *Ecrire en pays dominé*, (Paris: Gallimard, 1997) pp. 311–312.

51 Bateson, G., *Mind and Nature, op. cit*, p. 7.

PART THREE

Thinking Beyond the Divide

7

Affective Animal: Bataille, Lascaux and the Mediatization of the Sacred[1]

Felicity Colman

'An appetite for meat? Undoubtedly'.
(BATAILLE, *CIVILIZED MAN REDISCOVERS THE MAN OF DESIRE* [1953]).[2]

The state of being and or becoming sacred is an epistemological and economic movement. Philosophical accounts of the role that the non-human, and in particular the role the animal plays in the constitution of the world describe this movement of the sacred as an affective site. For Bataille, the sacred is a thing that appears with such intensive force that it can re-determine the world that it inhabits. The content of Bataille's work is most often summarized in terms of a focus on 'heterology'; 'in the intimate connection between the sacred and profane, between waste and luxury, between filth, beauty and eroticism'.[3] In addition to this, and, as scholars including Suzanne Guerlac, Stuart Kendall, Carrie Noland and Steven Ungar have suggested, underpinning Bataille's entire oeuvre is the tempering of the human by the animal – as concept, reality, and image that performs human consciousness.[4] These different figures and modulations of animality in Bataille's work provide instructions on the ethical organization of humans in social groups – from the absolute power held by prehistoric images of animals to aspects of use-values of the animal under capitalist market conditions.

Bataille charts the anthropocentric construction of the general economy of the animal, and the multiple terms of animality engaged by 'man' in his search for some structure of the forms of 'sensibility' that direct him-as-human.[5] Bataille will discuss the sacred nature of the animal, the animal as sacrifice, the animal as victim of the sacrifice, the animal as a ritual element, the use of the animal in festivals, the consideration of the animal as a horrific thing, or as an excess of nature, in terms of the 'horror of nature', the figure of the animal as a dialectic other for the human idea of the totality of being, becoming-consciousness, a way of structuring death, and as a concept for man-as-hunter to pursue.[6] Bataille rejects a phenomenological reduction of the materiality of the animal by the 'thickness' accorded it in the 'poetic capacity' of human language.[7] Instead, based on his study of animals, and in particular the prehistoric animal, Bataille's work provides a model for constructing a philosophy of consumption.

In this chapter I consider this philosophy of consumption, for the possibilities it offers in vectorizing anthropocentric thinking and the epistemology of matter into multiple states of immanence. Bataille's vectorial break with normative models of knowledge offers a model for philosophy that critiques the constitution of worlds, their forms, their inequities, and their ethical trajectories. The prehistoric images of the animal in cave art which Bataille explores afford an aesthetic dramaturgy, which, through their economic organizational ability to record, select and distribute knowledge, create and feed the various strands of what Bataille describes as the 'non-knowledge' of humans. To test Bataille's claims, in this chapter I consider some prehistoric and post-industrial images of animals, describing them as images produced as consumptive forms. As Bataille describes, particular animal forms hold an affective power over humans. In agreement with some of Bataille's propositions, my argument here is that images and symbols of animals provide paradigmatic media forms; they are images-in-process that are indicative of the affective range of states of the *mediatized evolution* of human consciousness. As one of the fundamental media platforms for human recording and human art, cave art provides evidence of the affective power of animals, not just at an emotional, or sacred level, but affective for the determination of labour and intellectual economies.

Bataille's study of cave art, and in particular his speculation on the affective forms of animals with some human figures in those caves, facilitates ideas that we see populating the general economy. Bataille's logic was to delineate the experience lived of life as the dialectic development of human activity which results in the creation of coded communities. In *The Accursed Share*, the theory of the general economy is detailed, descriptive of the affects of the consumption or expenditure of wealth (rather than the production of it).[8] The dialectic of this is the 'restricted economy' based on the workings of capital accumulation and profit. The waste factor of Bataille's theory of the general economy is dialectically generated by the use-value of the market restrictive economy.[9] In the consumption of the animal in community-specific economies, what are the excesses produced and to what end? Bataille's work is not concerned with profit-margins, but with the speculation on how human communities engage the agency provided by the affective animal encounter, generative of a breadth of paradoxical relationships, and different conditions for living. Repeatedly through his fictional and theoretical works, Bataille positions the art of animals as media that facilitate forms of human and non-human labour, and of consciousness.[10] The principles and ontology of what humans call animals are serviced, and are at the service of *various economic systems of societies*. As with every restricted economy, it is the images and conceptual abstractions of that system that are put to work to feed the determination of the aesthetic of the political ethics of any given era of human life.

Thus in trying to reach an account of the human 'spirit' or condition, Bataille wrote and lectured about anthropology not as a disciplinary study of mythology, ritual and the sacred aspects of collective communal experiences, but with regard to the disciplinary semiology of objects and materials of the anthropological. Bataille's anthropological study of life is set up as an affective, emotive, and anti-epistemological 'search'.[11] Bataille lectures on prehistoric art, reviews books on prehistoric anthropology, and publishes a series of essays on prehistoric art and anthropology throughout his career.[12] Bataille's knowledge is gleaned through this thirty-year study of prehistoric cave art forms, with a focus on the caves and speleological activities largely of the Vézère Valley in the Dordogne territory of south-western France. These contain hundreds of Palaeolithic era prehistoric sites and many decorated caves, including the Lascaux caves, and it is likely that many remain as yet 'undiscovered'.[13] Bataille referred to the sites in the Vézère valley as a place of the 'theatre of changes'.[14] He had begun writing about prehistory in relation to the visual arts in his surrealist journal, *Documents* (1929–30). Bataille's work on cave art appears after his volumes *The Accursed Share* (1949) and *The History of Eroticism* (1951), rewritten and published as *Eroticism* (1955).

In *Eroticism*, Bataille engages the way that prehistoric images of animals dramatize the nature of the human, where animality provides the necessary element of sacrifice, required for Bataille's thesis on anguish.[15] Bataille's notion of anguish is the dialectic product of a catalytic experience; sometimes non-human, but always in excess of normative structures for human consciousness.[16] What forms of anguish arise when the hunter finally kills and consumes his victim? Although, as Kendall argues, Bataille's focus is on the sense of a shared experience between hunter and victim, the affective states arising from this event are significant for Bataille's philosophy of consumption. As Bataille describes, the catalytic affect of sacrifice provides instances of where labour forms (of the hunter and of the victim), although driven by capital, refute the ideology of Marx's labour thesis as value-adding through 'profitable accumulation'.[17] Instead, Bataille situates the forms of fate and anguish – the affective outcomes of the labour of the hunter as complicit with destructive aspects of the capitalist system *and* also as political enabling of different embodied states of desire – of hunger and of the desire for self-consciousness. The politics of consumption affect a move away from inherited cultural positions, and a reversal of labour forms.

Bataille's somewhat anthropophagic approach articulates the dimensions and openings created by the active energies of the animal and human. Through the early 1950s, Bataille re-articulates his first visit to Lascaux, and the story of how it was 're-discovered'. Bataille describes Lascaux in terms of its anthropocentric accomplishment and the 'shock' not only of its discovery, but of the affective ability of each of the images of the caves to produce such an aesthetic collision of the prehistoric with the contemporary.[18] In his lecture on Lascaux in 1955 in Orléans, Bataille introduced a film that showed the discovery of the Lascaux caves in 1940 by noting that the paintings in Lascaux 'are the first to announce, by striking our sensibility and shocking it so completely, the presence of man on earth'.[19] As Henri Lefebvre pointed out, this presence is one that is determined by Lascaux as a place that holds a power that is accorded to other forms of 'cryptal art' where paintings are not made to be seen, but just 'to be' affective – in magical and occult ways.[20] The images preserved in these caves offer an alternative death-site to the everyday killing fields of the European war landscape of the 1940s. As Kendall points out, the pre-historians of Bataille's era – such as Abbé Henri Breuil and Raymond Lantier – describe cave art in terms of its magic, where the images are performed as a hunting ritual.[21] Bataille follows their work in certain aspects but in his comments on the images, a critique of the dominant anthropocentric mind-set begins. 'We are certain that [prehistoric man] confronted the animal not as though he were confronting an inferior being or thing, a negligible reality,' Bataille writes, 'but as if he were confronting a mind similar to his own'.[22] Bataille does not dismiss this aspect of the specialists work but develops his own less anthropologically-speciesist position to look at the products of affective intensities of encounters in different communities. His descriptors of the 'majestic sign' of Lascaux broaden to explore the affective economy of the animals of these images. In the conclusion of his Lascaux lecture, he notes that what 'pushes us past the initial moment, to see in these paintings a world of only an unfortunate sense of need – impenetrable to us – is linked to our inability to find a complete response to our desire in an animal world'.[23]

So for Bataille, (cave) art mediatizes the sacred affect of being human. Bataille situates the paintings within his vernacular situation: 'These hunters from Dordogne would better understand a housewife from Sarlat [Sarlat le Caneda, Dordogne] buying meat for lunch from a butcher shop than they would Leonardo da Vinci, or those drowned eyes intoxicated by his painting'.[24] But as Bataille further notes, what 'shatters' the everyday illusion given by the animal paintings is in fact the self-affective nature of the images. This state of self-affection is what Bergson termed 'durée' – the communication of a lived event, such as an experience of viewing art (and or images of things) – and is what holds an affective power. What Bataille and Bergson both describe is how it is the experience with the image[25] that affects their self-consciousness of their world – through a mediatization that is productive of an immanent self-consumption. Bergson is concerned to describe how consciousness is a product of movement that leads to an awareness of the indivisibility of the world, whereas Bataille draws upon the affective power generated by the consciousness of the position of the human being in relation to the animal – and that conscious awareness of the desires of consumption that drive and affect humans to devise his position on the world. If we describe the general economy of art as a mediatization that is expressive of consumptive excesses, after Bataille, then we have a methodology that provides the means for articulating different forms of art and the mediatization of lived experience as affectively absolute; physically situated, and not transcendent. Images produce particular ranges of perceptual epistemology through their modes of affectivity. The question this raises then is how the affective modality of the animal image of animality – *even through its mediatized market economy* – is able to offer another perspective for human capacity to account for lived experience, in a way that does not rely upon a merely human consciousness or a phenomenologically reductive account of the object, or speciesist 'thingness'. In order to think the terms of this animal-human economy of potentia, Bataille's logic of animality, where an other-than-human position resides, is where Bataille argues (through consideration of the animal), that 'human' 'consciousness only ever reveals objects'.[26] In this sense, Bataille's argument is that 'humanity' is in fact a false problem.[27] Bataille takes this proposition further in his address of the sovereignty of the incommensurable, where he provides an activist standpoint that rejects the status quo in favour of a more ethically sustainable and positive mode of being or mediatized activity. I say positive, in the face of criticism against

Bataille's turn to the position of 'nonknowledge', in the sense that the affects of the rejection of accounts of human consciousness of things reject patriarchal, heirarchized knowledge systems that facilitate acts of fascism and forms of cannibalism.[28] It is this position that can be taken as a key point in Bataille's philosophy of consumption, which developed through his thinking on the heterogeneity of life for humans, as posed by questions of animality.[29]

There is an animal aesthetic that is tied to every community's political and aesthetic acceptance – one that determines ethical use and codes of practice. The life of animals is used for the maintenance and comfort of humans, they exist within the restrictive human economies. Animals are farmed as products for human consumption at many levels; from scientific and psychologic experimentation, food production, medicinal uses, clothing and interior decoration, to use in entertainment, leisure and sports industries. The types of containment of animals in societies remain community specific, under all types of market processes, even under regulatory capitalist market drives towards homogeneity.

Human/animal relationships are dominated by economies of food, one of the most important of which is the containment and control of animals as food. The media dramatization of this relationship is perhaps nowhere more evident than in the story of the current global food crisis.[30] Man still hunts, but how does the affective power produced by the hunt that Lascaux registers continue to engender new forms, now that it has been dissipated by the genetic manipulation of animal farming, and robotic agricultural technologies? My argument is that different forms of animal affect are directed and controlled according to the mediated types of anthropomorphized labour forms, through which the animal and thus human form are metaphysically determined.

Animal Media: Lascaux, Bataille and Cattle Affect

To test these ideas concerning animal affect, I want to provide a focal point with a specific animal – one that is classified under the genus *Bos* – cattle – that includes the type of animal that is used for sports, hunted and raised for meat and dairy products and which appears on the walls of Lascaux: bison, cows, bulls, horses, bovids, aurochs, iboxes, ox, deer ,,. [Figure 7.1].

Commentators discuss Lascaux in terms of its function as a place of magic, of ritual; some call it art; others an archaeological record. Bataille refers to Lascaux as 'the cradle of humanity'. We can only speculate on the use-value the images had for the community that drew and maintained them. However, we can observe that the communal mediatization of the key things in the communities' life is nothing new. Today we have images that attest to a worship of information devices and recording equipment, but where are the affective images of the animals we depend upon to be found today, and what forms do they take? There are settler museums devoted to cattle images including the *Cattle Raisers Museum* in Fort Worth, Texas, USA and the *Australian Stockman's Hall of Fame* in Longreach, Central Queensland, Australia. Etymologically, *cattle* is a Middle English word, developed from the Old North French *catel*, meaning property and livestock. This animal genus has a long history in the human world,

Figure 7.1   Hall of Bulls, Lascaux. Back row: Abbé Breuil and Count Bégouën, on 24 October, 1940 at Lascaux. Seated front: the Lascaux discoverers Jacques Marsal, left, and Marcel Ravidat, right. N. Aujoulat © Ministère de la Culture et de la Communication/Centre National de Préhistoire.

from the vital part that *bos* played in sustaining Neolithic societies; their roles in the dramatization of life in Hellenistic mythologies (the cattle of Helios that Homer encounters in Sicily); *Guias* the Hindi cow, symbolic of Earth itself (similar to *Gaia,* the Greek goddess of earth); the bullfighting of ancient Rome and contemporary Spain. From the late 1800s, cattle played a determining part in many colonial projects.[31] As a central food item in American and European diets, at the end of the 1980s, a new disease resulted from human mis-management of farming cows – Bovine Spongiform Encephalopathy (BSE, also known in Britain as the mad cow disease).[32] Cattle continue to perform multiple important roles in societies, such as the spiritual and cultural roles in rural society of cattle in the Communal Lands of Zimbabwe.[33]

Some cattle forms have evolved by technological evolution that follows the human-assisted breeding programmes that have produced the *Belgian Blue Schwarzenegger* super muscle cow [Figure 7.2].

Along with the breed of Piedmontese, the Belgian Blues have been selectively bred so that they have super large muscles due to a mutation of the myostatin protein.[34] Myostatin is the protein that is

Figure 7.2 *Belgian Blue Schwarzenegger* super muscle cow. Drawing by Christos Zikos, 2011.

normally genetically coded to inhibit muscle growth after a biological time-framed sequence of development, and with its discovery in 1997 (by McPherron and Lee), scientists and animal geneticists were alerted to the genetic sequencing for how to control cell growth by its suppression or acceleration. Cows and other human-food farmed animals including sheep, pigs and chickens muscles are genetically manipulated so that a 'double muscling' occurs.[35] The Belgian Blues are described by *The American Belgian Blue Breeders Association* as 'the ultimate beef machine', and their breeding is totally managed for the benefit of human consumption.[36] In terms of an affective encounter with this animal, humans have produced living choice cuts through a bestial slavery where the animal is totally controlled.

The cow is also valuable for dairy products, and the mediatization of the diary product relies upon economic indices, which tend to present nostalgic, small farm 'rural' images of agriculture. Images of jersey patterned containers and cows roaming free to boost the sale of dairy products are distant from the reality of the conditions of dairy production. While hand milking is part of a general economy of organic farming, robotic machine milking has been standard in the industry since the 1970s and ranges from Herringbone milking parlours, parallel milking parlours, and the current industry favourite: carousel milking parlours [Figure 7.3].

The carousel cow milking method is globally used, and operates as a totally restricted economy. Milk is harvested by either partial or total automated milking; the cow steps onto a sensor and a robotic arm attaches the milking hose.[37] Restricted economies produce affectively restricted products, including affectively homogenous labour experiences for the [roboticized] worker. A CEO of Fair Oaks Dairy in Indiana, USA, says: 'we like the carousel because it brings the work to us'; the cow's udder is presented to the worker who simply has to hook up the robotic milking machine.[38] Fair Oaks Dairy (sort of like cow concentration camp, but which the company sets up as a mediatized theme experience for the human perspective along the lines of *dairy meets Disney*), takes animal consumption to an adventure-park-style thematized 'dairy-experience'. Cows step onto a rotating floor that takes 8 minutes to complete the milking process before they return to their sheds to eat and shit and give birth – where male calves are slaughtered to produce veal as a dairy

Figure 7.3 *Carousel milking* Drawing by Christos Zikos, 2011.

by-product, and female calves enter the Disney-dairy lifecycle and are inseminated, give birth, produce milk, and step back onto the carousel to be milked again and again and again until they die.[39] The animals are totally bound indoors by their human harvesters. If the humans fail in their attention, a swifter death awaits. In 2011, volunteer workers took images of hundreds of dead and starving dairy cows in ranches around the Fukushima I Nuclear Power Plant accident in Japan. The Japanese cows, along with other animals, were abandoned as their human managers were ordered by their government to leave and save themselves from radiation poisoning, and the images of the dead and dying dairy cows and their calves are all that remain.

Returning to the durational potential offered by the cave images of animals, another media form, 3D digital film, enables us to step inside another cave to 'experience' the affects of the images in a disembodied, but nevertheless, conscious way. Titled *Cave of Forgotten Dreams*, filmmaker Werner Herzog in 2010 documented aspects of speleology and some of the world's oldest known drawings discovered in 1994 at Chauvet Pont d'Arc cave, situated on a limestone cliff above the former bed of the Ardèche River in southern France.[40] Like Bataille, Herzog is struck by the consciousness-focussing affect of the images, remarking that 'the cave is like a frozen flesh of a moment in time'.[41] Herzog describes the animal images, particularly the panels where multiple horses appear, as a 'proto-cinema'. Similarly in Lascaux, Bataille described the sense of movement that the images affected.[42]

As these few examples illustrate, the use value for each community's situation of its cattle remains central for facets of self-determination of the perceived requirements of consumption. From Lascaux to carousel cow, humans need cattle. In the passage through these states, both human and animal species have changed, measurable in the forms of mediatization of cattle and their consumption by humans. Distinctions between the use of cattle by Paleolithic hunters of the Dordogne Valley of south central France, as depicted in the Lascaux caves, to the use of cattle in contemporary cow milking parlours provide the hetereogeneity of forms of this animal, despite its enforced measure by human articulated sovereignty. In Bataille's discussion of the Lascaux animals, he argues that the community that created and used this site revered the animals that it hunted. So they had a utilitarian function (they were edible; wearable) and an aesthetic function (they were to be worshipped). In addition, the cave provides a media platform that illustrates and is a component of the hierarchized culture of its present-day user-community. Bataille observes that animals in Lascaux provide a 'tool' function for humans:

> There is something truly unique here. For primitive human beings, the animal is not a thing. And this characterizes very broadly all of primitive humanity, for whom ordinary animality is rather divine. The thing is obviously not human. But the thing is on the side of humanity; it is a tool, which in the time of Lascaux is all that separated human beings from animals. In addition, if man is not a thing, he will become one when slaves appear, that is, men subjugated to work. Herein lies something that deeply underlines the meaning of the discovery of Lascaux.[43]

Bataille positions the Lascaux cave as an example of an affective animal media paradigm. This media paradigm is evolutionary in the sense that it vectorializes experience – in this case, the experience of the animal image – in relation to work. It is this aspect of labour that I want to raise in relation to the affective images. The cave functions in principle and in practice in terms of a general economy – it is a media form that as an intellectual or material condition displays the consumptive energies required and produced by the hunt. But Bataille describes 'the secret of Lascaux Man' as in fact providing a different sense of animal-human relations than with contemporaneous uses of the animal for food.[44] Bataille is certainly interested in the sexual life of [prehistoric] man [sic] – which he sees as offering a state unrestrained by social mores of his era, but is cautious about ascribing a material desire to the images. He notes that the images of Lascaux are 'within the provinces of both science and desire'.[45] In further essays and lectures, Bataille considers the few human figurative drawings in the caves, and on the small sculptural statuettes found in and in the vicinity of the caves, including the *Lespugue Venus* (dated at approx 24,000 years, in the collection of the Musée de l'Homme, Paris).[46] Like Herzog, Bataille is drawn to speculate on the sexual nature of the figurative form. Herzog goes so far as to structure *Cave of Forgotten Dreams* around the attainment of a Paleolithic money-shot, with the camera precariously hooked up to reveal a scene of interspecial sex/becoming-animal and becoming-human. However in both Bataille and Herzog, the figures indexically coded by the recognition of vulva, breast or penis contribute to a cycle of consumptive practices that colonize each thinker's position, and place a limit on precisely the forms of expanded consciousness they seek.

Bataille states that what concerns him in relation to the self-affective nature of the images are aspects of 'consciousness'– and 'consciousness of death' that anthropologists use to distinguish between *Homo faber* (the toolmaker) and *Homo sapien* (possessing consciousness).[47] It is the 'technical medium of magic' that Bataille charts as non-utilizable by the general economy of the hunt.[48] Perhaps unbeknown to Bataille, the excesses of the Lascaux images over time are productive of another system of growth. We can map Lascaux in terms of its site – Lascaux – its approximate date of creation (ca. 17,000 B.C.), its rediscovery in 1940 and closure to the public by 1963. In that mere twenty-odd year span in the life of these caves, tourism meant that the images and caves had been exposed to many visitors, and the introduction of electric lights and air conditioning systems as well as people have introduced new life forms into the caves. A 'bacterial and fungal colonization' and algae growth began destroying – and continues to destroy – the cave paintings. As a place it is a long way from the Lascaux Bataille described in the 1950s: 'If one goes to Lascaux during the winter it is easy to visit alone, or nearly alone'.[49] A replica of two of the cave halls form Lascaux— the Great Hall of the Bulls and the Painted Gallery — opened in 1983, 200 meters from the original, in Lascaux II.[50]

Much in the same way that cave art for different kinds of cultures has to function and cater for the tourist market and the labour forms created through tourism (such as the images of the white kangaroo in caves at KarbenadjarInglawe, Kudjekbinj, *Arnhem Land* Australia), the sites of Lascaux and Chauvet function as a mediatized ethological fantasy. In comparisons between the cattle of Lascaux, the carousel milkers and the Belgian super cow, some distinctions can be drawn in terms of the differences in affective labour that the containment of animals enables. Bataille's general economy is a condition that is the opposite of a restrictive or controlled economy. The excesses of Lascaux – the original use-value of the drawings, or even the fungal growths of the 1990s eating the images – cannot be utilized by humans at least, but a new plant and animal ecology can grow out of this excess. Perhaps the general economy only exists in terms of Bataille's position; for the tourist of ethnographic and indigenous art forms, whose perspective already has an epistemological framework designed to map an 'excessive' phenomenological, and thus anthropocentric, perspective onto the metaphysics of the experience, in this case, the animal experience.

Media forms like the Lascaux cave images, or a Channel 4, UK report on the Belgium supercow or the cow carousel farming unit theme experience, do not just collate and report biopolitical information on the practices of life; these media are the blueprints for specific communities' life forms. The affective nature of different media forms – written, visual, and the methods of producing them – are all approaches that Bataille learned from thinking about the affective impact of the animal in its encounter with humans, developed against contemporaneous anthropological methodologies, but proceeding from his work in surrealist constructed chance and limit test games, by experiments with the mind and with the physicality and chemistry of the body (see Clifford 1981).[51] In describing the breadth of cultural media produced in and of Lascaux, Bataille is charting the affective animal. He writes:

> Now let's imagine the hunt, on which life and death will depend, the ritual: an attentively executed drawing true to life, though seen on the flickering light of lamps, completed in a short time, the ritual, the drawing that provides the apparition of this bison. This sudden creation had to have produced in the impassioned minds of the hunters an intense feeling of the proximity of the inaccessible monster, a feeling of proximity, of profound harmony.[52]

Bataille effectively has an encounter with the hunter that affects and thus moves him to describe the state in which he finds himself. Who is the monster? This is a state of sanctity – of affective intensity – is 'transformational' for Bataille, in the sense that the value of Deleuze and Guattari's concept of 'becoming-animal' accords – which is not about identifying or imitating animals, but about a realization of other non-human positions.

Bataille's *realization* raises a number of issues, and I want to briefly highlight just two of them. First, Bataille's discussions of the affective power of the cave images provides him a theory of labour and a philosophy of consumption that he could use to articulate various states of being when investigating the affective nature of community practices and their absolute consequences. Lascaux offers an image and a consumptive topology of such a community, where the individual is free to choose how he/she might interpret or engage with those images. In the hunter, Bataille accords a freedom away from the profane nature of killing, and turns his experience into something sacred. Bataille himself critiques this position, noting that 'humanity's understanding of itself', is not a dialectic of the profane, but merely serves to demonstrate that 'we know nothing, ABSOLUTELY NOTHING'.[53] The sacred comes to be problematically described in terms of its affection of a sense of nostalgia or transcendentalism, for theory seeking to describe the qualities of *their* experience. Bataille wants to engage with the materiality of the sacred, and he goes on to discuss the inner and outer qualities of the sacred in the terms of its creation by a community.

States of the sacred are provisional states, specific to their contextual location and economy. Discussion of them in terms of a teleological knowledge is, in Bataille's philosophy, untenable, and limits our grasp of what constitutes the labour of expenditure of human activity.[54] In his development of the terms of general and restricted economies, Bataille thus manages to avoid the materialist turn that Marx and Engels make with regard to the division of 'man' from 'animal' in their book *The German Ideology*. Marx and Engels make a rather jocular comparison between the determined, and restricted life of a man's labour under capitalism, versus an unrestricted labour economy under an idealized communism, the point of comparison Marx and Engels use is an anthropocentric theory of hunting:

> as soon as the distribution of labour comes into being, each man has a particular, exclusive sphere of activity, which is forced upon him and from which he cannot escape. He is a hunter, a fisherman, a herdsman, or a critical critic, and must remain so if he does not want to lose his means of livelihood; while in communist society, where nobody has one exclusive sphere of activity but each can become accomplished in any branch he wishes, society regulates the general production and thus makes it possible for me to do one thing today and another tomorrow, to hunt in the morning, fish in the afternoon, rear cattle in the evening, criticize after dinner, just as I have a mind, without ever becoming hunter, fisherman, herdsman or critic.[55]

Marx and Engels have an entirely different sense of the value of the hunter than Bataille, and they are insistent on what they see as capitalism's inevitable drive of individuals towards consumptive, structuralist positions within the existing social hierarchy.

Second, the details of Bataille's general and restricted economy involve consideration of how the sacred of what I am here calling the communal processes of mediatization are in fact a mediated form of labour, a construction that is made by a specific set of circumstances, which perpetuate reciprocal relationships between animal and human.

These are the terms of the affective labour that the face and reversal of animal to human to animal provides in whatever mediated realm they might be encountered.

Bataille's distinction between forms of knowledge – on the one hand there are forms of *solidity*; on the other is *sovereignty* – provides the tools for closer examination of the mediatization of labour forms. While sovereignty is a notion that describes the ways in which laws of power are imposed by national figure heads, and which effect an absolute control over their subjects, Bataille's application of sovereignty speculates upon the nature of subservience. Bataille describes sovereignty in *The Accursed Share*, with Hegel's dialectic of master and slave in mind. Bataille says that the slave can only gain sovereignty through the *rejection* of work altogether, not through revolt, as Hegel suggests. Bataille rejects the *solidity* of humans' communal desire for their own sovereignty over the earth and their territory. If the enslaved animals (harnessed cows) reject their work through lack of production, they are simply killed. Does the animal hold the slave's 'fear' of death?

The End of the Work of Art, and the Consumption of Mediatized Labour

In the realm of food production for human species, the Lascaux caves are vectors for labour. They illustrate the conditions of the relationship between hunter and hunted – which Bataille and Herzog view as revelatory of an experiential high, but upon which we reserve ascribing experience beyond mediatization. Yes, these animal images are sacred, in the Bataillian terms of the informational economy that they represent for the community that created them; they are tools of communication. I do not think Bataille is looking for examples of instances of the truth of 'the sacred' (where 'truth' is to be found, as Arkady Plotnitsky has pointed out, the functioning of capital for Marx and Engels might provide the 'truth' of a particular material thing's labour) – rather, Bataille seeks to articulate the type of paradoxes that assert an affective control over humans' knowledge of the impossibilities and contradictions of their all-too-human existence.

Animals affect a certain degree of insanity into the human species. As Gemerchak argues, a fundamental issue in Bataille's work is 'to push the very limits of self-consciousness awareness'.[56] As such, and if we approach Bataille's general economy in more prosaic terms, then some way of critiquing the absolute position of the carousel cow may be addressed. Instead of an acceptance of Bataille's still anthropocentrically-grounded standpoint, what if we act upon the affective mediatization of animality with less than predictable results? At a textual level, what if we do not read Bataille's notion of the 'sacred' as a zone that gives an avant-garde 'authority' to ascribe it as a literalization of oedipalized erotica. Instead, what if we *convert* Bataille's call for a study of the conditions of the principles of the general economy that mediatized animal forms like those at Lascaux and Chauvet produce, to a study of animal affect that will flesh out a philosophy of consumptive practices that is adequate to address current issues of food sustainability and iniquitous labour relations? The sacred provides a study of the principles of media affect. This is Bataille's legacy via Lascaux; Bataille provides a law of animal mediatization affect. Instead of a drive for the relentless autoproduction of capital via a consumptive immanence of the eater and the eaten, what if there was a reversal of the terms of capital, where the 'goal' was not accumulation, but in fact the accursed share of the agency of the image, and the concept, and not the actual flesh and its products? Let me rephrase my topic sentence for this paragraph: Animals affect a certain degree of non-conscious agency into the human species. The image of the animal and its animal affect has a civic potential (as do all of media forms, including art forms), a potential that is realized in different animal-mediatizing and consumptive communities – where the specific organization of the animal *is* the absolute condition of the human, displayed in terms of that community's behaviour with the non-human.

Bataille describes the sacred by offering a critique of human obsession with the measure and capture of a 'privileged instant'.[57] Art is able to express the terms of the sacred, says Bataille, as it becomes 'aware of the created *share* that it had always added to the world it expressed'.[58] Art expands the already existent condition of time, or the instant, through its sacred addition to absolute worlds. This temporal addition is different from Bergson's sense of the dilation of a perceptual point into a virtual multiplicity.[59] According to Bataille, the sacred is 'only a privileged moment of communal unity, a moment of the convulsive communication of what is ordinarily stifled'.[60] Bataille thus presents the immanence of intensity, as something *that is* already and always within humans and animals. This intensity is not something imagined or something relationally produced. It is an affective intensity that art or experiences lived with and by animals can express or provide temporal mediation for current activities.

Notes

1 Different parts of this paper were first presented at the *Media, Communications and Cultural Studies Association* (MeCCSA) Conference, University of Salford, Manchester, UK., January 12–15, 2011 and at the *Human-Animal/Humain-Animal,* 20th/21st Century French and Francophone Studies International Colloquium, San Francisco USA March 30-April 2, 2011. I am grateful to the organizers, participants, and fellow panellists of both conferences for the invaluable support and feedback received. I want to thank the *Media Research Centre* at the Manchester Institute for Research and Innovation in Art and Design (MIRIAD) at the Manchester Metropolitan University, Manchester, UK., for its support of this work.

2 Bataille, Georges, *The Cradle of Humanity: Prehistoric Art and Culture. Georges Bataille* (New York, Zone, 2005), p. 81.

3 Botting, F. and Wilson, S. (eds.), *The Bataille Reader* (Oxford, Blackwell, 1997), p. 5.

4 Guerlac, S., 'Bataille in Theory: Afterimages (Lascaux)' in *Diacritics* 26: 2, 1996, pp. 6–17; Guerlac, S., 'The Useless Image: Bataille, Bergson, Magritte' in *Representations* 97, Winter, 2007, pp. 28–56; Kendall, S., 'Editor's Introduction: The Sediment of the Possible' in *The Cradle of Humanity: Prehistoric Art and Culture. Georges Bataille* (New York, Zone, 2005), pp. 9–31; Noland, C., 'Bataille Looking'. In *Modernism/modernity* 11.1, 2004, pp. 125–160; Ungar, S., 'Phantom Lascaux: Origin of the Work of Art' in *Yale French Studies* 78, 1990, pp. 246–262. See Bataille, *The Cradle of Humanity* and Bataille, Georges, 'Animality' in Calarco, Matthew and Atterton, Peter (eds.). *Animal Philosophy: Essential Readings in Continental Thought* London & New York, Continuum, 2004), pp. 33–36.

5 Bataille, *The Cradle of Humanity*, p. 58.

6 See Kendall, 'Editor's Introduction'; Bataille, *The Cradle of Humanity*; Bataille, 'Animality'; Botting, F. and Wilson, S. (eds.), *The Bataille Reader* (Oxford, Blackwell, 1997), p. 249.

7 Bataille, *The Cradle of Humanity*, pp. 34–35.

8 Bataille, Georges, *The Accursed Share: An Essay on General Economy* (New York, Zone, 1991), p. 9.

9 See Gemerchak, C.M., *The Sunday of the Negative: Reading Bataille Reading Hegel* (New York, State University of New York Press, 2003), pp. 80–90; Noys, Benjamin, *Georges Bataille: A Critical Introduction* (London, Pluto, 2002), p. 13; Staples, D., 'Women's Work and the Ambivalent Gift of Entropy' in Clough, P. T. with Halley, J. (eds), *The Affective Turn: Theorizing the Social* (Durham and London, Duke University Press, 2007), pp. 119–150: 138–140.

10 This position of Bataille's is similar in scope to Bergson's law of cinematographic evolution.

11 Bataille, Georges, *Georges Bataille: Visions of Excess Selected Writings, 1927–1939* (Minneapolis, University of Minnesota Press, 1985), p. 241; Kendall, 'Editor's Introduction'; Plotnitsky, A., *Reconfigurations: Critical Theory and General Economy* (Gainsville, University Press of Florida, 1993); Stoekl, A., 'Introduction' in *Georges Bataille: Visions of Excess Selected Writings, 1927–1939* (Minneapolis: University of Minnesota Press, 1985), pp. ix-xxv.

12 Bataille, Georges, *Prehistoric Painting: Lascaux or the Birth of Art* (Lausanne, Skira, 1955).

13 Bataille, *The Cradle of Humanity*, pp. 143–178.

14 Bataille, *The Cradle of Humanity*, p. 146.

15 Bataille, Georges, *Eroticism: Death & Sensuality* (San Francisco, City Lights Books, 1986), p. 86.

16 See Kendall, 'Editor's Introduction', p. 26; Gemerchak, C.M. 2009. 'Of Goods and Things: Reflections on an Ethics of Community', in A. J. Mitchell, J. Kemp Winfree (eds), The obsessions of Georges Bataille: community and communication (New York: State University of New York Press, 2009), pp. 63-81: 70.

17 Moore, P., *The International Political Economy of Work and Employability* (London and New York, Palgrave Macmillan, 2010), p. 33.

18 Bataille, *The Cradle of Humanity*, pp. 87–104

19 Bataille, *The Cradle of Humanity*, p. 92.

20 Lefebvre, H., *The Production of Space* (Oxford and London, Wiley-Blackwell, 1991), p. 254.

21 Kendall, 'Editor's Introduction', p. 20.

22 Bataille, *The Cradle of Humanity*, p. 49.

23 Bataille, *The Cradle of Humanity*, p. 84.

24 Bataille, *The Cradle of Humanity*, p. 82; comments originally published in 1953.

25 Bataille, *The Cradle of Humanity*, pp. 82–3; Bergson, Henri, *Creative Evolution* (Boston, University Press of America, 1983), p. 317; Bergson, Henri, *The Creative Mind* (New York, Philosophical Library, 1946), pp. 157–165, 191.

26 See the notes on 'animality' in Bataille, Georges, *The Unfinished System of Nonknowledge: Georges Bataille* (Minneapolis and London, University of Minnesota Press, 2001), pp. 239–242.

27 Carrie Noland provides a detailed account of the historical theoretical techniques on ethnography, prehistory and art history that provide fuel for Bataille's position on the cave images (Noland, C., 'Bataille Looking'. In *Modernism/modernity* 11.1, 2004, pp. 125–160.)

28 Bataille, *The Unfinished System of Nonknowledge*, p. 179.

29 Bataille, *The Unfinished System of Nonknowledge*, pp. 242–5.

30 The terms of the schizo-market place is one where media forms perpetuate modes of capitalist greed, causing imbalances in market quotas related to food production, and the devastation of certain animal ecologies either in the pursuit of a fashionable food form, or in the dumping of human waste forms. Mediatized production of forms of guilt remind consumers what they are doing in their obsessive and frenzied pursuit and consumption of all things and of all places – this is the 'State of the World'.

31 See Satya, L. D., *Ecology, Colonialism and Cattle: Central India in the Nineteenth Century* (Oxford, Oxford University Press 2004).

32 See Jasanoff, S., 'Civilization and madness: the great BSE scare of 1996' in *Public Understanding of Science* July 6 1997, pp. 221–232.

33 See Barrett, J. C., 'The economic role of cattle in communal farming systems in Zimbabwe, Pastoral Development Network paper No. 32b' (London: Overseas Development Institute 1992), http://www.odi.org.uk/

34 McPherron, A. C., and Lee, S J., 'Double muscling in cattle due to mutations in the myostatin gene'in *Proceedings of the National Academy of Sciences*, 94.23, 1997, pp. 12457–12461. [available online: http://www.pnas.org]

35 See Dickman, S., 'Gene Mutation Provides More Meat on the Hoof'. In *Science* 26 September Vol. 277 no. 5334, 1997, pp. 1922–1923.

36 See *National Geographic* programme discussion of this breeding, on the programme, 'Meet the Super Cow' (Season 208 episode 213) [Online: http://wn.com/national_geographic_world?orderby = viewCount]

37 Examples of milking parlours are at Bauer Livestock Technology http://www.bauer-technics.com/en/milking-parlours#rybinove-dojirny

38 Corbett, G., 'Fair Oaks Farms Adventure Centre – America's Heartland'(promotional video produced by 'America's Heartland' channel, 2009), http://wn.com/fair_oaks_farms_adventure_center__america%27s_heartland]

39 View Fair Oaks Farms Adventure Centre – America's Heartland'[promotional video produced by 'America's Heartland' channel]. [Online: http://wn.com/fair_oaks_farms_adventure_ center__america%27s_heartland]

40 The Cave of Chauvet-Pont- D'Arc: http://www.culture.gouv.fr/culture/ arcnat/chauvet/en/

41 Herzog, Werner (dir.), *Cave of Forgotten Dreams* Creative Differences/ History Films/ Ministère de la Culture et de la Communication/ Arte France/ Werner Herzog Filmproduktion/ More4, 2010.

42 See Noland, 'Bataille Looking', pp. 130–1.

43 Bataille, *The Cradle of Humanity*, p. 55.

44 Bataille, *The Cradle of Humanity*, p. 164.

45 Bataille, *The Cradle of Humanity*, p. 81.

46 Bataille, *The Cradle of Humanity*, pp. 105–119, 168.

47 Bataille, *The Cradle of Humanity*, pp. 149–150.

48 Bataille, *The Cradle of Humanity*, p. 166.

49 Bataille, *The Cradle of Humanity*, p. 97.

50 Reproductions of other Lascaux artwork can be seen at the Centre of Prehistoric Art at Le Thot, France. Lascaux II is also being destroyed by other fungal life forms, introduced by humans and their technological supports (Delluc & Delluc 1984). See also the interactive site of Lascaux: http://www.lascaux.culture.fr/?lng = en#/ fr/00.xml

51 See Clifford, J., 'On Ethnographic Surrealism' in *Comparative Studies in Society and History* 23, 1981, pp. 539–564.

52 Bataille, *The Cradle of Humanity*, p. 51.

53 Bataille, *The Cradle of Humanity*, p. 121.

54 Bataille, *Visions of Excess*, p. 118.

55 Marx, Karl. and Engels, Friedrich, *The German Ideology* (International Publishers Co., 1970), 'Private Property and Communism' n.p. [Online: http://www.marxists.org/archive/marx/works/1845/german-ideology/ch01a.htm]

56 Gemerchack, *The Sunday of the Negative*, p. 3.

57 Bataille, *The Cradle of Humanity*, p. 241.

58 Bataille, *The Cradle of Humanity*, p. 242.

59 Bergson, *Creative Evolution*, pp. 315–317; Mullarkey, *Bergson and Philosophy*, pp. 54–57.

60 Bataille, *The Cradle of Humanity*, p. 242.

8

Levinas, Bataille and the Theology of Animal Life

Donald L. Turner

Introduction

Our ambiguous times witness both a proliferation of 'animal studies' discourses reflecting increased (albeit overdue) concern for non-human animal questions and an enormous and ever growing tally of non-humans falling victim to factory meat and research machines. The complexity and alluring mystery of non-human animals' subjectivity prompts the first trend, while the radical differences between their forms of subjectivity and that of human beings is used by some people to justify the second. In this paper, I suggest blending the visions of sacredness described by Emmanuel Levinas, for whom humans encounter divinity when drawn to transcend their animal egoism, and Georges Bataille, for whom experiencing the sacred involves nostalgia for animal immanence, to help us better understand our ethical relationships with other species and advance these considerations beyond the familiar permutations of utilitarian and Kantian approaches. This model suggests new ways to think about and behave towards non-human animal life and points to a new understanding of the divine dynamics at play in human-animal encounters.

The Key Importance of Levinas

Despite Levinas's unapologetic anthropocentrism, his ethical philosophy is, once freed from its exclusively human focus, particularly well suited to advance pro-animal agendas, as commentators have shown by focusing on the asymmetry of his ethical model, his phenomenology of the face, and his notion of friendship.[1] His theological elements, however, have not been embraced by pro-animal advocates—an understandable reaction to Levinasian claims, such as the one that interhuman relations 'give to theological concepts the sole signification of which they admit'.[2]

Admittedly, Levinas is extremely reluctant to extend his ethical philosophy to include individuals of other species, and when he makes claims such as the one just cited, it is clear that he does not recognize divine appeals in non-human animals' faces. Still, his theology is very useful for pro-animal philosophy, despite his overt intentions. This becomes evident when we shift from what Levinas says about *where* the trace of God can be manifest to what he says about *how* the trace happens. With this orientation, it becomes clear how his theology blends a utilitarian concern with bodily suffering and a Kantian respect for the moral value of the individual in a way that helps advance the agendas of pro-animal thinkers such as utilitarian Peter Singer and rights-oriented Tom Regan, while avoiding certain problems intrinsic to these approaches.

Sensibility and the Cerebral

The Kantian mistrust of the sensibilities humans share with other animals forecloses fruitful possibilities one might locate in Darwinian and Nietzschean modes of thinking, and the Kantian position that humans deserve direct ethical consideration by virtue of their unique rational capacity has been disastrous for non-human animal life.

A similar (though less) problematic undervaluation of sensibility is evident in Tom Regan's rights-based pro-animal position. According to Regan, although suffering and the violent acts that cause it are wrong, the *fundamental* wrong is not 'the forlornness of the veal calf … the pulsing pain of the chimp with electrodes planted deep in her brain … the slow, torturous death of the raccoon caught in the leg-hold trap' but the philosophical view that grounds this violence, which defines animals existentially as human resources.[3] In other words, the fundamental wrong is not animal suffering but humans' incorrect metaphysical view of animal being.

A Heideggerian might find this Americanization of *Ge-stell* appealing, but the Levinasian utilitarian is understandably suspicious of a Kantian prioritization of concepts over sensibility.[4] In Levinas's very fleshy ethics, the trace of God occurs in embodied individuals; the suffering of his strangers, widows, and orphans takes physical form and requires material comfort. 'Starting from the analogy between animate bodies,' he writes, we arrive at the realization that 'matter is the very locus of the for-the-other', that the Other matters because she is matter, and her ethical significance is a function of her physical pain.[5] With Levinas and in line with pro-animal utilitarian Peter Singer, I agree that suffering is the fundamental problem, and its alleviation and prevention should be the ultimate concern.[6]

This conclusion leads to a related consideration of the role of emotion in ethical life. Regan repeatedly maintains that he employs reason, not emotion, to make his case. In Levinas's view, however, the self experiences the fundamental ethical phenomenon as a very emotional event: a fission of the self experienced as trauma, in which 'the stony core of [one's] substance is hollowed out,' in which the self suffers with the Other, as the Other's physical desolation reverberates in the self's consciousness, causing the self psychological distress.[7] Regan's description of being moved to tears by animals' plight, appended as an apparent afterthought at the end of an essay in which he discounts affective grounds for ethical argumentation, reflects an emotive experience that is more than just a morally dubious accompaniment to ethical thinking—it is a necessary factor and a prime mover.[8]

Making a point on how to think about a scientific experiment that will inflict suffering on a non-human animal, Singer asks whether one would be willing to perform the same experiment on a brain-damaged orphaned infant. To jar us from complacency into responsibility, Singer turns our attention to the hypothetical suffering of one helpless child—a very Levinasian move. Effecting ethical transformation by changing the way people think, an essential precursor to practical reform, requires a jolt: the kind one gets when one considers, with Dostoevsky, a system of happiness maintained by the suffering of a tortured infant. Or the kind one gets when walking through a chicken factory. The power of such an emotional assault is reflected in the steps we take to separate ourselves from the production of factory meat: we stamp sausage tubes with 'Happy Farms' logos with smiling pig faces. We fear being emotionally assaulted, yet ethics happens when people are thus moved, and animal abuse will decline as more people experience this religiously significant trauma.

Individualism and Egalitarianism

Notwithstanding the attention to sensuality and feeling that marks the accord between utilitarianism and my quasi-Levinasian animal ethic, I hold fast, in line with Levinas and Regan and in opposition to Singer, to a high valuation of the individual. As Regan and other critics of utilitarianism indicate, the theory's calculations can allow many violations to individuals in pursuit of others' benefit, a kind of thinking that appears in a simplistic defense of factory farming: the human benefits of cheap meat justify the non-human animal suffering its production involves. Like Regan's secular approach, Levinas's theologically based model protects the Other from such abuses; thinking this way demands our refusal to dignify factory farm torture with the idea that some human interest could make this the proper way to nourish ourselves. A strong valorization of the individual animal Other is required to counter utilitarian justifications of practices that should be beyond the pale.

Moreover, although the interests of the many must sometimes outweigh the interests of the few or the one, a Levinas-inspired approach will always maintain attention to the primary encounter between a singular self and a unique Other—a phenomenon that is sometimes lost in utilitarian statistical analyses. Adding numbers of sufferers certainly adds to the evil in the world, but it sometimes vitiates the effect on the observer. This is evident, for example, in a recent study in which subjects were more willing to make charitable donations, and gave more, when presented with a single individual's plight than when asked to help multiple others.[9] Similarly, in the classroom, I observe that many students react more powerfully to a single photograph of a veal calf than to staggering statistics, such as a million chickens an hour or ten billion chickens a year. Encountering suffering concentrated in just one other sufferer can supply the shock required to provoke Levinasian ethical responsibility, and it can do so more effectively than seeing similar suffering spread across numerous sufferers. The Levinasian God is brought to mind most pointedly by individual faces, not statistics.

My pro-animal position is also inspired by Levinasian attention to the significance of inequality and asymmetry between parties in the ethical relationship. Both Singer and Regan assume that granting non-human animals their due consideration requires that we recognize how they are like humans in some key way, establishing the genus of sentient beings (Singer) or subjects of a life (Regan). Of course, the ethically significant Other cannot be just any other entity, and entities designated as Others will surely have something in common, be it Singer's sentience, handy for its bodily focus, or Regan's subject of a life, valuable for the phenomenological richness it suggests.[10]

But both thinkers underemphasize the value of asymmetry. Singer's belief that (as he puts it, echoing earlier utilitarian Henry Sidgwick) 'from the point of view of the Universe,' the good of one individual is no more important than that of any other, threatens to blur important differences, and the absolute neutrality his method requires is absent in the quasi-Levinasian theological ethics I promote, where, when faced with the appeal voiced by the suffering of a particular embodied animal Other, I am thrust into obligation.[11]

Similarly, Regan's ethics is neatly reciprocal. He writes, 'My value as an individual is independent of my usefulness to you. Yours is not dependent on your usefulness to me'.[12] While affirming the second sentence, a Levinasian approach would remain attentive to the ways that one's value is a function of one's usefulness to the Other.

Singer and Regan argue as if asymmetry between humans and other species is either irrelevant to the question of the factory farm

(Singer) or a problem to be dispensed with on the way to theoretical symmetry between rights-bearers (Regan). By contrast, according to a Levinasian moral theology, the ethical life is born when the Other establishes asymmetry with me, commanding me with her powerlessness, provoking my response.

Importantly, Singer describes the ways that differences between humans and members of other animal species justify different treatment and different rights, but we need the Levinasian reminder that differences between species require different responsibilities. Non-human animals' incapacity to reciprocate, enter moral contracts, or universalize maxims—criteria used to deny non-humans ethical consideration and deemed irrelevant by some people who want to extend them such concern—are wellsprings of moral responsibility, as we follow divinity's traces along asymmetrical paths.

Love: Scarcity or Surplus? A General Economy of Ethical Life

Given the ways Levinas's model is appropriate to interspecies ethics and the problems it solves when so deployed, it is somewhat surprising that Levinas is reluctant to extend his model across species lines. Despite rare hedges[13], he consistently maintains that (1) non-human animals cannot rise above biological egoism to embody altruistic sensibilities of which humans alone are capable, and (2) they cannot provoke an altruistic response in the way humans can. As noted above, these two theses are linked with a troubling implicit 'therefore'—non-human animals cannot be ethical agents and therefore should not be ethical patients—that contravenes Levinas's general disavowal of setting criteria to delimit alterity.

One way to understand this perplexing situation is to see Levinas's approach as operating in what Georges Bataille calls a restricted economy or an economy of scarcity, in which a shortage of resources necessitates judicious allocation of assets for specific, carefully chosen ends, in contrast with a general economy, which includes attention to the ways societies and individuals squander surplus energy, concretized as wealth and consecrated through sacrifice.

I suggest that 'love,' involving positive regard and concern, can effectively stand in for energy, and material care can replace wealth. The question, then, becomes, does Levinas see positive regard and concern as in short supply, requiring judicious allocation towards circumspectly chosen ends?

I think one might trace the influence of this kind of thinking in Levinas's concern for the ways the self's enjoyment comes at the expense of Others' deprivation, and, on the flipside, in his constant rejection of egoism and his designation of self-assertion as the beginning of immorality.[14] Because concern and resources are seen as scarce, taking them for oneself requires withholding them from the Other, and giving them to the Other requires forgoing them oneself. I think it also shows up in his charting of the prevalence of 'the third'—a figure representing the people to whom I must deny attention in order to attend to the singular Other whom I encounter in the ethical relationship. I think the scarcity model is also implicated in his exclusion of non-human animals from the ethical inner sanctum. It is as if love is in short supply, and as long as there are suffering human Others who demand attention, focus on non-human animal concerns is misplaced, only becoming justifiable in the ethical eschaton when human relationships are perfected and human suffering eliminated.

If the ethical life must conform to the laws governing an economy of scarcity, then the case for denying non-human animals our attention would be stronger. But I am not convinced that it does, and I believe that in some ways it follows Bataille's general model. In Bataille's analysis, organic life receives more energy than is necessary to sustain or enlarge it, and this abundance prompts organisms to expend surplus energy and wealth in seemingly purposeless gestures without rational utilitarian return, either gloriously, as in the construction of enormous monuments and Northwest Native American potlatch, or catastrophically, as in war and Aztec hecatomb. If, as I suggest, energy and wealth become love and concern, this should mean that we would find Levinasian attitudes and actions useful as opportunities to give without return.

Is there any evidence that positive regard and concern operate not by rules of scarcity but by a system that must deal with surpluses? I would not reduce the love calculus to any one simple function, or presume my own experience to be either universal or unique, but I do see elements of this dynamic in my experience. One year, as I was preparing for a class session on animal ethics, a photograph of a desperate and forlorn veal calf struck me with the realization that humans are treated in a similar fashion, and if I was willing to undergo self-inflicted dietary inconvenience to prevent assaulting bovine life, consistency demanded that I make similar sacrifices on behalf of suffering humans, and I started supporting Amnesty International. It is not as if I had only 100 units of care and concern available, and upon realizing Amnesty International's ethical demand, had to reign in my concern for non-human animals, nor did I write a smaller check to Amnesty International because of my obligations to People for the Ethical Treatment of Animals. I simply wrote an additional check; I felt added care and was compelled to provide added concern. Perhaps something like this is involved when parents of multiple children report that the birth of the second child did not halve their concern for the first, as parity in a zero sum love universe would require. Instead, the new birth generates new cares and concerns, indicating that these might not be in short supply, but might be abundant to the point of surplus under certain conditions. Perhaps it is the nature of the ethical life, as it is the nature of organic life, to receive more energy than is necessary to sustain and nurture the individual Perhaps Levinasian Others provoke the production of excess love, which demands continual expenditures of care and concern.

Dietary Glory

Other features of Bataille's theory fill in remaining gaps in my quasi-Levinasian theology of animal life. Some critics claim that Levinas's radical altruism fails to grant due respect to the self, and, theologically, I think there is something to this. With Levinas, I recognize the trace of God in the face of the Other human, but is there not more than enough traceable material to go around, and might not an individual recognize her own manifestation of divinity without robbing the Other of his? Here, I think Bataille's notions of sovereignty and glory prove helpful.

Whereas for Levinas, the Other's powerlessness, manifesting the trace of God, takes the individual hostage and commands her response, for Bataille, the individual assumes divine status by virtue of her own excess energy, which she gloriously consumes through profitless expenditure. In Aztec sacrifice and Native American potlatch, it is society's richest members who can best afford to expend wealth through such rituals; people near the top of the glory hierarchy maintain their rank through the prestige obtained by being able to squander their resources.

Although Levinasian altruists might be dubious of the kinds of self glorification Bataille describes, concern for self and concern for the Other are not always opposing tendencies; sometimes they work in tandem. First, on a mundane level, to be able to tear bread from my mouth to give to the Other, I must have previously obtained bread; thus, some personal amassing of resources is necessary. In order to feel the imperative to give and to experience the radical giving as such, I must not only know the pain of deprivation, but also the fullness of enjoyment. In order to burn like the sun (one of Bataille's favourite images), which constantly expends its resources without return, one must amass fuel, and, though I do not offer here a full analysis of the mechanisms by which the ethical energy manifest in care and concern is produced, its sources may include both fellowship with others and a strong auto-affection.

These examples show how concern for self works to promote concern for the Other, but this Levinasian prioritization does not completely explain my experience. I adopt certain practices concerning non-human animals partly to pursue my own sense of personal glory, and here it seems that concern for the Other works to promote concern for myself. When, as sometimes happens, aromas of well-cooked meat provoke in me carnivorous cravings, I feed instead on the pride I take in conquering these forces, forgoing nutritional or gustatory benefit to obtain an aura of righteousness and to inspire admiration. Forgoing factory meat and dairy, then, can be like the potlatch—one sacrifices something useful for nothing but the glory obtained through the gesture.[15]

Nor is it the case, as it usually is with Bataille's analysis, that the generation of such glory requires others to witness the expenditure. One might think it necessary to flaunt one's vegetarianism, but in my experience, the highest forms of ethical glory do not depend on other people's plaudits, and forgoing others' reactions to conspicuous representations of one's elevated moral agency further enhances one's sense of personal splendour. In a manner akin to Bataille's analysis, where 'genuine luxury requires the complete contempt for riches', I generate self- admiration by avoiding opportunities to reap admiration from others.[16] If the Levinasian moments held exclusive sway, and the concern for the animal Other ruled everything, or if it was a question of receiving positive regard from others, as in most of Bataille's examples, I would spend more time proselytizing, decrying factory farming, and proclaiming dietary values. Instead, I refrain from missionary activity among carnivores—perhaps because I want to avoid souring relationships with otherwise cordial individuals, but also because I want to feed from the knowledge that I undertake, as best I can, to give without the return of others' recognition.

Closing

For me, Levinasian moments have chronological priority in answering questions about the ethical significance of animal life, because the sublime ethical pain I feel when presented with the Other animal's suffering provokes my benevolent response. The first two chapters of Singer's *Animal Liberation* made me a vegetarian, and returning each semester in my classes to the kinds of photographs and statistics he employs provides ongoing reinforcement.

Following a Levinasian dynamic, my resolve is buttressed by the periodic assaults I face when I bring factory farm brutality to my own attention, but my efforts are also fueled by my pride in maintaining the effort required to forgo the fruits of these assaults on animal life. There is a place for a sense of being taken hostage by inescapable obligation and of perpetual shortfall, as there is always an ethical deficit to be addressed, but there is also a place for a celebration of personal power from which orthodox Levinasians might shy.

I encounter divinity when provoked to responsibility by the Other's omnipotent powerlessness. Perhaps I also approach divinity when I assume a position of height with respect to an ethically inferior mode of being. The trace of God may exist both in the face of the suffering veal calf which in paradoxical asymmetry commands my response, and also in my assumption of openness to this possibility and my sovereign refusal to commit torture by proxy by enabling factory farming with my consumer dollars. Both movements work together for the betterment of humans and non-humans alike.

Notes

1 On asymmetry, see Clark, David, 'On being "the last Kantian in Nazi Germany": dwelling with animals after Levinas,' in Ham, Jennifer and Senior, Matthew (ed.), *Animal Acts: Configuring the Human in Western History* (New York, Routledge, 1997), pp. 165–198. On reciprocity and the face, see Diehm, Christian, 'Facing nature: Levinas beyond the human,' *Philosophy Today* 44, no. 1, 2000, pp. 51–9. On friendship, see Guenther, Lisa, '*Le flair animal*: Levinas and the possibility of animal friendship,' *PhaenEx* 2, no. 2, 2007, pp. 216–237.

2 Levinas, Emmanuel, *Totality and Infinity* (The Hague, Martinus Nijhoff, 1969), pp. 78–9. I have modified this translation slightly.

3 Regan, Tom, 'The case for animal rights' in Singer, Peter (ed.), *In Defense of Animals* (New York, Basil Blackwell, 1985), pp. 13–14.

4 Heidegger presents the notion of Ge-stell in the influential essay, 'The question concerning technology.' Often translated as "enframing," the concept connotes a framework into which reality is forced, according to which one recognizes only the practical use one might put things to or the energy one might extract from them. It suggests a crass, calculating process that dangerously threatens to foreclose other possibilities for revealing things differently, e.g., those involving poetic or artistic attunement. See Krell, David (ed.), *Basic Writings* (San Francisco, California, Harper Collins, 1993), pp. 307–341.

5 Levinas, Emmanuel, *Of God Who Comes to Mind* (Stanford, Stanford University Press, 1998), pp. 77 and 191.

6 We might resolve some of the tension here by distinguishing between two types of priority. Chronologically, we have a linear time-line of cause and effect: we make animals suffer because we see them as our resources. However, the question of degrees of wrongness points to another type of priority. A world with Kantians who outlaw factory farms because they think that cruelty to animals detracts from human dignity (and, thus, that non-human animals have only instrumental value and qualify only for indirect moral consideration) is preferable to a world full of people who affirm non-human animals' inherent value while somehow maintaining the torture factories.

7 Levinas, *Of God Who Comes to Mind*, p. 71.

8 Here this Levinasian approach is much more in line with Darwin than Levinas himself might have liked. Natural selection can easily be theorized to have favoured individuals and species who could feel the kinds of love and attachment found in some of the earliest social bonds between parents and offspring.

9 'Numbed by the numbers: tragedies in the news,' Narr. Neil Conan. *Talk of the Nation*. NPR. Washington, D.C. (17 July 2007).

10 Regan provides a partial list of the contents of a life: wants and beliefs, remembrance and expectation, satisfaction and frustration, existence and death.

11 Singer, Peter, 'All animals are equal' in Regan, Tom and Singer, Peter (ed.), *Animal Rights and Human Obligations* (Englewood Cliffs, New Jersey: Prentice Hall, 1989), pp. 148–162: 152.

12 Regan, Tom, 'The case for animal rights', p. 21.

13 For example, Levinas admitted during an interview with tenacious students that 'one cannot entirely refuse the face of the animal', opening the door to questions about which animals can and should be ethically welcomed, how they qualify, to what extent they qualify, etc. See 'The paradox of morality: an interview with Emmanuel Levinas' in Bernasconi, Robert and Wood, David (ed.), *The Provocation of Levinas: Rethinking the Other* (London, Routledge, 1988), p. 172. I think that this inconsistency is partially explained by the fact that non-human animals' ethical status was just not Levinas's question.

14 See, e.g., 'Ethics as first philosophy' in Hand, Sean (ed.), *The Levinas Reader* (Malden, Massachusetts, Blackwell, 1989), pp. 82–3; *Of God Who Comes to Mind*, p. 28; *Otherwise Than Being, or Beyond Essence* (The Hague, Martinus Nijhoff, 1981), p. 128; 'The philosopher and death' in *Alterity and Transcendence* (New York, Columbia University Press, 1999), pp. 164–5; *Totality and Infinity*, pp. 47, 63.

15 Here I do not mean to give the impression that I think it is appropriate to ride a high horse on this topic. First, it is not certain that a universally vegetarian humanity would cause less suffering than if we adopted any other dietary mode. See Michael Pollan's *The Omnivore's Dilemma* (New York, Penguin Press, 2006) for an argument that making beef our prime foodstuff would actually best promote this cause. Second, almost no one who eats can do so without causing pain and death to members of other species. Tractors that plow soybean fields kill rodents, and vegetarians annihilate insects with their scooter windshields on the way to the tofu store. And third, even if vegetarianism or veganism is the most morally appropriate dietary choice for most situations, this is only one of the million moral choices life requires, so this choice alone guarantees one no automatic moral high ground over other people. All of this notwithstanding, I am far from certain that humanity requires large scale consumption of mammalian and/or avian flesh, and I am completely certain that we do not have to have factory farming in the forms we have implemented for the past few decades.

16 Bataille, Georges, *The Accursed Share*, vol. 1 (New York, Zone Books, 1991), p. 76.

9

Degrees of 'Freedom': Humans as Primates in Dialogue with Hans Urs von Balthasar

Celia Deane-Drummond

Introduction

In the Christian tradition, the concept of humanity made in the image of God, *imago Dei*, has traditionally been taught as one that has shifted from a focus on ontological characteristics, such as rationality, to particular types of activity, such as human dominion of the earth. Both presuppose a measure of human freedom, which is one reason why theologians, such as John Zizioulas, characterize freedom as *the* characteristic that most distinguishes humans from other creatures.[1] Here he means positive freedom understood as freedom of will, rather than freedom from external constraint; but such positive freedom is to be exercised correctly only in acknowledgement of God's intentions for humanity, rather than simply a libertine and unbounded sense of individual free choice. His views challenge the growing tendency among those influenced by evolutionary psychology to characterize human moral agency as an adaptation that evolved in response to natural selection. [2] In the latter scenario, moral behaviour becomes tied to genetic traits, thus exposing a 'nativism' that even other biologists, such as Stephen Jay Gould or Steven Rose, find particularly offensive. [3] Yet before theologians congratulate themselves on resisting such tendencies, the history of the Christian tradition is replete with examples of the way the doctrine of predestination has been interpreted to elevate the freedom of God at the expense of mere human mortals, effectively suppressing free agency and thus crushing the genuine possibility of human free will even within certain limits. The language of human free will is itself problematic if it implies some sort of Cartesian dualism between the human mind and body. Such a presumption will lead to questions such as whether other animals have souls and so on. But once a dualistic approach to mind and body is left to one side, then the possibility of considering how animals act in accordance with their own good opens up new considerations of animal agency and its meaning.[4]

The purpose of this chapter is to consider in more depth whether it is possible to consider positive freedom understood as a capacity of animals other than humans, especially primates. This account is intended to illuminate not just how we think about ourselves in theological terms as distinct creatures, made in the image of God. It is also intended to show how the suppression of the possibility of free agency in other animals has served to encourage an anthropocentrism in the theological and philosophical tradition that effectively cut humanity off from the ground of creation in which it is embedded. Of course, such a focus on primate research should not give the false impression that *all* animals are like primates, or mammals for that matter – but I consider that paying close attention to our closest relatives enables particularly important insights to surface about the human condition. The work of Frans de Waal will be drawn on in most detail for his account of primate cognition and behaviour in order to glean what animal agency might mean from a biological and ethological perspective.[5] I will explore, in particular, the possibilities of (a) intention and (b) self-recognition (c) theories of mind, which include (d) perception of another's belief or knowledge.

The Question of Animal Agency

The first issue to be raised when considering the possibility of how other animals act in a self-directed way is a philosophical one, namely, in what sense animals might be considered as agents. Normally, agency is a broad term that designates the possibility for self-direction and includes terms such as 'free will' as part of the package identifying human beings as subjects.[6] Helen Steward has tackled the philosophical issues of animal agency and argues that non-human animals need to be considered as having a basic agency, drawing particularly on studies of early human development.[7] Her argument attempts to rule out the harsh line against animals as being agents of any sort, rather than suggesting that other animals are capable of sophisticated propositional attitudes. She argues against those, such as D. Davidson, who reject the idea that other animals could ever be intentional agents, based on the assumption that other animals do not have language.[8] However, rather than insisting on the capacity for communication or forms of language in other animals, Steward instead argues for a definition of agency that is more inclusive, so that it does not require complex versions of intention in the way that Davidson supposes. In particular, Davidson links intention with capacity for beliefs and ascribing beliefs to others. This seems to presuppose a theory of mind (TOM), and as a tautology, intentional agency seems to be a precondition for TOM.[9]

Early developmental analysis shows a capacity to distinguish animates from inanimates in early human infancy. Even infants as young as 7 months old could distinguish between living beings and those that required an external source of energy.[10] The basic division in this case was between objects that were or were not self-propelled. Propositional attitudes do not develop until the second year of life, when beliefs are attributed to others.[11] Steward uses these examples as a way of trying to situate herself between those philosophers who deny any agency to other animals and those such as Wittgenstein who interrogates the way folk culture reads human-like agency into animal behaviour.[12] But Steward comes down against the idea of animal responses, such as a cock calling its hens, as purely physical. Rather, she suggests that:

> We allow to an animal – and this is crucial, in my view, for the concept of agency – a certain freedom and control over the precise movements by means of which it satisfies those instinctual needs and desires. It decides, we think, precisely where it will go in search of food or shelter or to evade predators. Our natural inclination is to think of an animal as a creature that can, within limits, direct its own activities and which has certain choices about the details of those activities.[13]

Agency can be defined as having (a) the ability to move what we think of as its body, as (b) a centre of a form of subjectivity (c) where intentional states (such as trying, wanting, perceiving) are attributed (d) where movements of its body are non-necessitated events, originating in the agent, and only secondary to environmental triggers.[14] In this sense, agency is a prerequisite for the possibility of free choice, though ethologists are not known for using the language of freedom in describing animal behaviour. There may be examples of simple animal movement such as that of the paramecium that appear to have agency but on close examination are governed by physical forces.

Steward believes that attributing agency to other animals is resisted in the academic literature because of (a) cultural and religious forms of anthropocentrism (b) on the part of natural scientists because agency might seem to imply some form of dualism of body and mind (c) parsimony, where only simpler explanations are acceptable (d) an empiricist approach to consideration of other animals, which distrusts any form of what is perceived as misplaced anthropocentrism – in this case, reading into animal kinds habits of human society and (e) the influence of a rationalist Kantian ethic that presupposes that agency amounts to a complex form of moral judgement. Steward argues that instead the basic intuition that animals are capable of agency needs to be recognized. Nonetheless, by ignoring ethology, Steward's account is disappointing, for she opens up the philosophical space for animal agency but then does little to show what evidence might be accumulating in order to support it. She also stops short of attributing to animals anything like a TOM or pushing those areas of cognitive capacity to their limit in other social animals.

Mapping Cognitive Capacities of Other Animals

As I indicated above, straight observation of the behaviour of other animals is not sufficient to come to firm conclusions about the underlying capacities of other animals and their intentions. Historically, most scientists have taken a precautionary approach and assumed that animals *do not* have particular intentions in response to certain stimuli. Some standard texts use the hierarchical view of intentionality that Steward had reason to critique above, since it supposes zero-order intentionality for animals that do not exhibit beliefs and desires about either the world or the behaviour of others.[15] However, regardless of how intentionality might be mapped, it is clear that once beliefs about others or the world are present, then this is a capacity beyond that of internally directed responses. In this case, *first-order* intentions are said to be present, while if an agent considers the mental state of others, then *second-order* intentions are reached. This can be expanded further, so that one could consider the mental state of the person thought about by the person who is close by as the third order of intention, and so on. For example, the latter is something like this – I want my children to believe that I expect them to be waiting for me at the after-school club at a certain time of the day. While we may be naturally inclined to attribute second-order intentionality to other animals, careful ethological work research shows up in a more definitive way whether particular social cognition is involved or not.

Yet, assuming that intentions are *not* there may be problematic in that it fails to give what might be termed the benefit of the doubt to other animals and thereby sets up a sharp boundary between humans and other social animals.[16] In the area of intentionality, there seems no reason *not* to suppose that social animals are purposive in working out which actions to take in given situations. Examples of innovation in the cultures of social animals are not all that common, but there is a good case for social learning of given traditions among many different species of social animals, such as bird species, roof rats, bottlenose dolphins, and chimpanzees. Such learning seems to be spread by imitation of a neighbour, though it cannot be ruled out that there may be genetic predispositions to learn in a certain way.[17] The question becomes – how far can animals actively make choices other than those governed by affective states, including emotions, instincts, and learned desires?

Harvard philosopher Christine Korsgaard argues that humans have a deeper level of intentionality that allows them to make judgements in relation to particular norms or moral principles, so that we can choose actively either to follow such purposes or not. In this scenario, intentions do not simply exist in humans; rather, they are actively assessed and adopted.[18] However, the second aspect of her argument, namely, that *morality* is a function of the exercise of normative self-government, is itself based on the presupposition of a Kantian form of morality that could be challenged, depending on the particular definition of what morality entails.[19] She also acknowledges that there is nothing 'non-natural' about the capacity for normative self-government, but for humans, there is a *self-reflective* awareness of the motivation to act that she defines as 'reason' rather than merely 'intelligence'.[20] Frans de Waal also acknowledges that humans are unique in their capacity for disinterested judgement.[21]

To some extent, I do not think that acknowledging such distinctions between different animal kinds, including, for example, cultural differences between humans and other animals, is a problem. Only humans are capable of worrying about their own animality and its significance in relation to human self-identity; only humans discuss the fine points of what it means to express freedom; only humans are knowingly religious beings; only humans consider the possibility of trans-human or post-human futures. This distinctiveness should not cause too much concern. Such distinctions are also true of other animal kinds, that is, a biologist concerned with animal behaviour will pay attention to and be more aware of the unique characteristics of different animal kinds, as this, at least historically, forms the basis of classification systems. Some kinds of classification also seem to jar with others. For example, a scientific phylogeny of differences between different animal kinds will not necessarily map directly onto cultural distinctions between different kinds of creatures.[22] For example, a whale may appear to a child as a large fish, rather than a mammal. This means that human perception of animals and their differences from human beings will be predicated on how they are classified and in accordance with particular capacities and traits.

The ability to perceive another's belief or knowledge is necessary for the observed shift from emotional contagion characteristic of many primates and other social species to genuine empathy. The ability to recognize the mental states of another also presupposes a TOM. Chimpanzees, for example, seem to know that if another has seen food sources, then that other one knows such food sources exist; in other words, it is able to perceive another's knowledge by observation that it has seen the food. Although the reports suggesting TOM were sporadic in earlier research, de Waal resists the idea that all these can be dismissed as 'anecdotes', for 'If an experienced, reliable observer reports a remarkable incident, science had better pay close attention'.[23] Since then, more detailed experimental evidence has accumulated in addition to more readily understood stories that appeared in popular literature, though not all scientists are convinced that animals other than humans have the cognitive capacity for TOM.

An observation that points to its possibility was of an old male bonobo, Kakowet, who screamed frantically at the keepers when they started filling the moat with water and had not realized that several young bonobos were already in the moat, unable to get out. After such incidents, the moat was kept dry, but a chain was kept in place so that the bonobos could get up and down at will. On occasion, a younger male took hold of the chain when the dominant male was in the moat, and the adult female rushed to his defence, dropping the chain back and allowing him to get out. Such actions showed a considerable degree of *taking another's perspective*. There also seems to be a link between the ability to show genuine empathy and self-recognition, in that empathy seems impossible without self-recognition. Self-recognition implies a measure of distance between self and others so that the other's situation can be separated from one's own. The link between mirror self-recognition (MSR) and the ability to show empathy was first raised by Gallup in 1982, and since then, evidence has built up, not just in non-human primates but in young children, where MSR is linked with helping tendencies, and in phylogenetics, where helping and consolation behaviour is found in humans and apes but not monkeys. [24]

Behind all ideas about capacities of animals to act in ways that suggest self-directed agency and the ability to take another's perspective is the possibility of a TOM. Comparative studies with children are illuminating in this respect. Research suggests that children up to a certain age find it difficult to attribute thinking to others beyond what is concretely the case. The so-called acid test for a TOM is the *false belief test*.[25] A child passes this test if he or she can recognize that another's belief can be different from his or her own and from the way the world is. This can be done in the following way. A child is introduced to a puppet or puppet clown. The experimenter then hides a treat or toy in a particular (e.g., red) experimental box with the puppet clown observing. The clown leaves the room and the child sees the experimenter move the toy or treat into a different (green) box. The puppet clown now returns and the child is asked, 'Where will he look for the teddy/treat?' The reply is always in the box where the child knows the toy to be hidden, rather than in the one where the puppet originally saw the toy hidden. Early experiments involving chimpanzees and humans followed by experiments among co-specifics failed to provide firm conclusions that chimpanzees could pass a false belief test.[26] However, the way that TOM has been constructed in testing human subjects is one that is reliant on human language as that which underlies reasoning about the other's state of mind.

Yet, the image of the 'tower' of morality that begins in social animals and reaches up to human beings used by de Waal implies a superiority in humans that is somewhat unfortunate, given his consistent efforts to stress the continuities between humans and other social species. An overall philosophy of emergence is becoming particularly popular in discussion of religion and theories of mind. Philip Clayton, for example, speaks of the mind as 'having important precursors in animals' perception of their environment and especially in the signs of a rudimentary awareness of the other as other in some higher primate (call it proto-mentality)'.[27] Such an approach is reasonable as long as it is qualified by the recognition that humans are actually less specialized in evolutionary terms compared with monkeys. On this basis, emergence, if it implies evolutionary progression, is only descriptive of some traits in humans rather than others, since monkeys appeared to be more specialized in evolutionary terms. R. J. Berry comments tellingly that:

> There does not seem to be evidence of positive selection for genes concerned with brain development or function as a whole between chimps and humans, but one of the most intriguing results that has so far emerged from comparative molecular genetics is that since the human and chimpanzee line separated around six million years ago, a third more chimpanzee genes show signs of selection than do human ones .... There is no scientific support for the notion that we have been propelled towards a predetermined end by either a Blind or a Divine Watchmaker.[28]

It is a particular sense of *superiority* that almost unwittingly creeps into the discourse through acknowledgement of distinctive human characteristics that needs to be challenged. What is of particular interest in this context is that the possible difference in creaturely intention between humans and other social animals seems to be one of degree, rather than absolute, and so that a form of what we might term 'freedom' is still exercised in both cases, but in the case of humans, it is possible, but not inevitable, that it is scrutinized in relation to particular intentions according to given moral norms.

Human Freedom and Other Animals in Hans Urs von Balthasar

Hans Urs von Balthasar is one of the most influential Roman Catholic theologians of the twentieth century, and his treatise on human freedom sets out how freedom can be understood theologically. Balthasar's approach to the theological meaning of freedom is constructive in so far as he manages to avoid the shibboleth created by the opposite and equally problematic tendencies towards divine freedom as a vehicle for the denial of finite freedom, or the secular alternative in the humanist absolutization of human freedom understood as the absolute freedom of the individual to choose. Balthasar's motivation is strictly theological, for underlying the freedom of God is divine love that permits humanity its freedom. In the first part of his trilogy known as the *Glory of the Lord*, he discusses the metaphysical basis for freedom. Significantly, human freedom awakens as *freedom of consent* in the experience of another, for Balthasar this is the first awakening of the 'I' in relation to the 'Thou' of the mother.[29] Balthasar is naïve in as much as a baby's first smile may not imply the kind of self-recognition that he assumes is the case. Freedom of consent is a 'fundamental freedom that enables us to affirm the value of things and reject their defects, to become involved with them or to turn away from them'.[30] He also seems to recognize some kinship here with other animals, in that he allows for what he terms 'sub-human nature' being a 'singularly illuminating touchstone for the value of a metaphysics', rejecting the mechanical materialism of Descartes, while resisting the Hegelian continuity that views different forms of nature as ways or stages of the Absolute Spirit.[31] He rejects the former on the basis that it cannot interpret the 'glorious freedom of the essential forms', while resisting the latter on the basis that in 'Being' we find 'a superior and playful freedom beyond all the constraints of Nature'.[32] But for him, this freedom of Being is not self-explanatory, for 'the freedom of non-subsisting Being can be secured in its "glory" in the face of all that exists only if it is grounded in a subsisting freedom of Absolute Being, which is God', so its gloriousness is not hardened into a mathematical necessity but remains an 'event of an absolute freedom and thus of grace within its open ended sway in which each "pole" has to seek and find its "salvation" in the other pole'.[33] Within such communal relations of love, 'we have all been permitted entry … . Our mother too … . And the animals with which I play'.[34]

Here, Balthasar somewhat astonishingly seems to be allowing for the inclusion of companion animals within the core sphere of human freedom understood in terms of loving relationships, but he fails to consider social species that are not human companions. He also seems to envisage other animals as being included in our sense of freedom by the way that companion animals become involved in the lives of human beings, rather than any sense of other animals being subjects in their own right. Further, what he calls 'entry' is a reference to the light of being and love that is open to all creatures by the fact of their creaturely existence. Being, present as 'sublime and serene', is a metaphysical category hovering from the beginning to the end of human existence that, for him, puts even the terrors of this world into perspective. Even human beings are 'accidental' relative to the light of Being. Such metaphysics sounds somewhat unconvincing to ears tuned into contemporary scientific ways of thinking about the world, but at least it does have the beneficial effect of qualifying the stronger notes of anthropocentrism in his work.

Yet, before we reach the conclusion that his strong metaphysics of Being has forced him to adopt a continuity model between animals and humans characteristic of de Waal, even to a limited degree, a second important aspect of freedom as *autonomous motion* needs to be taken into account. This aspect of freedom is concerned with self-realization, and it is this that seems to be characteristic of humanity in a completely exclusive sense. Balthasar's view of autonomy is very different from humanist philosophy, in that it is not so much drawing on libertarian models, rather it is connected with obedience understood in relation to Christ. Using texts of the New Testament such as 2 Cor. 3.17, 'where the Spirit of the Lord is, there is freedom', he presents the case that freedom in the power of the Holy Spirit is the opposite of addiction, rather it is, citing 2 Cor. 5.15, 'to live no longer for themselves, but for him who died and rose for them'.[35] This, for Balthasar, issues in service, both for God and for others. Alongside this idea of freedom as autonomy, properly understood through the lens of service, he retains a traditional understanding of human image bearing, such that it 'raises man far beyond all other beings of the world', and moreover, these other beings are 'inferior beings', echoing his earlier assessment in his discussion of humanity as a microcosm.[36] Such anthropocentrism is in tension with other aspects of his thought that stress the creaturely basis for human life and its shared finitude alongside other creatures. Drawing on ancient interpretations of image bearing, he understands it as a 'making present' so implies a special relationship to God and a special representative of God that sets humanity apart from all other beings. Yet for him, the image-bearing nature of humanity is always incomplete in as much as it needs to be fulfilled through another in male and female relations, through the experience of grace, through humanity's response to God's call, and through relationship with Christ. All aspects touch on freedom in different ways, and the Christological dimension serves to shape the nature of the mission of humanity, which, for him, is a freedom that is the opposite of addiction, a freedom that is marked by service of God and others.[37]

One reason why Hans Urs von Balthasar's account of human freedom is problematic is that he retains a stereotypical view of women as associated with particular stereotypical roles in the home and bound to the natural world that leave much to be desired. Here, he speaks of man as being perfected by woman, who is his 'answer', and also, significantly, that man 'symbolises freedom, but now, how wound round he is by clinging ivy, which often threatens to choke him – by wife and children, home and profession and a knot of cares'.[38] His sexual stereotyping is particularly problematic and rests on a form of essentialism that is arguably the very opposite of what he is seeking to promote, namely, a way of thinking that resists reductionist tendencies in modernity. The trajectory in which he places humanity is therefore both anthropocentric and androcentric. For him, woman is fulfilled by man and all other species converge onto the human. He takes the latter position by supposing that humanity is a microcosm of all that is in the universe as a whole, so that 'All the realms and genera of living things converge in him; no animal species is alien to him. He contains them all, as superseded and discarded forms in which he can mirror himself and, as in fables, recognize the features of his own character'.[39]

Hence, while on the one hand he claims that other animals are not 'alien' to human beings, his mistaken trajectory of human evolution as one that leaves behind 'discarded' forms reinforces a strong sense of human superiority. For him, human beings are both 'the synthesis of the world' and at the same time 'above it'.[40] He dissociates humans from other animals by their ability to reason, so that 'animals are swept away by the waves of sexual drives which ebb and flow like the sea, whereas man can experience *eros* in a more inward, sublimated way and, through love, make for it a lasting abode in his enlightened heart'.[41] Here we have an attitude to other animals as driven entirely by sexual and other sensate instincts, presupposing a profound lack of agency. While I am not suggesting that other animals actively choose their sexual partners, to portray animals as driven by sensual instincts is stereotypically anthropocentric in as much as it assumes other animals do not have the capacity to willingly associate with others, form friendships, etc. His attitudes to animals have, as far as I can discern, received no attention, partly because he hardly ever mentions other animals, in spite of his frequent reference to creation and creaturely being, but also no doubt because of the anthropocentric bias of his commentators.

In the second part of his trilogy on *Theo-Drama*, Balthasar portrays the work of God's infinite freedom in Trinitarian terms in relation to human freedom as analogous to a theatre, where God is author, the Holy Spirit is the Director, and the central act of the *Theo-Drama* comes to be expressed through the incarnation, crucifixion, and resurrection of Christ.[42] In his later works, he spells out the specific task of human freedom in terms of mission. Human persons have a role to perform, but only when this role is united to their mission given by God, do person and role become fused in the manner found in the person of Jesus Christ.[43] Freedom is expressed, therefore, through practical action. The future hope and coming kingdom also looks to the transformation of human finite freedom into ultimate freedom by participation in infinite freedom. For Balthasar, the theological task is how to work out how finite freedom can act in relation to infinite freedom without being swallowed up by the latter and how infinite freedom can make room for finite freedom without surrendering its own nature as infinite.[44] While von Balthasar avoids the more extreme anthropocentrism by resisting the belief that only human souls are saved in heaven, his final vision of the future is one that is remarkably intellectual in tone, and free creativity is constricted and construed in intellectual and spiritual terms.[45]

If Balthasar had paid rather more attention to animals, other than somewhat cursory remarks about companion animals, and his limited discussion of sexuality, perhaps this tendency towards epic thinking would not have emerged.[46] Proper attention to animals can, therefore, act in the service of constructing a theology of freedom that remains suitably grounded in creatureliness. Moreover, I suggest that given Balthasar's understanding of freedom as primarily one that expresses agency, rather than simply theoretical judgement, then non-human animals can also be included in his notion of freedom as participation as well as in his notion of freedom as consent. The mission of humanity reflects the particular *density* of that participation in relation to freedom as autonomy. Perhaps we might even surmise that animal freedom in non-human kinds, in as much as it suffers less angst of the dichotomy of role and person found in humans, is also thereby closer to that freedom found in Christ, where person and role are united. Yet, there is also a distinction, for while it cannot be said that non-human animals possess an autonomy that is directed by a divinely ordained *mission* in the way that is possible for humans in Balthasar's thought, there is no real reason why they cannot be included in the participation in the divine life that is enabled by the grace of the Holy Spirit.

In theological terms, it is in the context of infinite freedom that these finite freedoms can flourish. We need to bear in mind also the different degrees to which different animal kinds might be capable of such participation, according to their own differential capacity for flourishing in different ways. It is also in the light of such infinite freedom that the relative difference between human and other animal freedom becomes one of degree. Both have the capacity to be free in a sense that is meaningful for that species. Yet, by linking together animal and human freedom, we are reminded again of the inadequacies of individualization; freedom is freedom in community, a community that includes all creaturely beings. Hence, lines of continuity and distinctiveness serve to emphasize the particular role of human freedom, and its capacity for good or ill is one that is joined with service for God and neighbour, where neighbour is understood in an inclusive, rather than exclusive, sense. Decisions about how to exercise our freedom in relation to these others become a moral and ethical one – but given the discussion so far, I would press for that good to be based on inclusive, rather than exclusive, parameters.

Humans in Animal Cultures

Balthasar qualifies his understanding of the limits of human freedom by situating his discussion in metaphysics that is itself qualified by an analogy of Being with the divine Creator. Religion will always therefore trump over forms of naturalism. Yet, if he had taken account of the cultural life of other animals, he might have had a more nuanced view of the natural restraints on the behaviour of humans and other animal kinds. There is no need, therefore, to assume that societies function through a kind of determinism or that individuals are entirely free of any form of restraint. Such has been the habit of naturalism and liberalism, respectively. Rather, by getting closer to what animal cultures signify, it might be possible to not only understand animals in their own worlds but also understand more fully the facets of human societal pressures. An examination of feral children is a good example of the crossing of human and animal societal boundaries. Although some scholars believe that in a globalized world children being brought up by other animal societies may no longer happen, the cases reported of this are remarkable for the light they shed on human and animal societies and their respective abilities to express different degrees of freedom. They show that particular capacities are related to particular contexts, that is, in some situations, capacities will develop in a particular way. Consider, for example, the case of adoption of young humans by animal societies, reported in about 50 cases in the last 600 years, mostly in Europe and Asia, but some in Africa.[47] Astonishingly, wolves, leopards, bears, a panther, a lion, monkeys, sheep, pigs, cattle, various species of birds, and gazelles have all been named as animals who have adopted vulnerable humans.

Most of the reports were more interested in the impact on the human beings and their accumulation of some of the habits of their host species, rather than the remarkable shifts in the animal society. Horrific accounts of how children were forcibly reintroduced to human societies, and in some cases mutilated so that they no longer carried exceptional capacities developed in the animal societies, show the extent of human hostility towards other animals.[48] In these cases, it would be interesting to see if such feral children are able, in spite of their origins in their truncated social environment, to pass the false belief test, for it would effectively remove the language variable in human communities mentioned above. So far, such observations have yet to be made.

Yet, it is interesting to note the observations of Jean Claude Armen, who discovered a boy who had been brought up by gazelles and, unlike other observers in such situations, made no attempt to bring the boy back to human society.[49] He found that imitating the licking contact of the gazelles improved trust. There was mutual affection between the boy and the gazelles, and he also observed particular signals of hoof, head, or ears that were used as a means of communication. The boy acted in imitation of these gestures, twitching his ears and scalp, sniffing in the air, as well as the food or dung in gazelle-like fashion. He also grazed plant food without using his hands. The boy could walk upright, and Armen believed this was because he had some contact with the Nemadi society from which he came. He also substituted some gazelle signals with other movements, such as twitching his face and tail signals with finger movements. Armen believed that to survive in such conditions was a sign of normality. The boy's agency was tuned into that of the gazelle herd in which he was placed, but he responded to the social rules in which he found himself. The animals had accepted the boy into their society in a remarkable way and showed the ability of humans and animals to adapt.

Some Tentative Conclusions

This chapter has argued that naming freedom as marking the boundary between humans and other animals assumed in much theological and philosophical literature fails on a number of fronts. First, it fails to recognize the common intuition of agency in other animals. While the precise degree of intentionality in a TOM for other primates is still under discussion, the possibility that social animals have complex cognitive capacities cannot be ruled out. Indeed, it makes more sense to give other animals the benefit of the doubt where the possibility exists. Hans Urs von Balthasar distinguishes between different forms of freedom; the freedom of consent is recognized by him as being open to other creaturely kinds. This acknowledges the relational aspects of freedom, and it is reinforced by the way other animals have been known to adopt vulnerable humans into their own societies. Freedom of autonomous motion, however, is a type of freedom that Balthasar seems to restrict to humans, but in this respect, he has a weak understanding of the level of sophistication of cognition in many social species. His understanding of freedom is also marred by a stereotypical view of women and animal kinds as inferior to men, elevated by their supposed superior rational capacities. I suggest that enlarging the acknowledgement of capacities of other animals so that they include the possibility of free agency shifts the ground of ethical discourse, so that it is built not just around compassion in the wake of cruelty, as those who press for sentience insist, but on mutual respect and recognition of the other. This opens up the possibility for a relational approach to animal ethics that Clare Palmer suggests is more inclusive of all other animals, both domesticated and in the wild.[50]

Notes

1 John Zizioulas, 'Preserving God's Creation', Lecture 3, *King's Theological Review*, Volume X111, No 1, 1990, pp. 1–6. He suggests that if we consider what is found in God and not in creation, then this 'forces us to seek the *imago Dei* in freedom', p. 2.

2 See Leonard D. Katz, *Evolutionary Origins of Morality: Cross Disciplinary Perspectives* (Bowling Green: Imprint Academic, 2000); W. A. Rottschaeffer *The Biology and Psychology of Moral Agency*, (Cambridge: Cambridge University Press, 1998); R. Joyce, Kevin N. Laland and Gillian R. Brown, *Evolutionary Perspectives on Human Behaviour* (Oxford: Oxford University Press, 2002), R. Joyce, *The Evolution of Morality* (Cambridge/London: MIT Press, 2006). Joyce takes this argument further and concludes that the logical outcome of the evolutionary origins of morality supports moral scepticism, namely, that we should not affirm or deny *any* moral stance.

3 Stephen Gould, 'More Things in Heaven and Earth', in H. Rose and S. Rose (eds), *Alas Poor Darwin: Arguments Against Evolutionary Psychology* (London: Jonathan Cape, 2000), pp. 85–105; Steven Rose, 'Escaping Evolutionary Psychology', in Rose and Rose, *Alas*, pp. 247–65. Mature reflection recognizes the importance of both genetics and environmental influences in behaviour, nature, and nurture, rather than one or the other.

4 For further discussion, see Sarah E. McFarland and Ryan Hediger, 'Appoaching the Agency of Other Animals: An Introduction', in S. MCfarland and R. Hediger, *Animals and Agency: An Interdisciplinary Exploration* (Leiden: Boston, Brilll, 2009), pp. 1–20. The disciplines represented in this collection of essays were English literature, history, science, and philosophy with no reference to religious studies or theology. The main issue discussed in this collection was how animals are perceived as agents in different literary contexts.

5 Examples of his work include Frans de Waal, *Good Natured: The Origins of Right and Wrong in Humans and Other Animals* (Cambridge: Harvard University Press, 1996); Frans de Waal, 'Morally Evolved: Primate Social Instincts, Human Morality, and the Rise and Fall of "Veneer Theory" in Frans de Waal, edited by S. Macedo and J. Ober, *Primates and Philosophers: How Morality Evolved*, (Princeton:Princeton University Press, 2006); pp. 1–75; Frans de Waal, *Our Inner Ape: The Best and Worst of Human Nature* (London: Granta Books, 2006); F. B. M. de Waal, 'Putting the altruism back into altruism. The evolution of empathy', *Annual Review of Psychology*, 59 (2008), pp. 279–300.

6 I have mentioned the problematic tendency for notions of free will to be disembodied in Cartesian forms above.

7 Helen Steward, 'Animal Agency', *Inquiry*, 52 (3) pp. 217–231.

8 D. Davidson, *Subjective, Intersubjective, Objective* (Oxford: Oxford University Press, 2001).

9 I will return to a discussion of TOM in more detail below.

10 See, for example, R. Gelman, 'First Principles Organize Attention to and Learning About Relevant Data: Number and the Animate-Inanimate Distinction as Examples', *Cognitive Science*, 14 (1990), pp. 79–106; D. Premark, 'The Infants Theory of Self-Propelled Objects', *Cognition,* 36 (1990), pp. 1–16; E.S. Speke, A. Phillips and A.L. Woodward, 'Infants Knowledge of Object Motion and Human Action' in D. Sperber, D. Premack and A. J. Premack (eds.), *Causal Cognition: A Multidisciplinary Debate (Oxford: Oxford University Press,* 1995), pp. 44–78. In this case, infants reacted to an object coming close to another object that then appeared to move of its own accord.

11 A. M. Leslie, 'A Theory of Agency', in D. Sperber et al, *Causal Cognition*, pp. 121–41.

12 Wittgenstein's *Philosophical Investigations* showed that sentences such as the cock called its hens by crowing presuppose a sophisticated communication among hens, so that the cock deliberately crows to attract the hens attention, and they know that this is what the cock wants, so come over to join him. Wittgenstein, *Philosophical Investigations*, 1953 §. 493, cited in Steward, 'Animal Agency', p. 224.

13 Steward, 'Animal Agency', pp. 235–6.

14 This helpful definition is taken from Steward, 'Animal Agency', p. 226.

15 See, for example, Sara J. Shettleworth, *Cognition, Evolution and Behaviour*, 2nd edn (Oxford: Oxford University Press, 2010), pp. 432–436.

16 Popularizers of animal ethology are inclined to push for giving other animals the benefit of the doubt. One such example is Jonathan Balcombe, *Second Nature: The Inner Lives of Animals* (New York: Palgrave/Macmillan, 2010).

17 Bennett G. Galef, 'Culture in Animals?', in Kevin N. Laland and Bennett G. Galef, *The Question of Animal Culture* (Cambridge/Mass: Harvard University Press, 2009), pp. 222–246. The author admits that any concrete link between the evolution of animal traditions and the emergence of human cultures has yet to be proven.

18 Christine Korsegaard, 'Morality and the Distinctiveness of Human Action', in de Waal, *Primates and Philosophers*, pp. 110–112.

19 I discuss this in more detail in 'Are Animals Moral? Taking Soundings Through Vice, Virtue, Conscience and Imago Dei', in *Creaturely Theology: On God, Humans and Other Animals*, edited by Celia Deane-Drummond and David Clough (London: SCM Press, 2009), pp. 190–210.

20 Korsegaard, 'Morality' p. 113.

21 Frans de Waal, 'The Tower of Morality', in *Primates and Philosophers,* p. 171; full text pp. 161–182.

22 The differential classification of other animals is discussed by John Dupré in his *Humans and Other Animals* (Oxford: Clarendon Press, 2002), p. 3.

23 Frans de Waal, 'Appendix B; Do Apes Have a Theory of Mind?', in *Primates and Philosophers*, p. 71.

24 See, G. G. Gallup, 'Self Awareness and the Emergence of Mind in Primates', *American Journal of Primatology*, 2, pp. 237–48; 1982, D. Bischof-Köhler, 'Über den Zusammenhang von Empathie und der Fähigeit sic him Spiegel zu erkennen', *Schweizerische Zeitschrift für Psychologie* 47 (1988) pp. 147–159.; C. Zahn_Waxler M. Radke-Yarrow, E. Wagner and M. Chapman, 'Development of Concern for Others, *Developmental Psychology*, 28 (1992) pp. 126–136. For further discussion, De Waal, 'Morally Evolved; Primate Social Instincts, Human Morality and the Rise and Fall of "Veneer Theory"', *Primates and Philosophers*, p. 36.

25 D. C. Penn and D. J. Povinelli, 'On the Lack of Evidence that Non-Human Animals Possess Anything Remotely Resembling a "Theory of Mind"', *Philosophical Transactions of the Royal Society*, B 362 (2007), pp. 731–744; A. M. Newton and J. G. de Villiers, 'Thinking while Talking: Adults Fail Non-Verbal False-Belief Reasoning', *Psychological Science*, 18 (2007), 574–79.

26 See, for example, J. Kaminski, J. Call and M. Tomasello, 'Chimpanzees Know What Others Know, But Not What They Believe', *Cognition* 109 (2008), pp. 224–234.

27 Philip Clayton, *Mind and Emergence: From Quantum to Consciousness* (Oxford: Oxford University Press, 2004), p. 98.

28 R. J. Berry, 'Biology After Darwin', in *Theology After Darwin*, ed. Michael S. Northcott and R. J. Berry (Carlisle: Paternoster), p. 17.

29 Hans Urs von Balthasar, *The Glory of the Lord, Vol. 5, Realm of Metaphysics in the Modern Age* (GL 5) trans. By O. Davies, A. Louth, B. McNeil, J. Saward and R. Williams, ed. Brian McNeil and J. Riches (Edinburgh: T & T Clark; San Francisco: Ignatius Press, 1991), p. 616.

30 Hans Urs von Balthasar, *Theodrama vol. 2, Dramatis Personae: Man in God*, (TD 2) trans. Graham Harrison (San Francisco: Ignatius Press, 1990) p. 211.

31 Balthasar, GL5, p. 621.

32 Balthasar, GL5, p. 621.

33 Balthasar, GL5, p. 625.

34 Balthasar, GL5, p. 635.

35 Hans Urs von Balthasar, *The Glory of the Lord: A Theological Aesthetics, vol. 7, Theology: The New Covenant* (GL 7), trans. B. McNeil (Edinburgh: T & T. Clark/San Francisco: Ignatius, 1989), p. 403.

36 Hans Urs von Balthasar, *The Glory of the Lord, Vol. 6, The Old Covenant*, trans B.McNeil and E. Leiva-Merikakis (Edinurgh: T & T Clark/San Francisco: Ignatius, 1991), p. 90.

37 Balthasar, GL7, p. 403.

38 See, for example, Hans Urs von Balthasar, *Man in History* (MH) (London: Sheed and Ward, 1968), pp. 308–309. His stereotypical views of women have been the subject of sharp critique, especially by feminist scholars.

39 Balthasar, MH, p. 43.

40 Balthasar, MH, p. 44.

41 Balthasar, MH, p. 44.

42 See Hans Urs von Balthasar, *Theo-Drama, Volume 1, Prolegomena*, tr. Graham Harrison (San Francisco: Ignatius Press, 1988).

43 Balthasar, TD2.

44 A. Nichols, *No Bloodless Myth: A Guide Through Balthasar's Dramatics* (Edinburgh: T & T Clark, 2000), p. 63.

45 See, for example, Hans Urs von Balthasar, *Theo-Drama: Theo-Dramatic Theory, Volume V, The Final Act*, tr. Graham Harrison (San Francisco: Ignatius Press, 1998), p. 474.

46 For a commentary on epic thinking in Balthasar, see Ben Quash, *Theology and the Drama of History* (Cambridge: Cambridge

University Press, 2005). Ben Quash describes Balthasar's own definition of epic thinking as 'an element of *necessity* at the heart of events and happenings that take place ... this is one way to choosing to read the interaction between God and his creatures ... At its worst ... . epic is the genre of a false objectification'. p. 42. Quash subsequently proposes that Balthasar has fallen into this trap of epic thinking himself, in spite of his denials. Quash, for example, comments that with respect to freedom, obedience has the last word in Balthasar, comparing him unfavourably with Barth in this respect, and Balthasar interprets obedience in an ecclesial way that leads to a lack of human creativity, pp. 158–9. While I agree that obedience in Balthasar comes over at times as cold and institutional, even claiming in a quite horrifying way that 'Every "dialogue-situation" was excluded – by a corresponding agreement of Adrienne's soul – so that it became experientially clear that the obedience of the Church can and at times must have all the reality and relentlessness of the Cross itself, both in the authority which commands and the faithful who obey', Hans Urs von Balthasar, *First Glance at Adrienne von Speyr*, translated by Antje Lawry and Sergia Englund, (San Francisco: Ignatius Press, 1968), p. 70. This rigid conservatism is not the only note in his theology, and elsewhere he speaks in a much more positive way about future hope including creativity. Ben Quash's association of Balthasar with epic, Hegelian thought has some justification in my view, but also for other reasons as well, namely, his tendency for a stereotypical view of the sexes and the intellectualization of freedom characterized as a male trait, with associated denigration of women (and animals). While Kevin Mongrain notes that Balthasar is influenced strongly by Irenaeus, it seems that, as far as his eschatology is concerned, this note becomes much weaker. See also Kevin Mongrain, *The Systematic Thought of Hans Urs von Balthasar: An Irenaean Retrieval* (New York: Herder and Herder, 2002).

47 Noske, *Beyond Boundaries: Humans and Animals* (Montreal/London/New York, Black Rose, 1997). p. 162.

48 For example, a Syrian child who had lived with gazelles had an exceptional capacity to leap from the first floor of his house to the street. The response by his 'benefactors' was mutilation by cutting his tendons. Such acts are best described as immoral and formed from distorted views of human supremacy over animals. See discussion in Barbara Noske, *Beyond Boundaries*, p. 164.

49 Jean Claude Armen, *Gazelle-boy: A Child Brought up by Gazelles in the Sahara Desert* (London: Picador, 1976).

50 Clare Palmer, *Animal Ethics in Context* (New York: Columbia University Press, 2010).

PART FOUR

Animal–Human–Machine–God

10

Inhuman Geometry: Aurochs, Angels and the Refuge of Art

Charlie Blake

The spider's web is certainly formed in a 'fly-like' manner, because the spider itself is 'fly-like.' To be 'fly-like' means that the body structure of the spider has taken on certain characteristics of the fly – not from a specific fly, but rather from the fly's archetype. To express it more accurately, the spider's 'fly-likeness' comes about when its body structure has adopted certain themes from the fly's melody.[1]

I am thinking of Aurochs and Angels, the secret of durable pigments, prophetic sonnets and the refuge of art. And this is the only immortality you and I may share, my Lolita.[2]

'Werewolves swarming 1730' … and so on.[3]

The God Machine

At the conclusion of his final volume of philosophy, *Two Sources of Morality and Religion*, published in 1932, Henri Bergson leaves us with a challenge and a provocation. He claims that humanity is now burdened by the weight of progress and is crawling and groping into an uncertain future but that, in spite of this burden, humanity as a species must decide collectively if they want to merely live or intend to make just the extra effort required for fulfilling, even on their refractory planet, the essential function of the universe, which is as a machine for making Gods.[4]

To suggest, as this sentence might initially appear to us to do from an early twenty-first century perspective, that we are as a species somehow aligned to a universal 'function', a programme whose underlying *telos* is the manufacture of deities, is, however, misleading. Such evolutionary teleology, whether aligned with the organic and the sentient, on the one hand, or the pre- and post-biological and possibly even the inorganic, on the other, is, of course, easy to caricature as little more than a desire for immortality inflated to a metaphysical principle. Has this not, after all, been the underlying narrative of countless eschatologies and their secular equivalents in the history of our species? Is this not at base merely some version of Sigmund Freud's drive to 'wish fulfilment' stripped of both its hypothetical status and its libidinal-economic value as fantasy and extrapolated into a cosmic or theological certainty? At face value, perhaps it is indeed such a reduction, such a deception, and this potential reading is certainly an important one to consider on a populist level in that it reflects a great deal of contemporary trans-humanist thinking, whether promotional, journalistic or explicitly fictional. But this is not, of course, what Bergson is suggesting in his mischievous philosophical coda. Indeed, the whole notion of teleology or finality is one that Bergson dismisses resolutely through concepts which have, arguably, and certainly in the influential Deleuzean reading of the philosopher,[5] what might be termed as an *internal* finality or drive, or pulsion, certainly, but absolutely no *end* as such, no *telos* in the Aristotelian sense, anyway. Thus, and in this view, change – continuous transition – is undoubtedly a constant in life and in the universe generally, as is creativity and the emergence or production of the new, with which it is sometimes, but not always, a cognate for Bergson and his most notable heir: but where that change leads or what that creativity might produce remains, for both of them, manifestly open ended. In this understanding, the idea of the universe as a 'machine for creating gods' should be considered as being less about a function or *telos per se* than as a tendency, or perhaps what the enigmatic and decidedly neo-Lamarckian French anthropologist, André Leroi Gourhan, described as a *tendance,* understood as a phenomenon with a universal if ungrounded manifestation, whether applied to phenomena as various as, say, tools, housing, transportation technologies or cosmetics and self-decoration (in the human world).[6] Borrowing rather loosely from Leroi-Ghouran here, it is a tendency or *tendance,* which Bergson, however, from a decidedly non-Lamarckian perspective, describes primarily through an image of universal force and flow rather than one of an object, machine, array or formation of either, of what he famously terms the *élan vital* and in this sense, and through this image as it is developed by Gilles Deleuze, finality, at least in the Aristotelian sense, is replaced by a Bergsonian-Deleuzian notion of virtuality or virtual multiplicity. Beyond his appropriation of Bergson, of course, Deleuze draws on the libidinal and existential economies of Friedrich Nietzsche and the exquisite and univocal geometries of Baruch Spinoza to construct a model of change and creativity through actualization and multiplicity that avoids what he describes as the 'maledictions' of philosophy and desire, specifically Cartesian dualism and its variants and Thomist analogy. Thus, multiplicities, for Deleuze, (and this is important when considering the trajectory of human evolution, as will be discussed below), whether objects, affects or actualizations become an aspect of singularity univocity, (whether we call this desire, substance or the will to power is unimportant here), and the *potentia* inherent in states of existence and anticipation become modes of expression of this singularity.

In terms of theories of natural selection and genetic (in)determinacy, this move effectively translates *telos* as virtuality rather than end, as pure past rather than ultimate future, with important consequences for the integrity or, otherwise, of what we call human. In this, and following Bergson, that which we perceive or experience as actual is a feature of an unstable present moving forever forwards, whereas the virtual belongs to all that is un-present, to the pure past as he calls it, which is shaped and constrained by the actualization of the present through the event. What, however, does this state of affairs, or configuration of concepts, actually mean in terms of our common scientific or quasi-scientific understanding of the processual nature of human evolution? Further, to talk as I have above of the human as a 'species' is surely, begging yet another question, or perhaps several questions at once. What do we mean by the term 'species' after all? Is it to be understood as some kind of singularity with clearly delimited boundaries, for instance – or possibly as a kind of ghostly assemblage, as ostensibly realist-materialist thinkers such as Deleuze and his sometime collaborator Felix Guattari might have it – within either case an external and objectifiable reality clearly in place aside from any mind dependency, as in the broader realist tradition? Or is it, alternatively, as many or even most idealist positions would probably argue and as many or most too who might be described less as idealists *per se* than as pragmatists, positivists or empiricists might indicate, merely a convenient fiction that we use to taxonomize the entities and adventures of sense and consciousness, the connections and definitions that we theorize as harmonious or relational entities, into cognitively workable patterns? Are we in fact dealing with a spectral or even a magical materialism, in other words, however disguised as a realism in its several variants? These questions resonate increasingly as we look into the nature of inscription and art (understood here through the broadly conventional categories of film, music and fiction, and – looking backwards (or possibly sideways, downwards or indeed, upwards) – the inscriptions, scratchings, scrapings, shapings and daubings of late Palaeolithic cave art) in their capacity as that which can be said to define what it is to be human, (or at least contribute persuasively to that definition), and accordingly, to configure the outlines of adjacent or overlapping notions of, say, animality, the inhuman, the non-human, the anti-human, the trans-human and the post-human, within the context of the broader conceptual canvas of time, evolution and necessity, signalled by Bergson's terminal provocation.

In non-realist terms, this is clearly quite a diverse and possibly recalcitrant collection of theoretical entities to structure into any kind of workable pattern.[7] To begin with, the question must be asked as to how inscription and art (and the *technics* upon which they rely) can be said to define what it is to be human? From there, the questioning will move on to look at Deleuze and Guattari's notions of refrain, monument and milieu and their conceptual forerunner in Jacob von Uexküll's influential theories of point and counterpoint and the musicality of the organism.[8] This will allow us in the next section to consider evolution less as a linear flow (or emanation) into the future than as an aspect of the neo-baroque, as it confers with and configures the musicality of correspondence and *umwelt* as described by Uexküll and developed, variously, by figures such as Martin Heidegger, Maurice Merleau-Ponty and Deleuze and Guattari, as well as through Michel Serres' reflections on temporal expediency of angels, statues and parasites and the god of information and communication and certain aspects of creation himself – Hermes. Finally, the ideas of angelic machinery and inhuman geometry thus raised will take us briefly into the realm of a cosmos of pure creativity, conjectured but yet to be generated from the fields of desire and temporality that determine the moment of the human and its excess.

From the Cave of Making to the Mirror of Dreams

As this chapter was in the process of being fabricated, the film-maker Werner Herzog released a 3D documentary, *Cave of Forgotten Dreams*, his eloquent study of the galleries of richly detailed and exquisite cave art discovered by Jean-Marie Chuavet in 1994 in the south of France, and subsequently closed off from the public gaze for preservation and analysis. As ever with Herzog, the film itself is something more than a 'mere' documentary recording of a place or an event, in that it poses questions about the 'who, when and where' of *us* as viewers, as well as that of the scientific participants in the study, as much as the 'who, when and where' of what we imagine we might be looking at. In adopting this transversal approach to its subject matter, the film confronts us with the deep human past at the same time as it probes what our limits might be as self-consciously 'human' in relation to what we think we see before and around us as also – but archaically – 'human' – liminally, phenomenologically or otherwise. Herzog's use of projectional 3D technology here, a decidedly retro-futurist technology of the moving image until comparatively recently, which has had a series of false starts since its inception in the 1950s, (and now, finally, seems to have found its techno-cultural moment) is highly significant, in that it manages simultaneously to illuminate and to perspectivize the paintings of cave bears and other animals extinct or absent from this region for millennia – and to perspectivize them also along with something akin to Stiegler's notion of the human as defined by *technics*, by the externalization of memory in language, tools and images, a process and set of skills and drives that differentiate our species from other animals.[9]

In the main, however, and for the community of experts and aficionados who descended into the cave system to study these images, the controversy surrounding the Chauvet discovery had to do primarily with the question of age. From radio carbon dating of the walls, it appeared that these paintings were nearly twice as old as similar examples previously discovered in Southern Europe, famously those of Lascaux or Altimira and as might be expected, this discovery of unexpected antiquity polarized archaeologists over a number of issues concerning procedure and paleontological specification, most specifically the procedures of carbon dating itself and the existence or otherwise in the region at this time of the cave bears and other creatures seemingly depicted. The main reason for this discovery's importance to this particular discussion, however, is not so much the specificity of evidence and hypothesis on the dating of origins, (though this does, of course, have complex philosophical as well as technical or scientific implications), nor the existence or otherwise in the region of particular mammals in particular periods, as it is the trace, reality and implications of sophisticated artistic expression and range apparently executed by our forbears some 30,000 to 32,000 years ago. It is important because our understanding of the origins of art is, as has been already noted, intricately woven into our understanding of the human itself. There is, in this sense, an underlying assumption here that defining the human is not merely a question of physical taxonomy, of the measuring of brows and jawbones and consideration of the advantages of opposable thumbs, for instance, nor is it the discovery of the control of fire or the power of the primitive tool or machine such as the wheel or the plough or the systematic violence enabled by an object transformed through human will, imagination and interaction into a weapon – though these are clearly crucial. Rather, it is the moment, however extended that moment might be in 'real' time, when our ancestors not only began to communicate in spoken language – an extended event that we obviously have no access to – but also to represent or express or inscribe images on wood, rocks and cave walls, creating – when the materials were right – visual events that still retain the power of affect for their distant descendants, and even hint at the possibility of trans-historical communication through magic or narrative, some thirty millennia on, that will be central. In this context, Herzog's use of 3D also, arguably, reminds us more indirectly of a distinction often made between the two major strands of artistic expression associated with the Palaeolithic, both in its mobile and so-called parietal forms, this being the flat two-dimensional form of the painting and the three dimensional carving or sculpture. That our predecessors could manipulate figures and images across dimensional planes transversally suggests to some theorists such as, for example, David Lewis Williams, that what the emergence of art represents is a fundamental alteration of consciousness:

> The whole of our evolution has been oriented towards placing outside ourselves what in the rest of the animal world is achieved inside by species adaptation. The most striking material fact is certainly the 'freeing' of tools, but the fundamental fact is really the freeing of the world and our unique ability to transfer our memory to a social organism outside ourselves.[10]

This process of externalization as a kind of emancipation of the *umwelt* or lifeworld from its paleo-organic constraints and facticity (and possibly even from itself through some combination of self replication, controlled mutation and participant evolution) hints at a number of themes which weave sometimes perilously, sometimes almost casually, through debates on the nature of the human and that which might lie beyond it, or – perhaps even more unnervingly – adjacent to it. 'Perilously', inasmuch as the subject-centredness that has so often been deemed as characteristic of what it is to be human in the first place, or at least one very important aspect of it, can be very easily displaced and even randomly so by certain versions of tertiary memory, whether existent or projected, from the forms of textualist and structuralist or poststructuralist antihumanism fashionable in Parisian salons of the 1960s, to the post-human speculations of more contemporary and geographically dispersed blogs and networks. 'Peril' is, of course, in itself, generally deemed to be a subjective notion, a perception of danger to the organism from the perspective of that organism, and from this rather limiting perspective the question of judgement when dealing with anti-humanism, trans-humanism or post-humanism becomes intimately tied to broader notions of the ethical and the aesthetic as categories of experience in which a mechanism of evaluation is central. In terms of the ethical, (and leaving to one side the possible criticism that might be levelled from, say, a Deleuzean perspective, against focusing on the 'organism' rather than a more immanent and dispersed singularity such as a Body Without Organs or machinic assemblage), the peril here might be ordinary or apocalyptic, and in terms of the aesthetic considerations, it might be a question of the momentary thrill of a funfair ride, on the one hand, or one of sublime transformation, on the other. In whichever case, however, and whether retained or abandoned experientially, value as affect – or as Nietzsche pointed out long ago – the process of evaluation, which is also affect, remains the mechanism of both measure and intensity.

That these are not merely philosophical concerns, or rather, the concern of philosophy should be evident from any consideration of film or fiction or animation or popular culture more generally. When considering the more literary projections of a post-human future or hybridized animality as suggested above, for example, as in the speculative fictions of writers as various as, say, Charles Stross, Greg Egan and Ursula La Guin or Angela Carter, Jeff Noon and Will Self, the central questions raised by these exploratory fictions, each of which dismantles and then reassembles human identity in various ways and to various ends at various socio-historical moments, and whether their apparent intentions are fantastical, epistemological, ontological or satirical, these questions ultimately remain those of judgement, and judgement of the ethical and the aesthetic, but particularly the latter. That this is the case surely has much to do with the way the aesthetic has a quality about, like perhaps the medieval *haecceity* so ardently re-engaged by Deleuze as a lightning strike or zig zag revealed by the dark precursor, or the *jenseit* of Walter Benjamin's messianic breach of history, that interrupts time's seeming progression and unidirectionality and extends itself across and beyond the temporal horizon it momentarily illuminates, becoming transversal rather than teleological. Like the Stoic idea of *chronos* that Deleuze also appropriates and adapts rather loosely to his own ends in his *Logic of Sense*, for instance, (before expanding these temporal syntheses for slightly different ends in *Difference and Repetition*), the aesthetic moment as it is understood here is one that stretches endlessly in all directions simultaneously, at least potentially, both past and future (as Deleuze suggests in relation to *chronos* rather than *aion*), but also in all those directions to which we give no name other than those vague delineations we gesture towards and attempt to ground in theology or physics or mathematics or poetry and fiction, such as the 'eternal' or the 'infinite' or the 'transfinite' or 'zero', or the 'outside' of Blanchot or 'impossible' of Georges Bataille.

In this extended sense, when Vladimir Nabokov's protagonist, the despicable *litterateur* and murderer and textually fabricated narrator of *Lolita*, Humbert Humbert, evokes aurochs and angels and the immortal image or lyrical butterfly net in his final elegaic epitaph to his love for the equally textually fabricated Dolores Haze, as cited in the epigraph at the head of this chapter, he also and quite deliberately calls attention to the fact that what it is to *be* human is inextricably bound up with what can be said to be *other* than the human and more pointedly to emerge *from* the human, not merely in the temporality of biological sequence, of sex and death and progeny, but through the fabricated eternity of art, invention and inscription, and the instruments that enable them. Accordingly, if Nabokov expresses this peculiarly human yearning for a quite possibly brief and thus faux immortality through the inscriptive powers of the literary event, he is also making a case, as the allusion to aurochs makes perfectly clear, for forms of inscription beyond this relatively recent invention, with all the aesthetic and evaluative impedimenta that it has accumulated in modernity and subsequently. He is making a case for a species of human action or expression, for what seems to be an aesthetic imperative, that may well take the form of what Aristotle called *poeisis,* but which is equally bound up with the more functional realm of *techne,* both of which are determined and conditioned as human making primarily by their relationship to time. Indeed, as Stiegler has argued so eloquently in *The Fault of Epimetheus*, drawing critically on the work of both Heidegger and Leroi Ghouran, that which defines what it is for us to be human is inextricable from both time and technics, as they are for that reason inextricable from one another. This observation has implications both for the forms of temporality we encounter in the acts of making or doing or connecting with others and for the kinds of temporality we abstract from these events and processes and either sediment as concepts or hypotheses, or project as maps of existential transformation or stasis; patternings which like the constellations so high above our needful primate exigencies become meaningful by virtue of our drawing them in to this desultory human orbit we share as both coordination and expression. This is an orbit which our later ancestors would, in due course, discover can be shrunk to the singular moment of a kiss or the prick of pin, or expanded to the event of a holiday or revolution or lifetime. It is also an orbit which can extend or conflate or spread and flatten out like a map our days, months, years, centuries, millennia or more into historical eras, palaeographic vistas or vast trans-historical aeons stretching back to our primal, Hadean origins as irradiated clusters of single cells beneath an infernal star: clusters of cells whose progeny would one day, billions of years on, gain both the powers of voice and the powers of inscription, not to mention the powers of violence, and name that star as their sun – and then worship it through sacrifice, plant, animal and human.

Of Music, Monoliths and Monuments

In geological terms, for example, and within this orbit as stretched and extended, metaphorically speaking, to encompass the evolution of the inorganic, the evolution of rocks and atmospheres, and to encompass thereby the predatory copulations of tectonic plates, and thus, through the infinitely slow accretions of geophysical desire, to encompass also the very different velocities of rivers, mountains, forests and archaic seas, it was a mere split second ago that the drawing rooms of late Victorian culture were simultaneously adapting to the exponential acceleration of technological change in the wake of the harnessing by machines and assemblages of mysterious and invisible forces and energies. At the same time, moreover, as these seemingly occult or at least occluded forces were being tamed through emergent communication, transport, matter and energy technologies, those same nineteenth-century drawing rooms were being haunted by new kinds of temporal ghosts and revenants – new spiritual activities. On one side, the more speculative and intellectually ambitious Victorian sensitivities were being taunted, both cruelly and seductively, by a nihilistic vision of the cosmic entropic machine gradually running down, the heat death of the universe as prophesied by Rutherford, but in the form of spectral traces flashing back to us prospectively from an unimaginably distant future as formulae and equations. On the other side, these same sensitivities were being haunted retrospectively by the ghosts of ancestral apes, calling to them and us from a more recent past through what we would, in the following century, recognize as the music of DNA. If we continue this temporal conceit, we find that it is only a second or so further back from where we now pause to that moment in which what we call writing first emerges in Mesopotamia, and prior to that, by maybe a minute, to that moment in which the first luminous representations or expressions of what we might now call either art or media – the latter of which can be defined here provisionally as any kind of communication at a distance, whether across time or space – appear in those curious and equally haunted psych-acoustic spaces of caves and caverns. This is the space that Georges Bataille argued as the source of both our sense of our humanity and of our animality and also of the sense of the sacred and the aesthetic that resulted from the ambivalence our ancestors felt about our simultaneous emergence from and spiritual consanguinity with the non-human animals with which we shared, at that time, a tiny portion of the Earth.

Indeed, between our forbear's first daubings of dogs, aurochs, horses, cave bears, mammoths, hairy rhinos, stick-figure humans with spears, various animal–human hybrids and abstract geometrical or 'entoptic' figures on cavern walls and the transmedial technologies of the present, the time of the human has indeed been brief and insubstantial. Now it seems, moreover, even before we have properly grasped what it is to be human in the first place, *pace* Bataille and Leroi-Gourhan and others, we are, according to the speculative explorations of trans-humanist thinkers such as Ray Kurzweil and Nick Bostrom,[11] on the verge of a supposed 'singularity' through which our augmented simian desires will, should we survive, transform elements of our species into a new kind of entity altogether – quite possibly a swarm-like post-human consciousness in which the distinction between the machinic and the organic, not to mention the corporeal and non-corporeal, dissolves into the generation of creatures beyond our current imaginings. And yet, at the same time as we contemplate this possibility, and however sceptical some may be of its wilder claims, we are as a species, or at least in certain enclaves of our speciality, reconsidering the notion of animality itself and the broader ecosophical parameters of the human in relation to the beast that we both are and have historically distinguished ourselves from.

Such reconsiderations and imaginations can lead to a certain ontological dissonance and conceptual chaos, albeit one that may end up being highly creative for some or indeed 'chaosophical' as the term has been derived from Felix Guattari's own assimilation of James Joyce's 'chaosmos' in *Finnegans Wake* to indicate the wisdom of chaos and schizophrenia.[12] This is especially important when we consider the ontological status of the human and its supposed predecessors and progeny, not to mention its more lateral alliances and mutations, for as Guattari's contemporary, Jacques Derrida, has noted in a mediation on his cat's gaze on his nakedness in the shower in *The Animal that Therefore I am*, and with affectionate allusion to the fading smile of the Cheshire Cat from Lewis Carroll's novel

> I no longer know who, therefore, I am (following) or who it is I am chasing, who is following me or hunting me. Who comes before and who is after whom? I no longer know which end my head is. Madness. 'We're all mad here. I'm mad. You're mad'[13]

If then – and to move from Derrida's feline cognitive disarray to an image of the post-simian that we define conventionally as human – if then, we have been suspended in some important sense in modernity and post-modernity 'between the apes and the angels', as certain Victorian commentators once put it, it would seem that we are now as a species at least partially enmeshed, (and bearing in mind the negative drift and drag of political and economic restraints), in something far more complex than a straightforward transition. It appears, that is, from a range of popular, technological and philosophical sources that we are in the process of becoming a baroque assemblage of potentialities and virtualities, a congeries of valences involving, by way of example: accelerating biotechnologies, pervasive nanotechnologies, aionic cryogenics, artificial intelligence, distributed consciousness, species hybridities, cybernetic augmentation, cosmetic mutation, genetic transposition and, most crucially behind all these developments, the guiding principle of participant evolution. That many of these potential developments would seem to arise from a paradigm shift in the human-technics relationship should nor surprise us, but there is of course a continuity in operation here as well as a series of discontinuities, and one that dates back to the origin of the idea of the future as technotropic in the late nineteenth and early twentieth-century writings of, most notably, Jules Verne or H. G. Wells. For when the conservative prime minister Benjamin Disraeli responded in 1864 to the twin Darwinian challenges of natural and sexual selection and the descent of man by posing the question: 'Is man an ape or an angel?' – and asserting by way of response: 'My Lord, I am on the side of the angels. I repudiate with indignation and abhorrence these new-fangled theories,' [14] he initiated not only a rather colourful Victorian cliché but also an image of human ontological suspension as one of choice rather than procession or purpose. Or, to put it another way, if the ontology of the human is identified primarily with the simian, it cannot in these Disraelian terms, be identified with the angelic, and vice versa. They are in direct contradiction to one another. Thus a static picture of the human as a being radically distinct from the animal but aspiring to the spiritual to which it potentially has ontological access by virtue of some divine or determined regulation is unequivocally asserted. For those, on the other hand, who had some sympathy with the Darwinian revolution, the transition or the bridge – to adapt a more Nietzschean image[15] – between the ape and the angel posed another conundrum – that of teleology. Was the human in some sense aspiring in evolutionary terms to a condition of the angelic or the superhuman, as certain neo-Lamarckians would have it and to some extent still do into the twenty-first century? In this understanding, was the process to be considered, then, as it often has been subsequently in certain political translations of natural selection, as one of an *ascent* (rather than a *descent*) of 'man' to some higher species or, in its Gnostic variant, a fundamental disembodiment or virtualisation of self or intelligence? Or was the essence of evolutionary change fundamentally random, mere *chance* rather than some kind of divine or genetic destiny or species determinism, as Darwin had clearly proposed? Between choice and chance, however, has emerged a third paradigm in which ontological boundaries blur and in which a dimension of technics that has characterized our simian descent from the ape-human to the projected post-human becomes illuminated – inscription.

One way of illuminating this is through the example of two related figures of monument and monolith, as they appear in the first instance in the writings of Deleuze and Guattari on art, music and territoriality, and in the second, the visionary echoes afforded by Stanley Kubrick's realization of Arthur C. Clarke's evolutionary and trans-human fable, *2001: A space Odyssey*. For Clarke, whose extraordinary projections of a human evolution controlled and managed by beings superior to us in all those ways that we have traditionally measured the supposed superiority of alien civilizations, whether ethically, conceptually or – most importantly – technologically, our progression towards an ever more refined form of hyper-intelligence proceeds by leaps, whether the sudden development of psychic abilities amongst children in the wistful *Childhood's End*, or the irruption into proto-human and human culture of obscure, black, non-reflective *monoliths* that signal a leap to be made, both conceptually and, in the case of Stanley Kubrick's filmic realization of *2001*, editorially. These extraterrestrial machines, which can teleport, self replicate, and, it is speculated, exist in more than the three spatial dimensions represented through the square of the integers 1, 2 and 3 which translate as a ratio of 1, 4 and 9, are both a plot device and an eloquent signifier of the strongly teleological implications of Clarke's vision. Drawing as much, it seems, on the neo-Lamarckianism of Teillhard de Chardin's omega point as the breath-taking futures of Olaf Stapledon's *Star maker*, Clarke's monoliths, for all their mysterious provenance, appear to indicate a direction for humanity to take, be it one of expansion or ascent, and in this the universe is indeed a machine for making gods in the most overtly unidirectional sense. The monuments are forms of inscription placed like grammatical markers in the sentences of time, to generate further inscription and replication into a future shaped and directed by specific notions of expansion and progression. In contrast, the *monument* of Deleuze and Guattari speaks of a very different approach to directionality and the production of the new. This is an image developed in *What is Philosophy* from the concept of the refrain which is itself an adaptation of the work of the bio-semiotician, Uexküll, and this requires a brief look at Uexküll's ideas on musicality and the lifeworld as the defining characteristics of the organism. For Uexküll, most famously in his image of the tick, the organism is surrounded by a skin which determines both its environment and its reality. Thus, the space peculiar to each animal, wherever that animal may be, can be compared to a soap bubble that completely surrounds the creature at a greater or less distance. The extended soap bubble constitutes the limit of what is finite for the animal, and therewith the limit of its world; what lies behind that is hidden in infinity.[16]

Along with this image of a bubble, Uexküll also deploys a range of musical images to clarify the orientation of living beings towards specific aspects of their environment, from the rhythm of cells through the melody of organs, the symphony of the organism, the harmony of organisms to the composition of nature itself.[17] Moreover, these two analogies are complementary rather than exclusive, for as Brett Buchanan has eloquently summarized, they

> offer complementary perspectives on the *Umwelt*. On the one hand, the soap bubble emphasizes how Uexküll sees the *Umwelt* as finite and spherical by encircling the organism within certain limits, and just as important, precluding us from ever penetrating into another organism's soap bubble to fully understand the significance of its *Umwelt*.[18]

The musical analogy, on the other hand, enables an understanding not of limitation but of expression and connection, the ways in which a musical score is created by each life form, not merely through sonic means, but through touch, vision, smell, taste, pressure, heat sensitivity and so forth, and the reception of impulsions and expulsions from other living organisms as their bubbles press upon our own and resonate with them, whether in consonance or dissonance or both.

Deleuze and Guattari take this musical idea and develop it through their notion of the refrain which arises from the rhythm of territorialization, such that the territory is by definition 'the product of a territorialization of milieus and rhythms.'[19] As Elizabeth Grosz has suggested, the refrain is the rhythmic adaptation of this need for regularity that allows a small patch of order amidst the chaos and thereby 'protects the body through the rhythms of the earth itself.'[20] Commenting on various rituals of colour, posture, gesture and sound in the non-human animal kingdoms, Deleuze and Guattari note that here we find the origins of art, the creations of blocks of colour and sensation or noise, which form refrains. Making the connection in *What is Philosophy* between these refrains and their deterritorialization in art, and thereby differentiating the human from the non-human animal, they at the same time note that the need in the artist to create monuments, to defy time with a note of faux eternity, both distances us from and illuminates the inner and spectral animality of what we are. Thus, 'the whole of the refrain is the being of sensation. Monuments are refrains. In this respect art is continually haunted by the animal.'[21] Moreover, 'A monument does not commemorate or celebrate something that happened but confides to the ear of the future the persistent sensations that embody the event.'[22]

This future-orientation of the monument should not be seen, however, as teleological, but rather, as expressive or creative. The essence here of the human as a creature, who not only hears the refrain but deterritorializes it and transforms it into art or music or fiction, bears corollary with the ways in which politics or evolutionary theory might also be understood as the real as virtual multiplicity which may or may not actualize as an event, but in doing so, goes against the grain of the virtual and must always be taken back into the pure past so that new futures can be continuously generated. These futures, however, are not generated progressively, so much as in a manner which might be described through the image of the baroque, as Deleuze has indeed done, of course, in his work on Leibniz in *The Fold*. To contextualize this baroque evolutionism, a brief visit to selected fiction and film created some thirty millennia after the art in the caves of Chauvet will conclude this chapter with a yet more brief return to Bergson and his notion of the circularity that composes what it is to be human projection.

Insects, Apes and Angels

This story begins in New York City in 1953, when an exterminator named Bill Lee discovers during the course of a job that his supply of insect poison has been severely depleted. Running into a pair of writers loosely modelled on Allen Ginsberg and Jack Kerouac, Bill then discovers that his wife Joan has been sampling the yellow powder on the sly and has seemingly become addicted to it. Returning to their apartment in the middle of the day he interrupts her in the act of injecting herself. 'You weren't supposed to see this,' she says, 'I'm shooting up your bug powder. You might like to try it.' On further enquiry, Bill learns from Joan that the insecticide, yellow pyrethrum, gives her 'a very literary high.' 'It's a Kafka high,' she continues, 'you feel like a bug.'

This is, of course, from the early establishing sequence of David Cronenberg's 1993 film adaptation – or perhaps more accurately, hybridization – of William Burroughs' 1959 novel *Naked Lunch*. That this re-inscription of Burroughs' text from book to screen might garner some negative criticism for its supposed aestheticization, post-modernization, de-politicization or 'un-queering' of the novel, as it indeed did, is hardly surprising for so inflammatory and unique a literary event.[23] In spite of intermittent interest and some tentative scriptings over some three decades, however, *Naked Lunch*, had generally been deemed unfilmable, and it is for this reason that Cronenberg justified his mutation of its subject matter, (with, it seems, the blessing of the author), as less an adaptation *per se* than a 'fusion' of two creative visions, in a manner not dissimilar to the fusion of the scientist and the fly as 'brundlefly' in his 1986 remake of the 1950s horror film, *The Fly,* or the merging or human consciousness and videoflesh in 1983's *Videodrome.*[24]

This notion of fusion or hybridization and the critical reactions to *Naked Lunch* are important for the discussion that follows for several reasons. To begin with, they indicate the ways in which modes of inscription that might be considered incommensurable also signal, however indirectly, an expression of incommpossible worlds delineated by those same dissonant modes of inscription. Or to put it another way, whether the 'art' of the book or movie in this context is treated as a representation, an expression, a sensation, an affect or possibly as an assemblage of precepts, the specific experience of its reception is delineated by its mode of inscription as that mode is understood to delineate a particular world or set of worlds thus inscribed. However, at the same time, and within a Deleuzean framework of univocality as will be discussed here, such distinctions may be viewed as mutations of degree rather than distinctions of kind, as may the distinctions one might make between species, phyla or genera. Or, as Burroughs puts it in *Naked Lunch* in relation to the human,

> Migrations, incredible journeys through deserts and jungles and mountains (stasis and death in closed mountain valleys where plants grow out of genitals, vast crustaceans hatch inside and break the shell of the body) across the Pacific in an outrigger canoe to Easter Island. The Composite City where all human potentials are spread out in a vast silent market.[25]

However, as Burroughs' image of the Interzone market suggests, these apparent incommensurabilities and incompossibilities, whether of degree or kind, also raise questions of choice and value in which the desiring production of text or image and what Burroughs called 'the algebra of need' fuse into a chimerical concept -affect as multiplicity, or as multiplicities, thus laid out as Burroughs puts it: 'in a vast silent market.' Also important in the fused *Naked Lunch* on the level of the 'literary high' mentioned by Joan in the film, is the intersection of obsessions between the writer and the director that highlight this chimerical concept-affect fusion and its generation of multiplicity. This is an intersection which on the level of articulation dramatizes the blurring of organic boundaries between species or other entities including the non-organic, between that which flows and that which channels those flows, between the organism and the machine, between the human and the insectile, but also between discourses of control, paranoia, addiction and desire. *Naked Lunch*, in this sense, (and I intend both of them here as fusion), can be positioned as an extended canvas of words and sensations and media echoes in which temporality, transversality and transmutation, concept, functive and affect, or in the figurative densities of the film – typewriter, asshole and insect – are effectively folds in a single ontological fabric. They are part of an ontographical regime in which mutation is more about emergence than taxonomy. Like Burroughs' fiction, Cronenberg's early work is full of transmutations of flesh and ontological dissonance, of entropic routines and passing economies of calibrated delirium and surgically or biologically enhanced lack, indicating that whatever the boundaries of the human might appear to be, these boundaries are decidedly permeable, even foldable, and that the human itself is driven less by will or desire than by what Burroughs has called, as signalled above, the 'algebra of need'. This may well be a 'literary' interpretation, or rather expression, of a potentially painful material reality, an 'aestheticisation', perhaps, of organic and non-organic life in a state of maximal hunger, and death, and thus the product of a 'literary high', as Joan describes the effect of the bug powder before Bill tragically, accidentally, shoots her in a game of William Tell. But if it is that, it is also a 'high' which re-perspectivizes, and which – as Deleuze and Guattari might have it – actualizes the virtual through events, in this case through events metamorphosing as loopholes in space, time and matter through which people can become bugs and bugs can become machines and in which all these metamorphoses or becomings generate milieus which in turn generate territories in which new refrains, events and entities can come into being. Here, then, is the rococo bestiary that both author and filmmaker deploy in *Naked Lunch* and elsewhere to elaborate a zone which can be home to talking centipedes, mugwumps, addictive poisons, bodies without organs, holey spaces, and typewriters that are also and simultaneously insects and human assholes. Here is a realm in which males and females of the same species apparently no longer belong to the same species, or even come from the same planet. Here is a world, effectively, in which the precession of evolution has dropped the conceit of being in any way linear or arboreal or even symmetrical and taken a rhizomatic spin into the neo baroque.

To assign an idea or affect to the baroque or neo-baroque necessarily requires a certain caution, for if as Deleuze has argued in *The Fold*, the baroque is less an artistic movement than a response to the nihilism that descends when the promise of reason is shattered, as it was for him in, for example, that moment that was simultaneously the decay of rationalism and its reassertion and that he associates with the proper name Leibniz, then the judgement of that response will also be subject to the rule of chaos, or at least *a* rule of chaos. It is a response, therefore, which may well extrapolate itself not as truth or principle, but as myriad if not infinite multiplicities of sense and non-sense, of spaces and sensations, of buildings and frenzies, of ephemeral skins and intricate folding, unfolding and refoldings. In architectural terms, it is described less as a chateau of reason or enlightenment than a 'baroque house'. Alternatively, it might be a labyrinth of chateaus of which the house of reason is but one element in a network as complex and uncontainable as the 'Book of Sand' from the story by Jorge Luis Borges.[26] If this is the case for the house or chateau, then the nature of what it is to be human or animal or vegetable or fungal or machine will also be elaborated along new lines of becoming, with new torsions and perspectives and symmetries. What is perhaps is most centrally at stake here is the whole question of the relation between the material and the temporal, in terms of directionality and adaptation as much as ontology.

We began with a quotation from Bergson's final monograph, in which he appeals to the notion of a universe as a machine for making gods. The image of the machine here is not in any way intended to suggest a crude mechanism, but rather, a divine mechanism which runs directly counter to the pseudo-evolutionary thrust of teleology and allows the virtual and the actual, and indeed, for Bergson, the spiritual and the material, to co-exist as a single and univocal force and field of desire and creativity. This at least is his hope for an alternative universe to our own. This is the mysticism that he begins to explore in this final work, in which, as Peter Hallward has argued, the fundamental impossibility encountered by Bergson is challenged by Deleuze through his own creative and baroque (and vehemently univocal) ontology.[27] It is a mysticism which, as with von Uexküll or Deleuze and Guattari, returns us to an image of music, rhythm, consonance and dissonance, as when Bergson contemplates a universe of pure creativity in which the virtual and the actual, as well as the material and the spiritual co-exist as complimentary, and in which materiality, as the opposite of divine spirituality, would simply express the distinction between being created and creating, between the multifarious notes, strung like pearls, or a symphony and the indivisible emotion from which they sprang.[28]

Unfortunately, this universe has not yet occurred for Bergson, this universe for creating gods, for the realm of matter and extension which dominates our own universe has limited scope and multiple velocities of the *élan vital* in a way that virtuality and intensity would not. Instead, humanity has been merely circling on the spot. For, as he puts it: 'The movement which started as straight ended as circular. In that circle, humanity, the terminal point, revolves.'[29]

This rather pessimistic vision leads Bergson to assert his late mysticism, but this does not mean that mysticism *per se* is the only way out of this terminal circling. Creativity, in the sense that Deleuze uses it to describe the production of the new, the metaphysical conditions which enable the production of the new, relies to some degree on a notion of time that is neither straight nor circular, but geometrical and baroque: conditions which are reminiscent of baroque typography or inscription as much as geometry as such. Alternatively, but in parallel with the inhuman geometry of Deleuze, in the writings of Michel Serres we encounter a form of angelic machinery that allows time to flow like a river across a delta that enables time to percolate and pool.[30] For Serres, the angel, like the figure of the statue or the parasite, has a value and valence including but also beyond conventional connotation and definition. The angel is a creature of hermetic code, of Hermes, of communication across time and space and planes of inference, of media itself. As the human becomes increasingly absorbed by its digital tools, we will become the media that once extended us to such a degree of intensity that the (extensive) times and spaces of biology, mechanism, teleology and primitive technics will become eclipsed by the (intensive) times and spaces of tertiary memory and internal finality. In this sense, it is, ultimately, though the reconfiguration of the human perception of time and technics, of life and inscription, of image and noise, brought about by the absorption of the organic into the divine (or perhaps celestial) machinery of the virtual and the multiple, rather than genetic modification *per se*, that our species will be able to grasp evolution creatively, if not quite as gods, then at least as angels.

Notes

1　von Uexküll, Jacob, *Bedeutungslehre*, Leibzig: Verlag von J. A.Barth, 1940. ('The Theory of Meaning' *Semiotica* 42, 1, 1982: p. 66). Cited in Buchanan, Brett, *Onto-Ethologies: The Animal Environments of Uexküll, Heidegger, Merleau-Ponty and Deleuze* (Albany: Suny University of New York Press, 2008), p. 34.

2　Nabokov, Vladimir, *Lolita* (New York: Vintage International, 1997), p. 322.

3　Deleuze, Gilles, *Negotiations*. trans. Martin Joughin, (New York: Columbia UP, 1990), p. 34.

4　Bergson, Henri, *Two Sources of Morality and Religion*, trans. R. A. Audra and C. Brereton. (London: MacMillan, 1935), p. 275.

5　Most notably in Deleuze, Gilles, *Bergsonism*, trans. H. Tomlinson and B. Habberjam, (New York: Zone Books, 1991).

6　Leroi-Gourhan, André, *L'Homme et la Matière*, (Paris : Albin Michelle, 1943).

7　Though, it should be stressed that the theoretical trajectory of this discussion is decidedly realist in its ontology, if not necessarily its methodology, that this does not infer a contradiction as will, I hope, become clear as the discussion progresses.

8　von Uexhill, Jacob, 'A New Concept of *Umwelt:* A Link between Science and Humanities,' trans. Gösta Brunow, *Semiotica* 134,I-4, 2001: pp. 111–123. The references to these concepts and those closely related to them are distributed through various parts of the work of Deleuze and Deleuze in collaboration with Guattari, but see especially, Deleuze, Gilles. and Felix Guattari, *A Thousand Plateaus: Capitalism and Schizophrenia*, trans. Brain Massumi, (Minneapolis: U of Minnesota P, 1986); *What is Philosophy*, trans. H. Tomlinson and G. Burchell, (New York: Columbia UP, 1994). See also, Grosz, Elizabeth, *Chaos, Territory, Art: Deleuze and the Framing of the Earth*, (New York: Columbia UP, 2008, *passim*).

9　Stiegler, Bernard, *Technics and Time 1: The Fault of Epimetheus*, trans. Richard Beardsworth and George Collins, (Stanford: Stanford UP, 1998).

10　Lewis Williams, David, *The Mind in the Cave: Consciousness and the Origins of Art* (London: Thames and Hudson, 2004). p. xx.

11　See, for example, Bostrom, Nick. and Julian Savulescu, eds. *Human Enhancement*, (Oxford: Oxford University Press, 2011); Kurzweil, Ray, *The Singularity is Near: When Humans transcend Biology*, (London: Penguin, 2006). See also the debate in Jay W. Richards. ed. *Are we Spiritual Machines? Ray Kurzweil vs. The Critics of Strong A.I.* (Seattle: Discovery Institute, 2002);

12 Guattari, Felix, *Chaosmos: An Ethico-Aesthetic Paradigm,* trans. P. Bains and J. Pefanis, (Sydney: Powerhouse, 1995).

13 Derrida, Jacques, *The Animal that Therefore I Am,* ed. Marie-Louise Mallet. trans. David Wills. (Fordham: Fordham UP, 2008), p. 10.

14 Frequently cited in many variants, but the most common is the following

'What is the question now placed before society with the glib assurance which to me is most astonishing? That question is this: Is man an ape or an angel? **I, my lord, I am on the side of the angels**. I repudiate with indignation and abhorrence those new fangled theories.'

- *Variant:* The question is this— Is man an ape or an angel? My Lord, I am on the side of the angels. I repudiate with indignation and abhorrence

- *Variant:* Is man an ape or an angel? Now, I am on the side of the angels! (Speech at Oxford Diocesan Conference (1864–11-25).)

See also, a short piece by Steve Jones in the Daily Telegraph, http://www.telegraph.co.uk/science/science-news/3344670/Charles-Darwin-Is-man-an-ape-or-an-angel.html accessed 29/06/11

15 An exemplary study of these themes in relation to Nietzsche, Darwin, Bergson, Deleuze and transhumanism may be found in Ansell-Pearson, Keith, *Viroid Life: Perspectives on Nietzsche and the Transhuman Condition,* (London: Routledge, 1997).

16 von Uexküll, Jacob, *Theoretische Biologie.* Berlin: J. Springer Verlag, 1926. (*Theoretical Biology,* trans. D. L. Mackinnon. (New York: Harcourt, Brace, 1926), p. 42.)

17 Uexküll, 'New Concept of the *Umwelt,*' p. 120.

18 Buchanan, p. 35.

19 Deleuze and Guattari, *A Thousand Plateaus*, p. 314.

20 Grosz, p. 52.

21 Deleuze and Guattari, *What is Philosophy?*, p. 184.

22 Deleuze and Guattari, *What is Philosophy?,* p. 176.

23 On the background to this debate, see Hibbard, Allen, Shift Coordinate Points: William S. Burroughs and Contemporary Theory, in Schneiderman, David. and Philip Walsh, eds. Retaking the Universe: William S. Burroughs in the Age of Globalization, (London: Pluto Press, 2004), pp. 13–28.

24 Rodley, Chris, ed. *Cronenberg on Croneberg,* (London: Faber & Faber, 1992). pp. 157–171.

25 Cited in Mottram, Ralph, *The Algebra of Need,* (London: Marion Boyars, 1977), p. 54.

26 Luis Borges, Jorge, 'The Book of Sand,' trans. Andrew Hurley, available at http://www.annecoale.com/web4pics/bookofsand.pdf - accessed 29/06/11

27 Hallward, Peter, *Out of this World: Deleuze and the Philosophy of Creation*, (London: Verso, 2006), p. 22.

28 Bergson, p. 255.

29 Bergson, p. 277.

30 For an incisive discussion of these figures in Serres, see Polizzi, Gaspare and Trina Marmarelli, 'Hermetism, Messages, and Angels' *Configurations*, Volume 8, Number 2, Spring 2000, pp. 245–270.

11

Articulating the Inhuman: God, Animal, Machine

Steven Shakespeare

Monstrous liaisons

'Since every truth is in-human, we can hardly hope to understand its genesis by poking around in the neurons of our brains!'[1]

I propose that it is only possible for us, today, to think God through the inhuman. This is not only because the recently declared 'inhumanity of man to man,' which takes the form of genocides, wars and capitalist catastrophes, has made the task of theodicy desperate, although that is indeed the case. It is also because the implicit and explicit logic of such events exposes the concept of humanity itself – universal, global, a bearer of rights or abstract object of manipulation – as a fragile, divided construction.

The inhuman is not therefore the simple opposite or absence of the human. It is its disavowed condition, its spectre. The human is defined by what it excludes: the divine, the angelic, the animal, and the artificial. However, these exclusions continue to inhabit, disrupt and solicit the human figure, a fact that becomes ever more pressing when the human as such becomes the frontier for ethics and politics.

To think the divine in this context demands a reckoning with this disfigurement of the human. The inhuman, of course does not present itself any more directly or immediately than what it conditions and haunts. As the monstrous, alien, bestial, mutant, superhuman and transcendent, it leaves its (mis)interpretable traces on our bodies.

What, then, is there between the animal, the machine and the divine? The question carries two senses. On the one hand, it concerns a space of separation or division, as when we say that 'something has come between us'. Equally, however, we are also speaking of a connection, some kind of significant relationship, as when we ask, with a suspicious or knowing tone 'Is there something between the two of you?' 'Something between': a liaison, a conspiracy, a distinction, an enmity, but above all, a history.

This chapter will draw out a number of the traces of that history left in the writings of philosophers, in the conviction that the questions of animality, technology and God are intimately interlinked. Hovering in the background will be the spectral figure of what seems to have been left out of this strange trinity: the human.

There is, of course, no shortage of contemporary discourses which seek to re-position the human, often by knocking it off its pedestal or removing it from the centre of our conceptual universe. If the slogan of humanism is that 'man is the measure of all things', the rise of all things post- and trans-human suggests that this measure is neither absolute nor innocent. The human is increasingly difficult to specify, materially or conceptually, and this is welcomed by those for whom an unexamined anthropocentrism is at the heart of imperial, sexual and environmental subjugations.

Donna Haraway famously argued that there are three 'boundary breakdowns' which make possible the emergence of a new way of understanding personal and political identities through the myth of the 'cyborg', that incorrigibly hybrid identity.[2] The first distinction which has proved 'leaky' is that between the human and the non-human animal. The field of 'animal studies' takes as one of its premises the questionable way in which the human has been isolated from and elevated above other animals by appeal to such traits as language, rationality and self-consciousness. The boundary breaks down from both sides:

non-human animals displaying use of complex symbolisms, memory, foresight, self-awareness; and human beings irrevocably defined by genetic, unconscious and embodied factors. Even more radically, we are witnessing an increasing insistence that non-human animals do not have to approximate to human ways of being in the world in order to be validated. In their very strangeness, the cephalopod, the arachnid and the amoeba constitute an other to the human which relativizes a certain way of constructing the world around 'us'.[3]

The second failing distinction is between the animal–human organism and the machine. When life becomes a matter of information transmission and coded behaviours, and when the possibility artificially created intelligence remains a live topic for debate, the machine cannot simply be resisted or celebrated in its remoteness from the human.

Finally, Haraway identifies the boundary between the physical and the non-physical as open to dispute. Whatever our precise degree of understanding, quantum physics has entered our cultural DNA. A world which can be analysed into the interaction of solid bodies according to 'mechanical' principles has only a relative reality. However, Haraway does not need to stress the quantum level to make her point. Rather, she focuses on the way in which the mechanical is transformed by being miniaturized and virtualized. The invisibility of this technology is as political as it is material, for the gears of manipulation are no longer obvious. Now strategies of power and resistance are created in its wake.

As this last point suggests, Haraway's acknowledgement of these transgressed borders is neither regretful nor utopian. The cyborg is a figure of new possibilities for hybrid identity, freed from the primordial Western myths of purity, oneness and control; but it is also a reality in part created by the militarized industry of nation states seeking an edge over their rivals.

One way in which Haraway underscores the scope and ambiguity of what is at stake in all of this is her use of religious imagery. As a socialist and feminist, she explicitly argues for a break with the story of Eden, that nostalgia for a lost perfection and innocence which also serves as a means of suppressing and containing alternative identities. However, she also addresses the religious aura surrounding the cyborg's emergence.

> Modern machinery is an irreverent upstart God, mocking the
> Father's ubiquity and spirituality ... Cyborgs are ether, quintessence
> ... Ultimately the 'hardest' science is about the realm of greatest
> boundary confusion, the realm of pure number, pure spirit,
> C3I, cryptography and the preservation of potent secrets. The
> new machines are so clean and light. Their engineers are sun-
> worshippers mediating a new scientific revolution.[4]

This does not imply any lessening of the need for a material analysis
and demystification of this aura. The new priest-engineers must be
exposed in all their grubby opacity. However, when the physical and
non-physical no longer constitute separate domains, there can be no
question of simply 'reducing' spirit to matter. A much more complex
and intriguing strategy is required.

Haraway's rejection of an innocent, original Eden finds its
counterpoise in the possibility that results of a cyborg utopia, a
removal of the waymarkers which once defined places and trajectories
of thought in order that the vertigo and promise of an unheralded
moment might be felt. Haraway's transgressive philosophy itself
remains contaminated with the unconditioned, or, to borrow Philip
Goodchild's phrase, 'compromised with God'.[5]

In abstract terms, this means that any attempt to delimit a 'purely'
immanent or material reality remains as complicit with a philosophy
of closed systems as the most 'ontotheological' metaphysics. Purity
is bought at the price of ignoring or suppressing the conceptual
(and political) act through which the system is closed. To think the
openness of the system is to allow thinking to be troubled by what
contemporary continental philosophy has variously named the 'other',
the 'event', the 'Real'.

To think the specific nexus of the animal, the machine, the human
and the divine is particularly significant in this context. It is all too easy
to circumscribe the openness of the system of thought, locating its
transcendental anchor in the human subject or its transcendent origin
in the divine mind. The animals and the machines – so often relegated
to mute subordination – have the power to interrupt this enclosure (not
least when they are entirely indifferent to the philosophical project).
They compel a thinking of a being in the world which is not limited to
human subjectivity, reflecting a pre-conceived ideal of divine intellect.

However, this is not simply about 'thinking animals', much less of rehashing doctrinaire statements about the end of man and the death of God. Rather, it is in our effort and failure to think animals and machines that a different *articulation* of what it means to think difference and unconditionality becomes possible.

Articulation – as method and topic – thus provides the focal point of what follows, which is no more than a preliminary sketch of where such an analysis might go. Haraway's work already suggests that the categories of animality/organism, machine and spirit are interrelated. The question of the animal cannot be pursued in isolation from technology and theology (in the broadest sense), whatever the temptations of a scholarly field as it develops its own canons, axioms and institutions. Articulation – variously thought by Derrida, Deleuze, Kant and Aristotle – offers a way for philosophy to avoid a premature romanticism which finds its ecstasy in voids, nihils and Godheads. Impure, precarious, expressive, disjointed in its embodiment, articulation is the openness of the system couched in systematic terms. It is thinking, contaminated by the unconditioned.

God Out of Joint: Aristotle

Aristotle is well known for his interest in the natural world and in particular for his writings on animals, which occupy a significant portion of his extant work. In the text, 'On the Movement of Animals', there is an extraordinary interweaving of the physical and the metaphysical. The treatise begins with a restatement of the argument that the only way in which to explain the origin of motion in the world is to posit the existence of an immovable prime mover, which is not itself a part of the ordered world.

Aristotle then goes on to apply this logic to microcosmic level

Now in the animal world there must not only be an immovable without, but also within those things which move in place, and initiate their own movement. For one part of an animal must be moved, and another be at rest, and against this the part which is moved will support itself and be moved; for example, if it moves one of its parts; for one part supports itself against another as though it were at rest.[6]

This is not all: the same principle is localized even further into the animal joint, of which Aristotle writes that 'a joint is the origin of one part of a limb, the end of another. And so nature employs it sometimes as one, sometimes as two'.[7] The joint is what articulates the animal, makes it able to move, because in the very act of flexing, it contains a point that is always at rest. The joint is a joining and a disjoining, and it can be this because it is articulated around a point of leverage.[8] This point, however, is not simply located in one internal space, but takes place differently according to the type of movement being exercised.

Within the animal joint is a trace of the unconditioned: the articulation which enables motion also connects the animal system to a metaphysical principle. This principle of the unmoved mover is both an outside one upon which the animal depends and an internalized facet of its own organization. Neither wholly outside nor purely contained within, the unconditioned traverses the animal body.

It is intriguing to note that Aristotle compares the animal body to automata. Bones are like pegs and iron, tendons are like strings. The difference is that animal parts can increase and decrease in size as they gain and lose heat, a change of quality that automatic puppets do not replicate. Nevertheless, there is a clear overlap between animal and machine parts. We can at least say that the organic in some way depends upon its machinic infrastructure. But we can venture more: it is the machinic infrastructure (and not the supposed organic quality) which links the animal joint to the unmoved mover. It is where the enclosure of the organism is interrupted by the automatic that the trace of the unconditioned can be read.

Articulating the Animal System: Kant

Aristotle's interruption of the organism is a surprising challenge to a significant tradition of philosophical thinking. In idealism and romanticism, the organic plays a key role as a privileged metaphor and instantiation of the absolute. This imagery leaves us a legacy of thinking the difference between life and technology which is still powerful today.

Idealism finds in the organism a privileged expression of self-relation preserved through growth and differentiation. The organism is more than a metaphor: it is an embodiment and anticipation of the living, absolute unity of Spirit in and for itself. Merely mechanical modes of explanation fail to grasp this vital complexity. As the Schelling of *The System of Transcendental Idealism* puts it 'One may say that organic nature furnishes the most obvious proof of transcendental idealism, for every plant is a symbol of the intelligence' and 'Organization in general is therefore nothing else but a diminished and as it were condensed picture of the universe.'[9]

However, the idealist projects are haunted by the unresolved frictions of Kant's philosophy, frictions which threaten to disorganize the harmony of Spirit's homecoming, the perfect circle of knowledge knowing itself.

Kant's first Critique established the bounds of the understanding as it constructed the world according to transcendental categories. The mind is no passive recipient of worldly sensation; rather, it is the world which is given form, objectivity and regularity by the modes of our knowing. The implication is that the only world knowable by the understanding is one governed by determined, mechanical cause and effect. The understanding shapes an iron-clad cosmos.

The second Critique then sought to build on hints in the first, to offer a deduction of moral agency and freedom. Although the world known by the understanding is mechanistic, the moral will is free. In order for genuine moral duty to be known and done, practical reason allows us to act as if the will were free, the soul immortal and the ultimate reconciliation of virtue and happiness secured by the existence of a moral God. However, we can have no cognitive, theoretical knowledge of any of these things. They are beyond the bounds of sense, beyond the scope of reason. But as practically indispensable for our moral, life, we live as if they were true, as if they traced a line of flight beyond the machine.

So far so good; but a systematic and prudent thinker like Kant could hardly be satisfied with this schism in thinking. He sweated over the problem of how to reconcile the inevitably mechanistic and deterministic way in which the understanding must explain the workings of the world, while preserving the freedom necessary for moral agency. Reason desires a system, an overarching organization of knowledge under certain principles. However, the bifurcation between our theoretical cognition of the world and our practical reason relating to moral duty makes such a harmony hard to come by.

When Kant's *Critique of Judgement* turns to the idea of purposiveness in nature and art, we are offered a set of themes which at once evade, complicate and confirm this division between mechanism and freedom. And it is the organism which is supposed to hold the clue to how this friction is to be smoothed.

According to Kant, nature appears to exhibit purposiveness. Neither the beautiful object nor the organism can be explained adequately in terms of mechanical cause and effect alone. The purposiveness of these phenomena, whether it is judged to be merely subjective and 'for us', or existing in some way in the object, elicits a distinctive yet valid response.

Kant describes the distinctiveness of the organism very clearly:

> Hence an organized being is not a mere machine. For a machine has only *motive* force. But an organized being has within it *formative* force, and a formative force that this being imparts to the kinds of matter that lack it (thereby organizing them). This force is therefore a formative force that propagates itself – a force that a mere ability [of one thing] to have [another] (i.e. mechanism) cannot explain.[10]

Mechanisms work by transmission of motor force in a linear chain. Organisms are self-forming and self-propagating. They behave purposively, and their various constituent parts are both the efficient and final cause of the activity of the whole organism. No part of the organism can be understood in isolation. As Kant puts it a little later '*An organized product of nature is one in which everything is a purpose and reciprocally also a means*'.[11] An organism, as a natural purpose, is '*both cause and effect of itself*'.[12]

It is arguable that when Kant distinguishes between aesthetic judgements of taste and teleological judgements about nature's purposiveness exhibited in organisms, this distinction is only relative. In neither case are we authorized to claim any theoretical cognition which justifies our judging. Beauty clearly does not have a cognitive content; it is the inner purposiveness, the harmonious play of our imagination and understanding merely provoked by an object's form. However, even the apparently objective purposiveness of organisms (and so of nature as a whole) cannot claim theoretical foundation. It is only a regulative idea, one we must use in exploring nature, but which can claim no absolute cognitive validity.

However, this solution begins to look rather tangled when we investigate matters further. The antinomy of teleological judgement we face is that we are compelled to use both mechanical and organic-purposive principles in making sense of nature, but these principles contradict one another. Kant's solution is that this contradiction is only apparent, because on the supersensible level beneath all appearances, they must be reconciled. The supersensible, by its very nature, remains impenetrable to our understanding, so the problem is shifted on to a level of reality to which our understanding has no access.

Kant's statements walk on the limit of the knowable and even the sayable at this point. On the one hand, he claims that 'We are quite unable to prove that organized natural products cannot be produced through the mere mechanism of nature'.[13] In other words, there might be some kind of supersensible mechanism which explains all appearances of purposiveness. On the other hand, the organism is said to be inexplicable because it points beyond nature conceived as a system of necessity. This quality of the organism, both within and yet beyond nature, therefore also points to the supersensible. The supersensible thus takes on the character of an unconditioned undecidability, an absolute machine-organism.

This antinomy cannot be resolved by theoretical thought, only by the strategy of the 'as if'. We must interpret nature as if it were susceptible to purposive explanation, and can ultimately only carry this though if we attribute its design to a divine designer, an intellect that creates and acts with purpose: God, but only 'as if', only as a ruse of reason, for the unconditioned cannot be thought in itself, cannot become an object of possible experience. God is the meeting of the machine and the organism in an imaginary technology of creation.

The strange success or heroic failure of Kant's project circulates around this point: in the gulf between nature and freedom arises the 'feeling of life', the intensity associated with beauty and the sublime, and the irreducible purposiveness of the organism. In each of these encounters, we are caught up in the unconditioned: the free play between imagination and understanding, the inextinguishable moral vocation aroused by the overwhelming experience of natural forces, the conviction that there must be a God to whom the world's purposes can be attributed. And yet in each case, the world folds up again within the knowing observer and the moral agent: it is simply that we are structured, articulated in such a way as to make these experiences inevitable. But they offer no route to the outside of our cognitive framework or moral imperatives.

The *Critique of Judgement* is Kant's unstable attempt to bridge the gap between the limits of theoretical reason and the demands of practical reason, and so complete his system. As such, it is an essay in fulfilling a lack in transcendental philosophy. In the final pages of the *Critique of Pure Reason*, Kant writes of the 'architectonic of pure reason', the systematic unity which raises it to the status of a science. Strikingly, he figures this unity in specifically organic and animal terms:

> The whole is thus an organized unity (*articulatio*) and not an aggregate (*coacervation*). It may grow from within (*per intussusceptionem*), but not by external addition (*per appositionem*). It is thus like an animal body, the growth of which is not by the addition of a new member, but by the rendering of each member, without change of proportion, stronger and more effective for its purposes.[14]

The irony, of course, is that Kant can only attain to systematic form at a price: the price of leaving reality in itself outside the scope of theoretical reason, invoking a supersensible basis for reconciling nature and freedom which can never be demonstrated and referring natural purposes to a God whose existence can only be assumed for regulative reasons. The system only functions because of what it attempts to exclude, what lies beyond the limits of sense it attempts to draw and cannot help but transgress. The appeal to organic unity is undercut by the ambivalence of the supersensible. The animal body is again traversed by the unconditioned, because it is the place where the friction between organic and the machinic is irreducible.

In other words, the lines Kant attempts to draw between the articulated and the aggregated, or the organic and the mechanical, fail to hold. Kant's brilliance lies in his acknowledgement that this is because the very articulation of these differences entails a reference to the unconditioned, to a supersensible that the human transcendental subject cannot delimit. Kant's critical acumen prevents him from turning this unconditioned into a metaphysical object. Rather, the unconditioned is the intrinsic openness of the system, even as it seeks theoretical and ethical expression. It is in fact the very possibility of theory and ethics.

In one sense, therefore, Hegel was right: Kant's transcendental subject is outflanked by the articulation of the absolute.

Beast, Sovereign, Machine: Derrida

Man *calls himself* man only by drawing limits excluding his other from the play of supplementarity: the purity of nature, of animality, primitivism, childhood, madness and divinity. The approach to these limits is at once feared as a threat of death and desired as access to a life without difference. The history of man *calling himself* man is the articulation of *all* these limits among themselves. All concepts determining a non-supplementarity (nature, animality, primitivism, childhood, madness, divinity, etc.) have evidently no truth-value. They belong – moreover, with the idea of truth itself – to an epoch of supplementarity.[15]

In Derrida's early work on Rousseau's 'The Essay on the Origin of Languages', we are faced with the problem of how human beings supposedly moved from the muteness of nature through the immediacy of natural cries, to the artificial constructions of language. For Rousseau, 'articulation' describes the development of language away from its natural, gestural and guttural origins, towards artificiality and convention. Both inevitable and yet regrettable, articulation is a corruption of immediacy and a betrayal of nature.

Derrida's reading aims to demonstrate the irresolvable tension in Rousseau's approach. The very articulation, which is supposedly secondary to and supplementary to our original natural state, is lodged in the heart of nature from the outset. Only because natural immediacy is disrupted from the beginning can the possibility of language and the ideas of 'nature' and 'man' arise. The artificial haunts the natural from its conception.

Man can only call himself man thanks to this supplementary structure of language. It makes it possible for man to conceive and articulate his essence. However, the supplement cannot play the role of a secure foundation, substance or essence defining the identity of man. As Derrida puts it, 'this property [*propre*] of man is not a property of man: it is the very dislocation of the proper in general.'[16]

Rousseau's claim that nature is inarticulate is belied by the natural process whereby language imperceptibly evolves and is articulated. Articulation is the possibility and the ruin of the proper. Articulation is disarticulation and vice versa.

To take up the question of articulation is therefore to engage with a fundamental dynamic of deconstruction. It is also, as Derrida hints in the quotation with which we began this section, to follow the frictional interaction of the various concepts which are supposed to ground supplementation. Among these, nature, animality and divinity are mentioned, alongside primitivism, childhood and madness. What these disparate ideas appear to share is an ability to surround and delimit the proper essence of the human. The human is what remains when these boundaries are drawn. It is the inviolable interior space of a unique concept. However, when we see this relationship between the human and its other not in terms of an excluding delimitation, but in terms of a dynamic articulation, a different approach to questions of truth is called for.

It is vital to note that Derrida, even at this early stage, is thinking the questions of the human essence together with artificiality, animality and divinity; and thinking them around the notion of 'articulation', a phrase which has linguistic, organic and mechanical overtones.

Articulation is not a 'pure' difference, but a frictional relationship achieved through mutual contact and separation. It is the way in which a system is 'organised' from complex parts, but also the opening of that system to unpredictable re-articulations. Articulation does not depend upon a single absolute centre organizing the whole, but is a dynamic, decentred process. What Rousseau regrets about articulation is its tendency to obscure and overlay a simple origin, leading the system into corrupt artifice. Derrida's point is the possibility of such artifice must already be insinuated within the origin. Articulation and disarticulation are two sides of the same coin, because the process by which a system is organized is also the inherent displacement of any absolute point of origin and return. The feedback loop is never entirely closed. Drift, frictional wear, errors and mutations of articulated systems are actually an essential part of their functioning.

All this might be taken to imply that we can no longer talk about the isolated essence of the human, the animal or the divine. It might be concluded that such essences are fictions, underneath which lies the only reality we have access to: the arbitrary play of signifiers, an indifferent relativism in which truth is dissolved into the flux of language.

Such relativism, however, hardly does justice to either Derrida's approach to truth, or to the nature of articulation in general. This is where we need to make a critical, if daring, move: Derrida's deconstruction of ontotheology itself harbours ontological claims, albeit in a strange way. The undermining of ideas of presence and divine simplicity is not – could not – be a simple rejection of those notions, as if there were an opposed alternative ('difference in itself', 'absence') which could do the same job of providing a purely transcendent or transcendental frame of reference for our truth claims. As Derrida puts it, 'In the deconstruction of the arche, one does not make a choice'.[17]

Nevertheless, this is still an ontological claim, not merely an epistemological one about the limits of our knowledge, how language works or how things appear to us. Articulation or difference is at work before language, before the distinction between reality and appearance is drawn. Of course, how we speak of this becomes difficult, not least because our conceptual resources are conditioned by the kind of foundational distinctions (truth versus appearance, form versus matter) that are parasitic on articulation. And yet articulation does not function as a new foundation, a new 'first thing'. The foundation and the first are the sedimented *results* of the process of articulation.

The relevance of this to a mutual consideration of the organic and the mechanical and to the borders between animal, human and divine have already been signposted. There is no question of simply eliding these differences. They have to be interpreted in their frictional relationship. And in this process, it still makes sense to speak of – to articulate – an otherness which is absolute and unconditioned.

Why? Because the articulated system never constitutes a purely self-referential organic or mechanical whole. *The very nature of articulation is to refer itself to what resists being incorporated into the interior of the system.* In Derrida's alternative idiom: 'Differance is also something other than finitude.'[18]

What is the ethical and political force of this way of thinking? In *The Beast and the Sovereign*, Derrida resists the notion that sovereignty is a conceptualization of a uniquely human mastery. The figures of bestiality and divinity, which always haunt the human sovereign, put this notion into contact with an otherness which fractures and disjoints the human economy (an economy that is as much linguistic, social and religious as it is financial): 'If sovereignty were (but I don't believe it) proper to man, it would be so much *like* this expropriating ecstasy of irresponsibility, like this place of non-response that is commonly and dogmatically called bestiality, divinity, or death.'[19]

Derrida's remark comes in the context of a discussion of Thomas Hobbes' characterization of the sovereignty of the state as Leviathan. As is well known, Hobbes argued that in a state of nature human beings lived in mutual warfare and constant insecurity. A resolution could only be achieved through a convention or contract, through which some sovereign body or individual was instituted and given a monopoly of the use of force, and the ability to impose and enforce law.

Hobbes refers to this sovereign both as an 'artificial man' and as Leviathan, the biblical monster apparently defeated by God in the establishment of a created order. The sovereign, as Derrida points out, is both, beast and artifice, organism and machine. Moreover, Hobbes maintains that the Leviathan is created in imitation of God's work in nature. The animal, the artificial/technological and the divine are gathered in an intriguing alliance.

Derrida develops the point by arguing against a common interpretation of Hobbes. According to this view, sovereignty is a purely human, secular construction. There can be no appeal to God as the basis for authority. However, Derrida shows that this humanism continues to have deep theological roots. As the creation of Leviathan mimics God's creation of nature, so the sovereign acts as an image or mediator – a lieutenant (literally, a 'place-taker') – of God's authority.

It is perfectly true that Hobbes claims that no convention or agreement can be made with either 'beasts' or with God. In neither case is there a shared language that would enable some kind of intelligible response to be given. Conventions can only be agreed among human beings, where meaningful words can be exchanged. God and the animals fall outside of the scope of dialogue.

Nevertheless, Derrida maintains that such distinctions and exclusions are unsound ('leaky', to use Haraway's word). First, we have to note the way in which the beast and God are drawn together, despite their apparent difference, as each sharing this lack of responsiveness to human language. Secondly, the result of human agreement, the sovereign, itself has both bestial and divine characteristics. The sovereign is above or beyond the law, beyond question. The sovereign cannot be called to account. It is marked by what Derrida calls 'expropriating ecstasy of irresponsibility'. The sovereign is a figure of God, of the animal conceived as bestial, and of the machine. The ultimate human construction attracts an inhuman, monstrous, mechanical and transcendent aura.

The connection between the otherness of the non-human animal and the otherness of God has been underscored by Derrida's formulation of the neologism *divinanimality:*

> Must not this place of the Other be ahuman? If this is indeed the case, then the ahuman, or at least the figure of some – in a word – divinanimality, even if it were to be felt through the human, would be the quasi-transcendental referent, the excluded, foreclosed, disavowed, tamed, sacrificed foundation of what it founds.[20]

What the further discussion in *The Beast and the Sovereign* makes clear is the link between this ahuman otherness and a technical apparatus of mechanization, artifice and reproduction. In other words, the 'other' can only appear as such thanks to a structure of repetition and representation. The other is at once singular, irreplaceable, translatable and communicable. To understand this point, we need to explore further an aspect of Derrida's account of language and meaning.

As Leonard Lawlor argues,

> [Derrida's] basic argumentation always attempts to show that no one is able to separate irreplaceable singularity and machine-like

repeatability (or 'iterability,' as Derrida frequently says) into two substances that stand outside of one another; nor is anyone able to reduce one to the other so that we would have one pure substance (with attributes or modifications). Machine-like repeatability and irreplaceable singularity, for Derrida, are like two forces that attract one another across a limit that is indeterminate and divisible.[21]

In support of this we could cite Derrida's discussions of tropes such as the poem, the date, the signature and circumcision. Each of these has a material specificity, an irreducible uniqueness, and yet each constitutes a sign or series of signs which are readable in the absence of their originating context. These different facets are neither merely contradictory nor simply unrelated. It is only by virtue of the mechanical, law-like repeatability of the sign that the singular event can arrive or the singular word can be spoken.

Two specific examples from Derrida's work enable us to see how this affects the performance of his philosophical activity. Both 'Circonfession' and 'Faith and Knowledge' use a mechanical technique precisely to evade the attempt to assimilate their meaning into a concept or intuition which could be securely and wholly grasped by the reader. It is significant for our purposes that both texts engage with – or are possessed by – a fascination with the nature of religious tropes and practises.

'Circonfession' is a work of disruption.[22] It forms part of a project shared by Geoffrey Bennington. The latter undertook to write a systematic account of Derrida's work to date, which would translate its themes into a philosophical language of such universal clarity, that there would be no need even to quote Derrida's own work. Derrida's 'response' appears running coterminously with Bennington's text at the bottom of each page.

It is not a conventional scholarly reply. Rather, it takes the form of an unpunctuated stream of consciousness. Circling around such questions as circumcision, secrecy, prayer, the death of Derrida's mother and his own experience of paralysis, the text is stubbornly unsystematic. It refuses to be incorporated into the clear light of scholarly comprehension. It plays between two versions of what Derrida names 'SA': on one side, *savoir absolu*, the absolute knowledge and mastery presupposed by Bennington's attempt to contain and decode Derrida; on the other side, St Augustine, the lover of God who does not know what it is he loves.

The persistent religious motifs perform a resistance to assimilation, but this is not in the name of a settled, dogmatic orthodoxy. More radically, the text uses a machinic conceit to achieve its disruptive aim: Derrida determined to follow an automatic code, writing 59 sections of an arbitrarily equivalent number of words without punctuation, simply breaking off when he reached the required amount. The text reads at once like the outpouring of a breath, a confession of faith, a prayer, a free association – and yet it is regulated by an extrinsic, repeated and arbitrary code.

The intertwining of faith and the machine is repeated differently in 'Faith and Knowledge'.[23] This text addresses the nature of the 'return of the religious' in the contemporary world. Derrida's analysis focuses on the 'autoimmune' reaction of religious institutions and discourses to a globalized world. A religious discourse on what is sacred concerns an absolute which is 'kept safe' from contamination with the materialism and instrumentalism of modern technological reason. However, the means used to preserve and communicate this sacred quality are inevitably tainted by that same instrumentalism. The sacred has to be coded and transmitted (often via cutting-edge media networks) if it is to be recognized, asserted and distinguished from other discourses, but there is no secure way of separating the content of the sacred from the way in which it is mediated. Fundamentalism stands as a refusal to acknowledge this unavoidable complicity of the sacred and the mediated.

Again, for Derrida, communication depends on iterability, which is indissociable from the mechanical. The language of faith and its referents cannot stand apart from this process. As Derrida puts it, 'No faith, therefore, nor future, without everything technical, automatic, machine-like supposed by iterability.'[24]

'Faith and Knowledge' encodes this becoming-technical of faith in its own structure: an arbitrary division into fifty-two sections, perhaps echoing the division of the cycle of the year into weeks. This cyclical/ linear structure brings the incalculable nature of faith and the future into contact with impersonal mechanisms of counting. One cannot be *articulated* without the other, where articulation encompasses *both* the expression of a meaningful content *and* the mechanical structure needed to encode and transmit such expression.

Again, it is this question of *articulation* that is key to Derrida's construal of the relationship between faith and reason, the sacred and the technological, the unpredictable event of the future and the inescapable condition of iteration. As we are discovering, it is this motif which can organize and rupture philosophical thinking, where it seeks a systematic comprehension of the modalities of being (including what might be said to lie 'beyond being'). For our purposes, these modalities include the unconditioned, the mechanical and the organic, with the divine, the technical, the animal and the human variously distributed among the three. When the articulation of these modalities is understood as bringing them into contact in some way, they lose their aura of self-contained, essential purity. This is not an invitation to passive relativism; however, the point is to think about the specificities of these articulations, not to dissolve them in an undifferentiated morass of relativity. The rupture of form is not merely the absence of form.

As we have already seen with Hobbes, these linkages can play a decisive role in philosophical thinking and they carry with them ontological commitments. The languages of animality, technology and divinity are not reducible to surface decoration or illustration of some more fundamental realm of being. Could we say that they are the modes in which being unfolds, unravels, ruptures, becomes other than itself, with no guarantee of being retrieved or gathered in any humanistic or conceptual resolution? If so, it is no longer possible to put into straightforward opposition the technological and the natural, the mechanical and the organic, the automatic and the spontaneous. Each inhabits, conditions and corrupts the other.

Even the 'purest' immanence betrays this structure.

Judgements: Deleuze/Guattari

According to Deleuze and Guattari, 'God is a Lobster'.[25] The surrealism of their statement is not exactly eliminated when understood in the context of the section in which it appears in *A Thousand Plateaus* ('10,000 B.C.: The Geology of Morals'). For our purposes, however, it stands as a compressed thesis on the articulation that haunts the philosophical texts we have considered.

In their analysis of the formation of geological strata, Deleuze and Guattari identify a 'double articulation', in which, form and substance interact in mutually reciprocal ways. More or less stable molecular substances are ordered and connected by forms, and forms or structures are actualized in new large scale 'molar' compounds. In other words, there is no simple hierarchical relationship between form and matter (or, in terms deployed later in the analysis, between expression and content).

As the argument unfolds, it becomes clear that the articulation of strata is not limited to a self-contained geological realm. It is repeated, albeit with differences in organic, animal/reproductive and human/ linguistic strata. Each stratum has different ways of expressing its content and using this expression as the basis for forming new content: sedimentation, crystallization, segmentation, genetic repli- cation and linguistic signification. The distinctiveness of these relationships is not denied, but all are involved in the ebb and flow of deterritorialization and reterritorialization. A stable centre is formed, but only as a basis for further accretion, offshoots, divisions and progeny. These destructurations harbour 'lines of flight', an escape from defined territories and standardized, sedimented, centralized modes of being.

To think this dynamic, thought itself must become decentred, which is not to imply that it must be merely random. A dispersed, always self-transgressing organization characterizes this articulation. We should no longer privilege the individual discrete substance, organism or machine as an organizing fulcrum for philosophy. Rather, 'we must always think in terms of packs and multiplicities'.[26]

The phrase echoes the argument of the previous section, '1914: One or Several Wolves?' In the classic Freudian case history, the so-called 'Wolf Man' dreamt of six or seven wolves sitting in a tree staring at him. However, Freudian analysis interpreted this in terms of a single traumatic incident, centred on the Wolf Man seeing his parents having sex. The whole Oedipal edifice is founded upon that interpretation. However, for Deleuze and Guattari, this analysis rests on a fundamental misreading, a refusal to hear the multiplicity in the dream. The wolves are a pack, not a single individual. They cannot be confined within the settled boundaries of a single organic body, and so cannot be captured by a theory which imposes such limits. The pack strains against the skin which would hold it firm.

In this context, to 'become animal' is not to imitate a wolf, a horse or an insect in their singular essence; it is to become associated with a pack in such a way that such essences are disrupted and disturbed and it is no longer possible to discern where humanity ends and animality begins, *because those categories are no longer at one with themselves.* Earlier in his career, Deleuze's analysis of Bergson had signalled this desire to think 'beyond the human condition'.[27]

While space does not allow a full analysis of the complexities of *A Thousand Plateaus*, we must note a residual absolutism curled in the heart of this celebration of the multiple: 'what is primary is an absolute deterritorialization, an absolute line of flight, however complex or multiple – that of the plane of consistency or body without organs (the Earth, the absolutely deterritorialized)'.[28]

This is a strange absolute: a line of escape from all that defines a territory, a stratum, an organism, but not towards any transcendent reality. It is a flight to pure immanence, beyond representation and metaphor, with their assumption that there could be distinct levels of being. No, 'The plane of consistency is the abolition of metaphor; all that consists is Real.'[29]

We should not mistake this 'body without organs' or 'plane of consistency' as an absolute chaos, however. As the authors insist 'the body without organs is opposed less to organs than to the organization of organs insofar as it composes an organism.'[30] Localized modes of organization are not opposed to the immanent Real; rather, they constitute points of friction within a dynamic process which cannot be resolved into the self-contained figure of the organism.

This is further suggested by the naming of the plane/body as the 'abstract machine'. Immanence is approached via abstraction from organized centres, but what is arrived at is not some kind of pure transparent essence of spirit, but a machine. The abstract machine is at work in all local processes of drift, deterritorialization, pack behaviour and so on. But at the most general and abstract level of all, it seems to coincide with the plane of consistency, the Real.

We are accustomed in post-idealist philosophy to count the mechanical as a limited, non-conscious, instrumental mode of being.

It falls short of the holistic mode exemplified by the organism, in which whole and parts exist in reciprocal, developing interaction, allowing the organism to act purposefully. While this purposefulness may not be conscious, it opens the way towards the emergence of a richer, self-reflective form of consciousness, which is able freely to shape and commit to its own purposes. In the move from the machine to the organism, there is hidden a whole philosophical commitment to the freedom of the absolute subject, the divinization of the subject as purposeful being.

Deleuze and Guattari circumvent this elevation of the spiritual-organic to the highest level in the hierarchy of being. In writing of the abstract machine, they suggest an absolute, which functions in terms of immanent flows, frictions and intensities and cannot be gathered under the heading of a subjected body or the body of a subject. It is not an Other that stands dualistically opposed to stratified reality, but an abstraction that is effectuated in concrete forms by so-called 'machinic assemblages'. The net result is that 'There is no biosphere or noosphere, but everywhere the same Mechanosphere'.[31] Neither biological life nor the free, knowing mind constitutes the foundation or telos of the Real.

The abstract machine is therefore not a mere chaos, but an *absolute structuring deformity*:

> The plane of consistency, or planomenon, is in no way an undifferentiated aggregate of unformed matters, but neither is it a chaos of formed matters of every kind. It is true that on the plane of consistency there are no longer forms or substances, content or expression, respective and relative deterritorializations. But beneath the forms and substances of the strata, the plane of consistency (or the abstract machine) *constructs continuums of intensity*: it creates continuity for intensities that it extracts from distinct forms and substances. Beneath contents and expressions, the place of consistency (or the abstract machine) *emits and combines particles-signs* that set the most asignifying signs to functioning in the most deterritorialized of particles. Beneath relative movements, the place of consistency (or the abstract machine) *performs conjunctions of flows of deterritorialization* that transform the respective indexes into absolute values.[32]

The abstract machine constructs, combines, conjoins; what is held discrete and separate in stratified, organic life *is disorganized in a specific way*: not into undifferentiated chaos, but into a productive intensification of flows of creative desire.

It is of course notoriously difficult to construct a philosophy of pure immanence. It would be easy to plot the tensions that exists between Deleuze and Guattari's refusal of any form of hierarchy or dualism with their recourse to language of absolute and relative, the abstract machine on the one hand and the machinic assemblage which 'effectuates' it on the other.

Granted, we should not neglect the way in which these thinkers unravel a particular conceptual knot: the absolute is associated neither with ontological plenitude, nor with the void, nor with utter chaos. The abstract machine is an *articulated* absolute, and it is articulated in such a way that it cannot be defined by any single or simple organizing principle.

Such a view cuts across the classical metaphysical view of the simplicity of God or the One. It also militates against the teleological form of absolute idealism, which historicises the absolute without abandoning the ultimately holistic and organic form of Spirit. Division and alienation are recuperated in the course of Spirit's self-alienation and self-recognition. Deleuze and Guattari's line of flight proposes a thinking of the absolute as the moment of departure from 'Spirit' in this sense.

On this view, 'God' is not so much rejected as relativized, reduced to being a limited aspect of the immanent plane. In their account of the 'body without organs' (the 'BwO'), Delueze and Guattari make plain the association of God with the prison of the organism.

> The BwO is not opposed to the organs; rather the BwO and its 'true organs,' which must be composed and positioned, are opposed to the organism, the organic organization of organs. The *judgement of God*, the system of the judgement of God, the theological system, is precisely the operation of He who makes an organism, an organization of organs called the organism, because he cannot bear the BwO, because He pursues it and rips it apart so He can be the first, and have the organism be first.[33]

Their philosophy thus performs a necessary blasphemy, defying the 'judgement of God' as the force which constrains life into closed forms. As John Protevi argues, the statement that 'God is a Lobster' is a refusal of any transcendent organizing principle or power: 'the Lobster-God is neither transcendent, nor is he all of nature, but only one aspect of nature as abstract machine of stratification *and destratification. The partiality of the Lobster-God.*'[34]

However, this relativization of God is precarious. The articulation that is evident in the lobster is not merely a local phenomenon. Articulation is what structures and de-structures the whole. It is the expression of life and the conflict of life with itself, where both expression and conflict refer us to an irreducible excess, an outside, and, yes, a transcendent.

Strange as it sounds, the Lobster-God names the moment when immanence is unlocked by the transcendent, a transcendent which makes possible the articulation and affirmation of immanence.[35] The Lobster-God is neither simply organism nor merely mechanical nor purely different. It is the friction between these surfaces which creates the possibility of relating to the unconditional, to the future, to the event, to the other. As such, it is 'something other than finitude'.

God is implicated in the animal, in the purposiveness of the organism, which cannot take place without the multiplicity of packs, the dissolution of fixed territories and the machinic repetition which paradoxically opens the otherwise closed system to the incalculable. It is when the animal and the machine are thought together that we can also think the articulation and disarticulation of life and language.

Moreover, the interplay of these surfaces reawakens the possibility of agency, whether it be hermeneutical, ethical or political. The very possibility of expressing such distinctions and *taking an attitude towards them* ruptures the smooth surface of immediacy and immanence. Not all bodies without organs are to be affirmed; not all states of the organism deserve to be dissolved. The question is: what allows the friction of a genuine meeting to take place?

Conclusion

We have been attempting to pursue several lines of thinking at once. It is clear that hard and fast distinctions between animal, human, machine and the divine cannot be maintained. However, far from leading to a relativistic soup, this line of thinking opens up another possibility: that of considering the ontological (and indeed ethical) implications of the way in which being is articulated.

Articulation is a break with natural immediacy, but it is not simply the opposite of the organic. In thinkers as diverse as Aristotle, Kant and Deleuze/Guattari, articulation makes the organic possible, but also opens it to a kind of transcendence, to a non-assimilated outside. It is striking that in each of these philosophical projects, the shadow of God, the unmoved mover or the unconditioned is cast precisely where this fault line is exposed. Ironically, the overcoming of dualism demands a reference to the transcendent, because only such a reference is able to articulate differences in their interaction and interpenetration, their compossibility. Without such a reference, differences in their purity are simply annulled.

Derrida's exploration of animality, iteration and sovereignty provides the pivot for this analysis. His reading makes it clear that the questions he raises about grammatological meaning cannot be divorced from the issues about what is proper to man, how the otherness of the animal interrupts our humanisms, and how we understand the indispensable risk of the machinic to our thinking of being and ethics.

As Derrida asks, what happens when 'the articulated a gathering up of oneself, coherence, responsibility' can no longer rely upon a simple unity, a harmony of time with itself? When time itself is out of joint, 'Is not disjuncture the very possibility of the other?' If so, we need to think two different 'dis-adjustments'. One would be that of the unjust, the tragedy of unredeemed wounds. The other would be a justice which exceeds any calculation or law, 'justice as the incalculability of the gift and the singularity of the an-economic exposition to others'.[36]

Thinking the 'animal' is therefore not merely a subdivision of the academic factory farm, conceptually domesticating and processing new representations of the other. The animals refuse to stay on the side of the object and the other, but swarm into the movements of thinking itself. As they do so, we find that neither wholly organic nor wholly mechanistic models are adequate to what is thought. It is in their strange attraction and repulsion that the chance of transcendence arises, enabling us to affirm and become different.

The transcendent is not merely the purity of a judgement that fixes things in a sealed organic form, but the taint of a crisis that stretches our powers of articulation and disorganizes our essentialisms. Perhaps this crisis is what it means to be 'human' today: to be human for the sake of a more disciplined, more discerning, inhuman hospitality.

Notes

1 Badiou, Alain, 'Philosophy, science, mathematics. Interview with Alain Badiou' in *Collapse. Philosophical Research and Development* Volume I, 2006, pp. 11–26.

2 Haraway, Donna, *Simians, Cyborgs and Women. The Reinvention of Nature* (London, Free Association Books, 1991).

3 See, for example, Fellenz, Marc, *The Moral Menagerie. Philosophy and Animal Rights* (Illinois, University of Illinois Press, 2007).

4 Haraway, *Simians*, p. 153.

5 Goodchild, Philip, 'Why is philosophy so compromised with God?' in Bryden, M. (ed.) *Deleuze and Religion* (London, Routledge, 2001), pp. 156–166.

6 Barnes, Jonathan (ed.), *The Complete Works of Aristotle Volume One* (Princeton, Princeton University Press, 1984), p. 1090.

7 Barnes, *The Complete Works of Aristotle*, p. 1093.

8 For further analysis of Aristotle's understanding of leverage, see De Groot, J. 'Dunamis and the Science of Mechanics: Aristotle on Animal Motion' *Journal of the History of Philosophy*, 46.1, 2008, pp. 43–67.

9 Schelling, F. W. J., *System of Transcendental Idealism (1800)* (Charlottesville, University Press of Virginia, 1978), pp. 122 and 123. Of course, this is only a superficial aspect of Schelling's project of a philosophy of nature. His exploration of the dark ground in God, of all that resists conceptual elucidation, make him a potent resource for delineating the limits of idealism and humanism. See Zizek, Slavoj, *The Indivisible Remainder* (London, Verso, 1996) and Hamilton Grant, Iain, *Philosophies of Nature After Schelling* (London, Continuum, 2006).

10 Kant, Immanuel, *Critique of Judgment* (Indianapolis, Hackett, 1987), p. 253.

11 Kant, *Critique of Judgement*, p. 255.

12 Kant, *Critique of Judgement*, p. 249.

13 Kant, *Critique of Judgement*, p. 269.

14 Kant, Immanuel, *Critique of Pure Reason* (London, MacMillan, 1929), pp. 653–654.

15 Derrida, Jacques, *Of Grammatology* (Baltimore, Johns Hopkins University Press, 1976), pp. 244–245.

16 Derrida, *Of Grammatology*, p. 244.

17 Derrida, *Of Grammatology*, p. 62.

18 Derrida, *Of Grammatology*, p. 68.

19 Derrida, Jacques, *The Beast and the Sovereign Volume I* (Chicago, University of Chicago Press, 2009), p. 57.

20 Derrida, Jacques, *The Animal That Therefore I Am* (New York, Fordham, 2008), p. 132.

21 Lawlor, Leonard, 'Jacques Derrida', *Stanford Encyclopedia of Philosophy* (2006), http://plato.stanford.edu/entries/derrida/

22 Derrida, Jacques, 'Circumfession', in Bennington, Geoffrey and Derrida, Jacques, *Jacques Derrida* (Chicago, University of Chicago Press, 1993).

23 Derrida, Jacques, 'Faith and Knowledge' in *Acts of Religion* (London, Routledge, 2002), pp. 42–101.

24 Derrida, 'Faith and Knowledge', p. 83.

25 Deleuze, Gilles and Guattari, Félix, *A Thousand Plateaus* (London, Continuum, 2004), p. 45.

26 Deleuze and Guattari, *A Thousand Plateaus*, p. 59.

27 Deleuze, Gilles, *Bergsonism* (New York, Zone, 1991), p. 28; for a sustained analysis of this trajectory, see Ansell Pearson, Keith, *Germinal Life* (London, Routledge, 1999).

28 Deleuze and Guattari, *A Thousand Plateaus*, p. 63.

29 Deleuze and Guattari, *A Thousand Plateaus*, p. 77.

30 Deleuze and Guattari, *A Thousand Plateaus*, p. 34.

31 Deleuze and Guattari, *A Thousand Plateaus*, p. 77.

32 Deleuze and Guattari, *A Thousand Plateaus*, p. 78.

33 Deleuze and Guattari, *A Thousand Plateaus*, p. 176.

34 Protevi, John, 'The organism as the judgement of God: Aristotle, Kant and Deleuze on nature (that is, on biology, theology and politics)' in Bryden, *Deleuze and Religion*, p. 39.

35 Compare the point made succinctly by Philip Goodchild: 'the criteria for absolute immanence and absolute transcendence are the same: they consist in removing all pretenders from the role of the absolute. They are ways of thinking the unconditioned as unconditioned without restriction' (Goodchild, Philip, 'Why is philosophy so compromised with God?', p. 158).

36 Derrida, Jacques, *Specters of Marx* (London, Routledge, 1994), pp. 22–23. Derrida goes on to discuss Heidegger's analysis (in 'The Anaximander Fragment') of the Greek notion of *Dikē* as 'joining, ad-joining, adjustment, articulation of accord or harmony' – a reminder that the present chapter is merely preparatory to a fuller analysis which encompasses Heidegger and other thinkers.

12

Transforming the Human Body

Gareth Jones and Maja Whitaker

Human Anatomists' Views of Bodily Transformation

One may be forgiven for thinking that human anatomists would view the human body in *status quo* terms. After all, one of the quips about teaching macroscopic anatomy, that is, anatomical structure that can be seen with the naked eye, is that the anatomy remains unchanged from one generation to the next. In contrast to cellular or molecular biology, with their rapidly changing data and even concepts, macroscopic anatomy gives the impression of being the quintessential example of all that is static and unchanging. How then can anatomists possibly contemplate the transformation of the body as suggested by the title of this chapter?

The truth is of course that the impression given by studying the body from the outside is only one aspect of the whole. Even pathology demonstrates very clearly that the body is capable of surprisingly large amounts of change. Broken bones heal remarkably well, wounds close up and repair as a matter of course, large segments of organs can be removed and reconstituted, and organs can be transplanted from one individual to another. All these processes may be regarded as natural processes, even if the repair is sometimes made possible by a range of sophisticated medical procedures.

Imperceptibly, as the sophistication of the procedures has increased, they have begun to incorporate elements we regard as artificial. This may be repairing something like the gut in non-physiological ways, that is, in ways that are not found 'in nature', perhaps to bypass a section that has had to be removed as a result of a tumour. More obviously artificial is the replacement of a degenerating hip joint with an artificial one – a prosthesis.

These ways in which the human body is transformed cause no consternation; they may even be considered uninteresting. After all, they are nothing more than a routine aspect of modern medicine. They all fit into the category of therapy in its most straightforward guise. Illness or incapacity is being replaced by a return to health and a sense of well-being; chronic pain or limited movement is being consigned to the past. In no way are they viewed as threatening one's sense of self-identity. While the human body is undergoing transformation, albeit minor rather than major, the integrity of what we are as persons is not under threat. The intrusion of the artificial into the human body in these instances is an adjunct to what might be termed the normal body. The artificial aids rather than challenges the body, both structurally and functionally.

What is the essential difference between an artificial limb and a crutch? The former is far more efficient and gives the appearance of (semi) permanence, and this is to be welcomed. Nevertheless, it contains within it elements of a human-machine interface, however rudimentary these may be, and these are beginning to transform its nature. This is taken much further when the limbs, particularly an arm and hand, begin to come under the control of the individual's own brain. The interface now is far more intrusive and, theoretically, far more effective. And yet, this particular interface is doing nothing more than replicating what goes on normally in the human body. The part of the brain that usually controls the arm and hand is being brought into play to control a prosthesis.

If we have not been discomforted by this trajectory, we have already accepted some intrusion into human life of the artificial. But, it may be contested, this has not even begun to address the profound issues raised by radical transformation of the human body – processes

enabling us to live significantly longer lives, disease-free lives, cognitively enhanced existences, with abilities we neither currently possess
nor can even imagine. The acceptance of a neurally controlled hand is
not the same as the desire to live in a dementia-free, memory-improved
state for hundreds of years.[1]

This is true, because the crucial divide is not between the artificial
and the natural. The illustrations we have given so far of the intrusion
of the artificial into human life have been actual ones, ones already
in clinical practice. The radical transformation being surmised
by some bears no resemblance to reality. The vistas of the trans-
humanists are precisely that – vistas, grand scenarios. This is where
anatomists begin to stumble, because for them the human body is
not an infinitely malleable piece of machinery. Its limitations are all
too evident. Talk of living a dementia-free existence is appealing, but
for those living close to clinical reality, the challenges required to be
overcome before anything even remotely resembling such a state is
achieved are formidable. Overcoming Alzheimer's disease, let alone
the myriad cancers that plague us or even the normal ageing that
proves enervating, constitute challenges of immense proportions. By
all means transform the human body, but it will not be accomplished
by glib assertions.

The Artificial in Historical Perspective

In order to explore where we have come from, we have to go back to
consider developments that have become part of our daily experience.
One way of doing this is by tracking life expectancy. While this is a
crude measure, it points to significant underlying trends.

In the mid-nineteenth century in the United Kingdom, life
expectancy at birth was around 41 years, and it only rose to 46 by
the end of the century.[2] Throughout this period, all the largest cities
recorded life expectancies well below the national average. Some
northern industrial towns had life expectancies of around 30 years.
The most pressing causes stemmed from infectious diseases, poor
diet and hygiene, contaminated water, and inadequate sewage
disposal. These problems were all external ones that had to be
rectified if mortality rates were to decline and life expectancy was to

increase. It was intervention in the environment that laid the basis for controlling the spread of diseases such as cholera and dysentery.

However, control of the external environment was accompanied by another factor – one that is highly relevant to the subject of this chapter, notably modifying individuals themselves. The thrust of this intervention was to equip them to respond to infectious agents. This was accomplished by vaccination, which is nothing less than a means of combating disease by altering healthy people. No matter how readily accepted vaccination may be today (although it still continues to elicit controversy in some quarters), its introduction was revolutionary and elicited considerable opposition. Something was being inflicted upon healthy people, in the hope of protecting *in the future* from certain infectious diseases. This 'something' was a muted disease, its aim being to give to healthy individuals a sub-clinical illness; no wonder there was initial opposition.

What is taken as commonplace today had its origins in a dramatic change in medical therapy.[3] With this, medicine moved from the external realm of public health and the environment into the inner workings of the human body. And yet, it is only when these two operate together that the quality of human life and the possibilities of human living are transformed. The overall consequence is that life in contemporary Western societies bears little resemblance either to life in these same societies 100 years ago or to life in the developing world today. Life expectancy at birth approaches 80 years in many developed countries, although in many of the majority world countries, it is in the 40s and, in some, is as low as the 30s.

These developments are a long way removed from the world of trans-humanism. Life expectancy in the 70s or 80s seems puny compared with 300 or even more, and yet, the contrast with the 30s or 40s is life transforming.[4] This is also a realistic transformation. Its repercussions are felt in our outlook on the world, our expectations and aspirations, and ultimately our dignity. Human well-being depends upon this intimate connection between the two interventions – environmental and internal. It is important to note the role played by environmental factors, because discussions on modifications to the human body have a tendency to focus solely on the body as if it could be isolated from its environment. In our view, this is seriously misleading.

The significance of these historical episodes for the present discussion is that medicine has already moved from the external realm of public health and the environment into the inner workings of the human body. It has moved into an artificial realm, in the sense that the body has been cajoled into functioning in a way in which it would not act apart from this intervention.[5] These episodes also highlight the continuum from a barely technological world to the far more sophisticated technologically driven societies of which many are a part today.

The question confronting us is how far we are along this continuum. The contribution of procedures such as vaccination, the replacement of limbs, and the neural control of artificial joints demonstrates that we have commenced on a journey, but how far might this journey take us? What criteria do we possess for determining how much further we wish to travel, or have we already gone too far? What is it that is pulling us further in the artificial direction? Is it a desire to transcend our humanness, on the ground that the limitations inherent to normal human living can and should be overcome? Or is it the hope that this will improve our functioning as human beings?

In this chapter, we shall concentrate on three areas: human-machine interfaces including brain implants, the related world of cyborgs, and the unlikely prospects opened up after death by the preservation technique known as plastination. In their differing ways, these approaches provide entrée into the domain of radical alterations to the human body by an extreme merger of human and machine. With the sudden explosion in machine intelligence and rapid innovations in gene research and nanotechnology, the distinction between biological and mechanical and physical and virtual realities is becoming blurred. While the prospect of maintaining our bodies post-death by highly sophisticated technological preservation techniques is not usually considered in this context, the impression it conveys that individuals can live on in a dissected state forces us to contemplate whether there is a form of technological 'life' after death. Hence, its designation as 'post-mortal' existence.[6] These various technological approaches have one feature in common, namely, they are all striving after a new kind of life, albeit following death in one instance. It is a form of life that is technologically driven and technologically sustained.

Human-Machine Interfaces

As touched on above, there are varying degrees of human-machine interfaces in present use or envisioned in the not-too-distant future. These all point to symbiotic partnership between body and machine. While these interfaces have cyborgian overtones, they themselves occupy a significant place in their own right and are worthy of analysis before entering the more futuristic world of cyborgs. This is because human-machine interfaces have already entered the lives and experiences of real people in actual clinical situations. The realm of science fact and clinical treatment should not be glossed over in a rush to consider science fiction and idealistic speculation.

While the applications that fit into this category are recognized independently, they major on the brain. They can therefore be collectively referred to as *brain implants*. However, we shall look at them separately. The applications are dominated by deep brain stimulation (DBS), cochlear implants, retinal implants, and brain-machine interface-based motor prostheses.[7]

Deep Brain Stimulation (DBS)

DBS is used in patients with Parkinson's disease, in whom electrical signals generated in a subcutaneously placed unit are sent to electrodes implanted in the motor region of the brain. The aim of these is to stimulate the function of the motor regions that have been detrimentally affected by the loss of the neurons producing the neurotransmitter, dopamine, in an attempt to control motor activities. It is used when routine treatments have become ineffective, although care has to be exercised because it may have negative side effects including personality changes.[8] Worldwide, more than 80,000 patients have been provided with these implants. DBS is also used as an experimental treatment for intractable depression, obsessive compulsive disorder, and Tourette syndrome.[9] While not all patients respond to the treatment, in many patients, the primary symptoms are substantially improved with rare adverse effects.

A range of post-operative neuropsychiatric symptoms has been reported when DBS is used for Parkinson's disease, including depression and apathy, though most are transient and treatable.[10] If side effects of this nature are minor, the alleviation of the crippling motor deficiencies will be welcomed. The balance between the positives and the negatives will weigh strongly in the positive direction and will be assessed as clinically acceptable. The underlying assumption is that there are no noticeable effects on the patients' identity. Of course, the removal of a debilitating neurological condition will in all probability have some effects on self-identity, although one imagines that these are minor and the removal of the symptoms using DBS will restore the patients to their usual self. The change is strictly therapeutic and equates with any other form of therapy to alleviate the troubling symptoms, whether drug based or by the use of neural grafts (or in the future, possibly the use of stem cells).

While there is still a great deal to be learned in this area, DBS is an example of a relatively successful neural prosthesis, and hence, it serves to illustrate a melding of brain and machine. This may be far removed from our usual perception of cyborg existence, but it shows nicely the path along which we are moving.

Cochlear and retinal implants

Cochlear implants occupy very similar territory. They are used in those whose auditory nerve has been damaged. Appliance acoustic signals are recorded by an external microphone and sent to a speech-processing unit outside the skull where electrical signals are generated. These are transmitted wirelessly to a receiver inside the skull, and they stimulate the auditory nerve at an interface with an electrode implanted in the cochlea in the inner ear. Modern devices are now so refined that the average sentence recognition is near perfect, particularly in quiet environments.[11] An alternative kind of implant is under development for patients with an absent or destroyed cochlea or auditory nerve. These implants bypass the cochlea and connect directly with the brainstem by penetrating the ventral cochlear nucleus.[12]

The hardware of the implant dynamically interacts with the 'wetware' (the patient's nervous system), and neural plasticity means that appropriate training and rehabilitation are crucial to the success of the implant. Congenitally deaf children who receive their implants before 1 year of age develop near-normal speech, whereas those who receive them as adolescents derive only limited benefit.[13]

The tension here is whether this is enhancement or therapy. For the hearing, the answer may seem obvious – it is therapy. However, for some members of the deaf community, this is far from the case, because for them deafness is normal and hearing is an enhancement. While this particular issue lies beyond our concerns in this chapter, it underlines the centrality of what we mean by 'normal' and the justification for using prostheses. Does resort to any one of them inevitably mean we are going beyond the bounds of normal human experience, even when the rationale for their use is ostensibly therapeutic? This question, while framed within this much focused context of deafness, has far broader implications. Normal human experience for each of us is a constrained experience, bounded by the parameters of our genetic and functional endowments, our upbringing, educational and allied possibilities, and our beliefs, hopes, and fears. The interplay of these results in what we are and what we are known to be – to ourselves as well as to others.

For most subjects, cochlear implants have no effect on their personal identity, although care should be taken in assuming that this is never the case. Overall, the implant probably aids the expression of the subjects' identity and facilitates personal flourishing without compromising their holistic integrity. If this is so, it is largely unproblematic on philosophical grounds,[14] bearing in mind that there will be exceptions.

Similar queries are raised by the use of retinal implants, development of which is at a more rudimentary design stage.[15] The aim is to restore sight to certain blind individuals. Since there is not a blind community intent on retaining blindness as a norm, some of the ethical and identity issues raised by cochlear implants are not encountered in this instance. Visual signals are recorded through light-sensitive electrodes on a miniature video camera mounted on the individual's glasses. The data are converted to an electronic signal that is then transmitted to the remaining viable secondary neurons via a microelectrode implant tacked to the retina. These cells process the signal and pass it on via the optic nerve to the brain where a visual image is synthesized. Another approach is to bypass the eye completely and directly stimulate the visual cortex.[16] No matter which method is employed, any success is due to the prosthesis and the human-machine interface. The first device, trialled in 2002, had 16 electrodes. More recent versions have over 60, and even greater numbers are planned, with consequent increases in acuity and sensitivity. Perhaps one day a retinal implant may outperform 'normal' natural vision.

An interesting, if highly speculative, query is to ponder how society will respond to those who might one day prefer a retinal implant to their own natural vision? Even if this were to eventuate, it does not seem to raise any particularly new philosophical questions. Intrusion of the artificial into normal existence for no compelling therapeutic reason raises ethical and resource issues, and it is these that elicit serious debate.

Brain-machine interface-based motor prostheses

Neuroprostheses directly implanted into the motor cortex of paralyzed individuals have allowed them to manipulate a cursor on a screen by directing their thoughts to a specific action.[17] This can then allow the individual to interact with a computer: sending emails, controlling a television, etc. When used by locked-in patients, this could allow them to communicate with the world in an unprecedented manner.[18] Dramatic as developments of this order may turn out to be, their sophistication should not belie their therapeutic intent.

A group of American scientists has recently reported on their attempts to decode the brain signals associated with spoken words. The brain signals were recorded from a microelectrode array placed on the surface of the subject's brain (who was undergoing epilepsy surgery at the time). The signals could be associated with the correct word 28 to 48 per cent of the time – better than chance. At this stage, it is only proof of concept, and the technology needs to be greatly refined to be accurate enough to be used to translate a paralyzed person's thoughts into words.[19]

Neuromotor prostheses have also been used to control the movement of a robotic device.[20] Motor signals are recorded through electrodes implanted in the brain and sent to a unit that computes and generates signals to direct an artificial limb. Research is continuing with monkeys to develop a procedure that would allow neural signals recorded from a multielectrode array implanted in the motor cortex to control a robotic arm to manipulate objects, in particular food for self-feeding.[21] Here, there are two levels of artificiality – the limb and the interface in the brain. Along similar lines, one can think of spinal implants to help paraplegics walk.[22] The risks associated with such an invasive approach and the long-term care required for such an implant are considerable, although it is hoped that further research will eliminate the need for wires to pass through the skin.[23]

Examples such as these may not elicit undue concern, because they are aiming to replace functions and abilities that have been lost. In regaining lost function, the patient is liberated and normalized. It is possible that the mechanical nature of the intervention may have an alienating effect, although even this may be temporary and the disadvantages may pale into insignificance compared with the functional advantages. Adapting to the newness and unusual nature of the artificial devices involved may be no more demanding than learning to live with an artificial limb or renal dialysis.

The above examples pose no threat to our humanness. But as technology is increasingly internalized, does this threaten the integrity of the human body? How much transformation is too much and how is one to determine where the limits of normality lie? Kevin Warwick, Professor of Cybernetics at the University of Reading, has conducted a series of self-experiments, which have taken the internalizing of computers one step further.[24]

In 1998, Warwick had a silicon chip transponder temporarily implanted in his upper arm. It transmitted a signal, which was received by the computer network at his work and would open the appropriate doors, activate his computer, and track his movement through the building. Experimental as this work certainly is, it is apposite to be reminded that radio-frequency identification tags are becoming increasingly mainstream. They have found use as the keys that can never be lost and even as a form of implanted credit card. In some European nightclubs, 'chipped' patrons can order their favourite drinks, and pay for them, simply by walking in the door.[25]

In 2002, Warwick had a second implant inserted and directly linked to the nerves in his arm – signals from an external computer could be transmitted to the nerve fibres and readings from the nerves then transmitted to the computer. By transmitting his neural signal over the internet, he could control the movements of a robotic arm on another continent. His (obviously very agreeable) wife had a similar implant inserted in her arm. They were able to send signals from one person's nervous system, across the internet, down into the other person's nervous system, eliciting movement. These experiments open up the possibility of remotely controlling a robot, or even another person's movements.

The Warwick experiments have little to do with therapy. Their aim appears to be at least two-fold: to demonstrate what may be possible by pushing the limits of the technology and to explore the human-machine concept. What is not clear is where technology of this order will take us, and whether it will have any impact on self-identity. The prospect that one day humans could become a curiosity for the machines, as Warwick has claimed, appears to be an unhelpful exaggeration.[26] The present developments may be fascinating, but their justification can be seriously questioned. Internalizing technology is all very well, but unless its potential far outstrips that of equivalent external technology, its future would appear to be limited.

Warwick's experimentation takes us some distance into the realm known as invasive brain-machine interfaces (BMIs). In general, medicine shies away from using invasive technology when non-invasive means of obtaining comparable results are available. This is on account of the substantial burden placed on patients, the risks of infection and rejection, their stability and reversibility, and body integrity concerns. Any such concerns are multiplied exponentially when the users are healthy, and hence a therapeutic rationale is missing. In these circumstances, it is preferable to employ non-invasive BMIs, such as those based on electroencephalography (EEG). The use of non-invasive BMIs by healthy users is being explored primarily in computer gaming and associated forms of entertainment, but also in education, security, and training.[27]

The line between entertainment and therapy has been blurred by hyperactivity reduction therapies for children with ADHD via the playing of BMI-controlled video games that reward user relaxation efforts.

BMIs could also be used as alertness detectors to monitor workers in intensive workflow situations, such as airplane pilots, air traffic controllers, operators of industrial plants, or security personnel.[28]

When considering the use of BMIs in healthy subjects, the safety bar should be set very high. This is especially the case when using them on young people. This is because of the plastic nature of the brains of young people.[29] The thrust of this concern centres on the fact that the brains of those in the first few years of life are still developing, and so imposing any form of neural manipulation may have much more extensive repercussions than in older people. While this is a theoretical concern, it suggests that a cautious approach should be adopted. Of course, the same stipulation applies to any form of neural manipulation that is applied over a long time period, including pharmaceuticals.

Assessing brain-machine interfaces

The interfaces alluded to above fall within the bounds of our experiences, even though some of them are pushing the boundaries and fall outside the experiences of most people. We are capable of envisaging them and thinking around their implications. Ethically, we are aware of the centrality of fully informed consent, especially where the processes of interest are experimental in nature and lack even a hint of a therapeutic driver. Informed consent also comes to the fore if children are the subjects of any of the experiments. However, debate on BMIs tends on occasion to be far more expansive than this. Consider the following quote:

> There is both a sense of human fulfillment and of human transgression when BMIs are imagined, both a sense that BMI is a form of transcendence that will allow us to realize heretofore unknown aspects of our humanity and a sense that eventually BMI will eclipse humanity altogether.[30]

With this quotation, we have entered the realm of hypothesis and speculation. We have to admit to scepticism when entering this territory, because debate readily moves away from hard examples or even readily imagined examples. One has to ask whether such speculation is profitable. Putting this reservation to one side, and indulging our imagination for a while, we emerge with questions along the following lines.

How would the interaction between mind and machine impact on personhood? Does mental enhancement by BMIs alter the personality of the user? Might there be unwanted consequences for the individual's personality? We have seen that this is not the case at present, but with the development of increasingly sophisticated and intrusive interfaces, this may change. Could the day come when there will be direct interaction between internalized computers in our brains and a person's neural processes and decision-making? After all, our brains are physical objects and are amenable to modification and manipulation. The involvement of machine interfaces could perhaps alter an individual to such a degree as to threaten personal identity persistence.[31] This may have flow-on effects for the attribution of moral responsibility.

We remain to be convinced that questions of this order lead to productive debate, because the crucial consideration is why the procedure is undertaken in the first place. If it is to overcome a pathological deficit, the use of BMIs could well prove beneficial, in the same way as conventional therapies are viewed. They may increase autonomy by restoring a lost capability. On the other hand, if used for insubstantial reasons, the opposite may be the end result: jeopardizing autonomy and serving as a threat to well-being. But these are hardly unique ethical considerations. The European Group on Ethics in Science and Technology concluded that because of 'the right to respect of human dignity, including the right to the respect of physical and mental integrity', information communication technologies should 'not be used to manipulate mental functions or change personal identity'.[32] It is not clear what reasoning was used to reach this conclusion.

Approaches to BMIs and other examples of man-machine interfaces elicit the same considerations as in most other areas where human beings are being manipulated. As with any form of manipulation, we need to ask whether they will

- be used for therapeutic or dubious enhancement purposes
- alter the personality of the person concerned, either for good or bad

- allow one person to control another, thereby contributing to injustice and exploitation

- be used to enhance quality of life, by allowing people to fulfil themselves

- improve or detract from human relationships

- diminish or accentuate the divide between the privileged and the underprivileged

- be used for the common good or for devious purposes.[33]

Each of these is a judgement call, and each demands careful moral, spiritual, and scientific discernment. Developments are gradual, and the decisions to adopt new procedures are generally taken by the population at large. True, the developments themselves are brought about by scientists and technocrats, but once available, they are seized upon by ordinary people. They appear to meet some felt need.

As with practically all the technological possibilities we encounter, we are not generally faced with a simple good or bad dichotomy. Judgement and wisdom are prerequisites for assessing and weighing up where we are to go, what is of value and what is dross. General as are these comments, they are as important in the human-machine interface area as in any other.

Cyborgs

The move to cyborgs represents a gradual transition from the forms of interfaces we have just been considering. This is an important starting point because it directs us to view cyborgs within a much broader context and helps dispel some of the myths surrounding them. The image of part-human part-machine is the essence of the image of cyborg, although as we have seen, there are numerous illustrations already in existence of mainly human, part-machine. In all probability, most individuals with prostheses, even with just one, or with a brain implant, would be alarmed to be referred to as cyborgs. With these provisos in mind, let us turn to some prevalent views in the cyborg literature.

Ray Kurzweil, the inventor and futurist, is one of these. In his book, *The Singularity Is Near*,[34] he foresees a theoretical future period of extremely rapid technological progress when accelerating technology will lead to superhuman machine intelligence that will soon exceed human intelligence. According to him, human existence on this planet will be irreversibly altered. This will be due to a combination of brain power with computer power. The effect of this, in his view, will be a transformation of the knowledge, skills, and personality quirks that make us human, enabling us to think, reason, communicate, and create in ways unimaginable today.

For Kurzweil, the merger of man and machine, coupled with the sudden explosion in machine intelligence and rapid innovation in the fields of gene research and nanotechnology, will obliterate the distinction between the biological and the mechanical and between physical and virtual realities. The opportunities opened up by these developments will, in his words,

> allow us to transcend our frail bodies with all their limitations. Illness, as we know it, will be eradicated. Through the use of nanotechnology, we will be able to manufacture almost any physical product upon demand, world hunger and poverty will be solved, and pollution will vanish. Human existence will undergo a quantum leap in evolution. We will be able to live as long as we choose.[35]

Kurzweil describes what he calls the 'Human Body 2.0'.[36] A modified, updated human body where nanobots, robots the size of blood cells, have provided the means to conceptually redesign every body system. He continues:

> We are becoming Cyborgs. We are rapidly growing more intimate with our technology. Computers started out as large remote machines in air-conditioned rooms tended by white-coated technicians. Subsequently they moved onto our desks, then under our arms, and now in our pockets. Soon, we'll routinely put them inside our bodies and brains. Ultimately we will become more nonbiological than biological.[37]

Eventually he sees the line between humans and machines blurring as artificial intelligence develops and humans embrace cybernetic implants.

Kurzweil's projections may be far removed from what will actually eventuate, but that is not the point. Minor errors are irrelevant for our purpose. The genesis of his imagined world is, as we have seen, already reality. The origins of all the possibilities Kurzweil has predicted are with us. The brave new world is here, and we are living in it whether we realize it or not.

This vastly expanded trajectory à la Kurzweil is, of course, not inevitable. Possibilities, which appear eminently reasonable today, may soon be seen to be irrelevant or even obstructionist. The charting of scientific progress is an unenviable task. The world predicated by Kurzweil may prove illusory. Most will hope that it does. But let us imagine that cyborgs will exist and will walk our streets and perhaps even the corridors of power. What then? Will that demonstrate that the scientific possibilities with which we have been dealing are fraught with horrendous problems and aberrant possibilities that we should resist with all our might?

Discussions of this ilk suffer from a crucial problem: the definition of cyborgs is unclear. There is an assumption that the definition is self-evident, but as we have attempted to demonstrate, there is a continuum from the merest presence of the artificial at one end to a melding of human and machine at the other. However, what this latter might entail is difficult to fathom. Is it a 50:50 mixture of human and machine, or a 60:40 ratio? Or are such ratios irrelevant? Or is it when the machine or the artificial encroaches on the core of what makes us human? This may occur when the interface directly intrudes into the brain and then when the intrusion significantly alters the person. Gillett refers to 'a non-human mode of relationship and reaction or response to others'.[38] Hence, it may be wise to refer to cyborgs only when the intrusion of the artificial into the human results in significant functional differences cognitively. This will probably involve implants in decision-making brain regions. It is within this context that we encounter concerns that cyborgs will disrupt normal moral categories,[39] although one imagines that the machine element would have to be a dominant one before anything of this nature emerges.

Even surmising like this points to the inherent definitional problem. Are cyborgs innately worrisome because we do not know how to define them? How different is so different that one is no longer human? How much artificiality can be incorporated before the subject has moved from the category of human to that of cyborg?[40]

Andy Clark proposes that we are natural-born cyborgs – the drive to incorporate technology is so much a part of our human nature that technology cannot truly be separated from our essential selves.[41] Tools such as language, written text, digital encodings, etc. are 'not just external props and aids, but they are deep and integral parts of the problem-solving systems we now identify as human intelligence. Such tools are best conceived as proper parts of the computational apparatus that constitutes our minds'.[42] Routine use of cell phones, computers, and even diaries constitutes cognitive enhancements of some degree. But for Clark, these enhancements are a natural extension of our human nature, and the integration of technology will not stop at external aids. He writes, 'Human-machine symbiosis, I believe, is simply what comes naturally. It lies on a direct continuum with clothes, cooking ('external artificial digestion'), bricklaying, and writing. The capacity to creatively distribute labor between biology and designed environment is the very signature of our species'.[43] External computers and cybernetic implants are thus different only in degree not in kind.

Consider the rapid rise in personal electronic equipment, iPods, iPhones, Blackberries, and so on. The modern person is increasingly reliant on these, particularly for social networking and often to the neglect of face-to-face relationships. A dead battery in one's cell phone, the loss of a laptop, or even lack of access to Facebook poses a temporary disability and a degree of social isolation. Our partnership with computers today is far more pervasive than most realize, because our use of them leaves data shadows; they 'remember' us in a way in which a photocopier does not. This can be, and has been, commercially exploited; the privacy concerns raised by the increasing mingling of our computer use and personal identity are significant.[44] In other words, even now our partnership with computers is a symbiotic one.[45]

As long as computers remain external to the human body, society is largely unconcerned about the implications, even though as external appendages, they have enormous implications for what we are as people. Comparing computers to artificial limbs is instructive. It is when technology is internalized that alarm bells start ringing in our collective consciousness and images of cyborgs arise without summon. But why should cochlear or retinal implants be inherently more troublesome than artificial limbs?

Even before computers are fully internalized, there are unsettling degrees of assimilation to be encountered. MIT's wearable computer project envisions a future where computers are a clothing accessory, almost seamlessly augmenting daily living. 'A person's computer should be worn, much as eyeglasses or clothing are worn, and interact with the user based on the context of the situation. With heads-up displays, unobtrusive input devices, personal wireless local area networks, and a host of other context sensing and communication tools, the wearable computer can act as an intelligent assistant, whether it be through a Remembrance Agent, augmented reality, or intellectual collectives'.[46]

One gets the impression that the possibilities opened up by cybernetic transplants take us to the limits of our imaginations, and yet, we repeatedly return to the same fundamental queries: What are they for? What effects will they have on normal human functioning – what indeed is normal human functioning? Will they be associated with a major transformation in human self-identity? Will they be implemented voluntarily or coercively? The futuristic aspects of cyborgs reflect surprisingly traditional ethical questions.

The outcome of these deliberations is that the notion of cyborgs should not prove nearly as forbidding as often suggested. The cyborgian revolution is a gradual evolution, so that at each point along this evolutionary pathway, there is the opportunity to stop and question the justification and possible repercussions of the latest technological possibility. Whether or not we will take this opportunity or rush headlong in a hedonistic direction is the perpetual challenge from which there will be no escape.

Body Worlds

After the world of cyborgs, the move to the dead body will appear strange and will be unexpected. And yet, the invasion of technology into the human body is occurring even following death. In fact, this is radical transformation of the human body, with the use of preservation techniques that give the impression that individuals continue to live on in a dissected state. In the *Body Worlds* exhibitions, whole-body 'plastinates' are presented with a welcoming, almost life-like visage and serene facial expressions. The result is transformation of the corpse into the 'post-mortal body' giving the impression that the dead are still alive. Even more remarkable is the fact that these dead bodies have been dissected to display muscles, organs, and nerves. Nevertheless, these whole-body dissections, these plastinates – more plastic than human – have overtones of physical permanence. Their 'immortality' is technologically derived and constitutes a new category of human body, neither fresh corpse nor decaying remains.[47] The artificiality of these bodies could be described as cyborgian, even if the machine is non-functional.

This unexpected topic provides another perspective on corporeal identity and the outcomes of the intrusion of the artificial into the human body. The *Body Worlds* exhibitions are the creation of Gunther von Hagens, who invented plastination, a process by which body tissue can be preserved, free from decay, in a dry, odourless, and poseable state. *Body Worlds* features two types of plastinates. The first is the dissected body regions illustrating basic physiological functions and disease processes, which poses little concern to anatomists. In contrast, the whole-body plastinates are moulded in poses immediately familiar to the public: running, skateboarding, playing baseball or soccer, and even playing poker or the saxophone.

Plastination is a method of preserving human or animal tissues by replacing the tissue fluids with plastic. The specimens preserved in this manner are dry, odourless, and durable, thereby making them much easier to handle, while at the same time, the process retains the natural structure of the tissues. Hence, a deeply perplexing question: Is the plastinate any longer a human body? After all, 70 per cent is now plastic. Barilan points out that while water and fat have been removed in the process of plastination, more 'significant' constituents such as proteins and nucleic acids remain.[48] However, he also adds that the 'significance' of these constituents is culturally determined. Kuppers asks, 'Does the plastic preserve the flesh, or is the flesh gone?'[49] The plastinate certainly retains many human qualities and much of the cadaver's physical substance, but a considerable transformation has taken place. Individual identity is retained, and this is perhaps a significant clue to the most appropriate category for the plastinate. It is not simply a plastic model; each plastinate is based on a real individual, so that all plastinates are different. But are the plastinates as much the work of the master technicians responsible for dissection and subsequent plastination? It is difficult to escape from concluding that the dead body has been shifted along a continuum from conventional dead body towards technologically modified tissue with distinctive features of plastic model or even sculpture. One gets the impression that they occupy a semi-human category, with some remaining features of personal identification alongside dim memories of the individuals they once were.

The intention of *Body Worlds* is not to present dead bodies in their 'deadness'.[50] The later exhibitions in particular are designed to be less about dead bodies and more about the dynamic and living body. The plastinates are given a welcoming, almost life-like visage, as if the plastinates are fulfilled by the 'life' they are now living. They appear to be one of us but cannot respond as one of us.

There are two opposing conceptual movements occurring in the preparation and display of the plastinates in exhibitions such as those of von Hagens. The cadaver is initially depersonalized by the removal of the skin and external identifying information and also by the substitution of much of the tissue with plastic. Thus, the plastinate is made physically approachable and emotionally acceptable as it (according to von Hagens at least) is no longer a decomposing body to be mourned. This is followed by the repersonalization of the plastinate by the addition of naturalistic poses and familiar accessories (whether chess set or cell phone). It is this second transformation that is both disquieting and supposedly necessary – at least for von Hagens.[51] The repersonalized plastinate engages the viewer by its life-likeness, even though it is not only dead but also largely plasticized.

It is interesting to reflect that life-likeness does not demand real human bodies. Very life-like sculptures (as in those by Ron Mueck), accurately depicting human features in very precise detail, are equally engaging. What they lack is individual identity, although even here they can be modelled on actual human beings.

It is in these processes of depersonalization and repersonalization that the identity of the body is radically transformed. The donated body is entirely anonymized by the removal of the 'exterior face' (the skin) and the absence of any identifying information. Then the plastinates are given new identities via the characteristic poses and accessories. Together these processes highlight the artificiality of the resulting plastinates. This is where the cyborg features come to the surface, but with a difference. The link of human and machine in order to produce a new sort of functioning organism is replaced here by an entity in which human has been largely replaced by machine. Perhaps it would be better to refer to plastinates as non-functioning cyborgs.

Though von Hagens' institute seeks the donors' input on how they wish to be displayed once plastinated, it is unclear how much say the donors ultimately have. One gets the impression that the poses and activities in which plastinates are 'engaged', hence their post-mortal identities, are determined by their new creator, von Hagens. He shapes their bodies and thus their identities in perpetuity.

These new poses suggest a new ability with which the individuals have been gifted in their 'post-mortal' life. The transformation from what may have been a non-athletic person to a sporting plastinate parallels the gaining (or regaining) of function via a technological prosthesis. Whatever the donors were in life, plastination ensures that they are slimmed down and fitted out with the appearance of physical skill and fitness. The character of the donor has been transformed by the intrusion of the artificial under the creative direction of von Hagens.

For von Hagens, the plastinates are examples of the 'post-mortal body'.[52] He considers that he, through plastination, has transformed them and, in doing so, has moved them beyond death. Von Hagens describes the plastinates as 'frozen in time between death and decay',[53] for they will never decompose, and thus have achieved a form of immortality. This is immortality, not in any spiritual sense but of physical permanence. This is very much a post-Christian, secular form of immortality.[54]

One has to ask whether running throughout all von Hagens' endeavours there is not an attempt to escape from the reality of death, by giving the impression that these cadavers are continuing to exist in much the same way as when they were alive. The artificial has triumphed, having eradicated decay and disease; it may even have attained eternal bliss. We can live on as plastinates, with our post-mortal bodies. While this is not the ageless existence that transfixes trans-humanists, plastinates appear to have attained their own form of everlasting existence. It is a shame they are unable to reflect on this artificial nirvana. In acquiring a form of everlasting existence, plastinates have ceased to be human, which has been totally eclipsed by the artificial.

Concluding Thoughts

The contrast between plastinates and cyborgs is immense, and yet in a strange way, this discussion of plastinates has proved to be prophetic for our consideration of cyborgs. There are discernible limits to the extent to which the artificial can intrude into human existence before core features of human life are lost. There are limits to the transformation of the human body. General as this statement is, unexpected as it may be, it provides a framework for our discussion.

In moving from the way in which the artificial has been incorporated into human life over the past few centuries, to more explicit human-machine interfaces and on to cyborgs, we have followed a trajectory. Most of these developments have been driven by finding ways of controlling disease and overcoming illness; they have been therapeutic in intent. While the border between therapy and enhancement is tenuous, the movements we have encountered have been largely uncontentious – in hindsight if not always at the time. However, as we have contemplated the inroads projected by cyborgs, and the somewhat different vistas presented by plastinates, we have moved into uncharted territory – murky in scientific terms, let alone ethical and philosophical ones. The role of therapy is receding as the role of philosophical exploration takes over. Overarching all such exploration is the degree to which the human body can be transformed in practice. It will not allow anything like as much manipulation as that in which human philosophizing indulges. It may be a salutary exercise if we took seriously the caution of human anatomists, because the human body will have the last laugh.

Notes

1 Such visions are promulgated by a number of theorists, including Aubrey de Grey and Nick Bostrom. See Bostrom, N., 'Why I Want to be a Posthuman When I Grow Up' in Gordijn and Chadwick (eds.) *Medical Enhancement and Posthumanity*, (Dordrecht; London, Springer 2008); McCall, B., 'Do you want to live to be 800? This man says that you can', *The Times Higher Education Supplement*, 10 March 2006.

2 Szreter, S. and Mooney, G., 'Urbanization, mortality, and the standard of living debate: new estimates of the expectation of life at birth in nineteenth-century British cities', *Economic History Review*, 51, (1), 1998, pp. 84–112.

3 Jones, D. G., 'The biomedical technologies: prospects and challenges' in Jones and Elford (eds.) *A Glass Darkly: Medicine and Theology in Further Dialogue*, (Bern, Peter Lang, 2010).

4 Bailey, R., 'Anyone for tennis, at the age of 150?' *The Times*, 8 April 2006, Available: http://www.timesonline.co.uk/tol/comment/columnists/guest_contributors/article703117.ece Accessed 18 October, 2007; McCall. 'Do you want to live to be 800? This man says that you can'.

5 Jones 'The biomedical technologies: prospects and challenges'.

6 PRNewswire, 'Anatomist Dr. Gunther von Hagens Reiterates His Mission of Public Health Education to Press Corps in Guben, Germany'. 30 November 2006, www.prnewswire.co.uk/cgi/news/release?id = 185453 Accessed 20 September 2010.

7 Clausen, J., 'Man, machine and in between', *Nature*, 457, (7233), 2009, pp. 1080–81.

8 Glannon, W., 'Stimulating brains, altering minds', *Journal of Medical Ethics*, 35, (5), 2009, pp. 289–392.

9 Kuhn, J., Grundler, T. O., Lenartz, D., Sturm, V., Klosterkotter, J. and Huff, W., 'Deep brain stimulation for psychiatric disorders', *Deutsches Arzteblatt International*, 107, (7), 2010, pp.105–13.

10 Voon, V., Kubu, C., Krack, P., Houeto, J. L. and Troster, A. I., 'Deep brain stimulation: neuropsychological and neuropsychiatric issues', *Movement Disorders*, 21 Suppl 14, 2006, S305–27.

11 Fallon, J. B., Irvine, D. R. and Shepherd, R. K., 'Neural prostheses and brain plasticity', *Journal of Neural Engineering*, 6, (6), 2009, 065008.

12 Colletti, V., Shannon, R. V., Carner, M., Veronese, S. and Colletti, L., 'Progress in restoration of hearing with the auditory brainstem implant', *Progress in Brain Research*, 175, 2009, pp. 333–45.

13 Fallon, Irvine and Shepherd 'Neural prostheses and brain plasticity'.

14 Gillett, G., 'Cyborgs and moral identity', *Journal of Medical Ethics*, 32, (2), 2006, pp. 79–83.

15 Chader, G. J., Weiland, J. and Humayun, M. S., 'Artificial vision: needs, functioning, and testing of a retinal electronic prosthesis', *Progress in Brain Research*, 175, 2009, pp. 317–32.

16 Dobelle, W. H., 'Artificial vision for the blind by connecting a television camera to the visual cortex', *ASAIO Journal*, 46, (1), 2000, pp. 3–9; Tehovnik, E. J., Slocum, W. M., Smirnakis, S. M. and Tolias, A. S., 'Microstimulation of visual cortex to restore vision', *Progress in Brain Research*, 175, 2009, pp. 347–75.

17 Hochberg, L. R., Serruya, M. D., Friehs, G. M., Mukand, J. A., Saleh, M., Caplan, A. H., Branner, A., Chen, D., Penn, R. D. and Donoghue, J. P., 'Neuronal ensemble control of prosthetic devices by a human with tetraplegia', *Nature*, 442, (7099), 2006, pp. 164–71; Ryu, S. I. and Shenoy, K. V., 'Human cortical prostheses: lost in translation?', *Neurosurgical Focus*, 27, (1), 2009, E5.

18 Birbaumer, N., 'Breaking the silence: brain-computer interfaces (BCI) for communication and motor control', *Psychophysiology*, 43, (6), 2006, pp. 517–32; Fenton, A. and Alpert, S., 'Extending our view on using BCIs for locked-in syndrome', *Neuroethics*, 1, 2008, pp. 119–32.

19 Kellis, S., Miller, K., Thomson, K., Brown, R., House, P. and Greger, B., 'Decoding spoken words using local field potentials recorded from the cortical surface', *Journal of Neural Engineering*, 7, (5), 2010, 056007.

20 Hochberg, Serruya, Friehs, Mukand, Saleh, Caplan, Branner, Chen, Penn and Donoghue 'Neuronal ensemble control of prosthetic devices by a human with tetraplegia'.

21 Velliste, M., Perel, S., Spalding, M. C., Whitford, A. S. and Schwartz, A. B., 'Cortical control of a prosthetic arm for self-feeding', *Nature*, 453, (7198), 2008, pp. 1098–101; Pohlmeyer, E. A., Oby, E. R., Perreault, E. J., Solla, S. A., Kilgore, K. L., Kirsch, R. F. and Miller, L. E., 'Toward the restoration of hand use to a paralyzed monkey: brain-controlled functional electrical stimulation of forearm muscles', *PLoS One*, 4, (6), 2009, e5924.

22 Fong, A. J., Roy, R. R., Ichiyama, R. M., Lavrov, I., Courtine, G., Gerasimenko, Y., Tai, Y. C., Burdick, J. and Edgerton, V. R., 'Recovery of control of posture and locomotion after a spinal cord injury: solutions staring us in the face', *Progress in Brain Research*, 175, 2009, pp. 393–418.

23 Ryu and Shenoy 'Human cortical prostheses: lost in translation?'.

24 Warwick, K., 'Cyborg morals, cyborg values, cyborg ethics', *Ethics and Information Technology*, 5, 2003, pp. 131–37.

25 Graafstra, A., 'Hands on: how radio-frequency identification and I got personal', *IEEE Spectrum*, 44, (3), 2007, pp. 18–23.

26 Pasternack, A., 'Cyborg professor looks to future of bionic technology', http://edition.cnn.com/2010/WORLD/europe/09/21/vbs.cyborg/index.html Accessed 5 October 2010.

27 Nijholt, A. and Tan, D., 'Playing with your brain: brain-computer interfaces and games', *Proceedings of the international conference on Advances in computer entertainment technology*, Salzburg, ACM, 2007; Tamburrini, G., 'Brain to computer communication: ethical perspectives on interaction models', *Neuroethics*, 2, 2009, pp. 137–49.

28 Kohlmorgen, J., Dornhege, G., Braun, M., Blankertz, B., Müller, K.-R., Curio, G., Hagemann, K., Bruns, A., Schrauf, M. and Kincses, W., 'Improving human performance in a real operating environment through real-time mental workload detection' in Dornhege, Millán, Hinterberger, McFarland and Müller (eds.) *Toward Brain-Computer Interfacing*, (Cambridge, MA, MIT Press, 2007).

29 Tamburrini 'Brain to computer communication: ethical perspectives on interaction models'.

30 Spezio, M. L., 'Brain and machine: minding the transhuman future'. *Dialog: A Journal of Theology*, 44, (4), 2005, pp. 375–80.

31 Tamburrini 'Brain to computer communication: ethical perspectives on interaction models'.

32 The European Group on Ethics in Science and New Technologies, 'Ethical Aspects of ICT Implants in the Human Body, opinion 20', p.32 ec.europa.eu/european_group_ethics/docs/avis20_en.pdf Accessed 14 September 2010.

33 Jones, D. G., *Designers of the Future*, (Oxford: Monarch, 2005) p. 165.

34 Kurzweil, R., *The Singularity Is Near*, (New York: Viking, 2005).

35 Kurzweil, R., 'Reinventing humanity: the future of human-machine intelligence', *The Futurist*, March-April 2006.

36 Kurzweil, R., *Human Body Version 2.0*, 2003, http://www.kurzweilai. net/meme/frame.html?main = /articles/art0551.html Accessed 20 September 2010.

37 Kurzweil, R., *Human Body Version 2.0*, 2003,

38 Gillett 'Cyborgs and moral identity'.

39 Haraway, D. J., *Simians, Cyborgs, and Women: The reinvention of nature*, (London, Free Association Books, 1991) pp. 149–155.

40 Gillett 'Cyborgs and moral identity'.

41 Clark, A., *Natural-born Cyborgs: Minds, Technologies, and the Future of Human Intelligence*, (Oxford: Oxford University Press, 2003).

42 Clark, A., *Natural-born Cyborgs: Minds, Technologies, and the Future of Human Intelligence*, pp. 5–6.

43 Clark, A., *Natural-born Cyborgs: Minds, Technologies, and the Future of Human Intelligence*, p. 174.

44 Clark, A., *Natural-born Cyborgs: Minds, Technologies, and the Future of Human Intelligence*, pp. 169–174.

45 Board for Social Responsibility of the Church of England, *Cybernauts Awake!*, (London, Church House Publishing, 1999).

46 MIT Media Lab, *Wearable Computing at the MIT Media Lab* http:// www.media.mit.edu/wearables/ Accessed 23 September 2010.

47 Jones, D. G. and Whitaker, M. I., *Speaking for the dead: The Human Body in Biology and Medicine*, (Farnham, England, Ashgate, 2009), p. 104.

48 Barilan, Y. M., 'Bodyworlds and the ethics of using human remains: a preliminary discussion', *Bioethics News*, 20, 2006, pp. 233–47.

49 Kuppers, P., 'Vision of anatomy: exhibitions and dense bodies', *Journal of Feminist Cultural Studies*, 15, (3), 2004, pp. 123–56.

50 Skulstad, K., 'Body Worlds draws large crowds – and controversy'. *Canadianchristianity.com*, November 2006, www.canadianchristianity.com/cgi-bin/bc.cgi?bc/bccn/1106/18body Accessed 20 September 2010.

51 Walter, T., 'Plastination for display: a new way to dispose of the dead', *Journal of the Royal Anthropological Institute*, 10, 2004, pp. 603–27.

52 PRNewswire. 'Anatomist Dr. Gunther von Hagens Reiterates His Mission of Public Health Education to Press Corps in Guben, Germany'.

53 Schulte-Sasse, L., 'Advise and consent: on the Americanization of Body Worlds', *BioSocieties*, 1, 2006, pp. 369–84.

54 Stern, M., 'Shiny happy people: 'Body Worlds' and the commodification of health', *Radical Philosophy*, 2003, p. 118.

Bibliography

Adorno, T. W. *Aesthetic Theory* (London: The Athlone Press, 1997).

Ansell-Pearson, K. *Viroid Life: Perspectives on Nietzsche and the Transhuman Condition* (London: Routledge, 1997).

von Balthasar, Hans Urs. *Theo-Drama, Vol. 1, Prolegomena*, trans. G. Harrison (San Francisco, CA: Ignatius, 1988).

—. *The Glory of the Lord: A Theological Aesthetics, vol. 7, Theology: The New Covenant* (GL 7), trans. B. McNeil (Edinburgh: T & T. Clark and San Francisco, CA: Ignatius, 1989).

—. *Theodrama, Vol. 2, Dramatis Personae: Man in God* (TD 2) trans. G. Harrison (San Francisco, CA: Ignatius, 1990).

—. *The Glory of the Lord, Vol. 6, The Old Covenant*, trans B. McNeil and E. Leiva-Merikakis (Edinurgh: T & T Clark and San Francisco, CA: Ignatius, 1991).

—. *Theo-Drama: Theo-Dramatic Theory, Vol. V, The Final Act*, trans. G. Harrison (San Francisco, CA: Ignatius Press, 1998).

Barnes, J. (ed.). *The Complete Works of Aristotle Volume One* (Princeton, NJ: Princeton University Press, 1984).

Barthes, R. *Mythologies* (Paris: Seuil, 1957).

—. *Mythologies* (New York: Hill and Wang, 1972).

Bataille, G. *Georges Bataille: Visions of Excess Selected Writings, 1927–1939* (Minneapolis, MN: University of Minnesota Press, 1985).

—. *The Accursed Share: An Essay on General Economy* (New York: Zone, 1991).

—. *The Unfinished System of Nonknowledge* (Minneapolis and London: University of Minnesota Press, 2001).

—. *The Cradle of Humanity: Prehistoric Art and Culture* (New York: Zone, 2005).

Bateson, G. *Mind and Nature, a Necessary Unity* (Cresskill, NJ: Hampton Press, 1979/2002).

Berger, J. *Ways of Seeing* (London: Penguin Books, 1972).

Bergson, H. *Two Sources of Morality and Religion*, trans. R.A. Audra and C. Brereton (London: MacMillan, 1935).

Bernasconi, R. and Wood, D. (ed.). *The Provocation of Levinas: Rethinking the Other* (London: Routledge, 1988).

Botting, F. and Wilson, S. (eds). *The Bataille Reader* (Oxford: Blackwell, 1997).

Bryden, M. (ed.). *Deleuze and Religion* (London: Routledge, 2001).

Butler, J. *Bodies That Matter: On the Discursive Limits of "Sex"* (New York: Routledge, 1993).

Calarco, M. and Atterton, P. (eds). *Animal Philosophy: Essential Readings in Continental Thought* (London and New York: Continuum, 2004).

Cavell, S., Diamond, C., McDowell, J., Hacking, I. and Wolfe, C. *Philosophy and Animal Life* (New York: Columbia University Press, 2009).

Clark, A. *Natural-born Cyborgs: Minds, Technologies, and the Future of Human Intelligence* (Oxford: Oxford University Press, 2003).

Clayton, P. *Mind and Emergence: From Quantum to Consciousness* (Oxford: Oxford University Press, 2004).

Coetzee, J. M. *The Lives of Animals* (Princeton, NJ: Princeton University Press, 2001).

Daston, L. and Gregg, M. (eds). *Thinking with Animals, New Perspectives on Anthropomorphism* (New York: Columbia University Press, 2005).

Davidson, D. *Subjective, Intersubjective, Objective* (Oxford: Oxford University Press, 2001).

Deane-Drummond, C. and Clough, D. (eds). *Creaturely Theology: On God, Humans and Other Animals* (London: SCM Press, 2009).

Deleuze, G. *Negotiations*, trans. J. Martin (New York: Columbia University Press, 1990).

—. *Difference and Repetition* (New York: Columbia University Press, 1994).

Deleuze, G. and Guattari, F. *A Thousand Plateaus* (London: Continuum, 2004).

DeLoughrey, E., et al. (eds). *Caribbean Literature and the Environment. Between Nature and Culture* (Charlottesville, VA: University of Virginia Press, 2005).

Derrida, J. *Of Grammatology* (Baltimore, MD: Johns Hopkins University Press, 1976).

—. *Specters of Marx: The State of the Debt, the Work of Mourning, and the New International* (New York: Routledge, 1994).

—. In Marie-Louise, M. (ed.), *The Animal that Therefore I Am*, trans. David W. (Bronx, NY: Fordham University Press, 2008).

—. *The Beast and the Sovereign Volume I* (Chicago, IL: University of Chicago Press, 2009).

Freccero, C. *Popular Culture* (New York: New York University Press, 1999).

Fudge, E. *Animal* (London, Reaktion Books, 2002).

Galloway, A. and Thacker, E. *The Exploit* (Minneapolis, MN: University of Minnesota Press, 2007).

Gemerchak, C. M. *The Sunday of the Negative: Reading Bataille Reading Hegel* (New York: State University of New York Press, 2003).

Gordijn, B. and Chadwick, R. (eds). *Medical Enhancement and Posthumanity* (Dordrecht and London: Springer 2008).

Grant, I. H. *Philosophies of Nature After Schelling* (London: Continuum, 2006).

Grosz, E. *Space, Time, and Perversion: Essays on the Politics of Bodies* (New York: Routledge, 1995).

Guattari, F. *Chaosmos: An Ethico-Aesthetic Paradigm*, trans. P. Bains and J. Pefanis (Sydney: Powerhouse, 1995).

Hallward, P. *Out of This World: Deleuze and the Philosophy of Creation* (London: Verso, 2006).

Ham, J. and Senior, M. (ed.). *Animal Acts: Configuring the Human in Western History* (New York: Routledge, 1997).

Haraway, D. *Primate Visions: Gender Race and Nature in the World of Modern Science* (New York and London: Routledge, 1989).

—. *Simians, Cyborgs and Women. The Reinvention of Nature* (London: Free Association Books, 1991).

—. *The Companion Species Manifesto: Dogs, People and Significant Otherness* (Chicago, IL: Prickly Paradigm Press, 2003).

—. *When Species Meet* (Minneapolis, MN: University of Minnesota Press, 2008).

Hearne, V. *Adam's Task: Calling Animals by Name* (London: William Heinemann Ltd., 1987).

—. *Animal Happiness* (New York: Harper-Collins, 1994).

Hegel, G. W. F. *The Philosophy of Fine Art* (London: C. Bell and Sons, 1920).

Imanishi, K. *A Japanese View of Nature – The World of Living Things* (London: Routledge Curzon, 2002).

Jones, A. (ed.). *The Feminism and Visual Culture Reader* (London and New York: Routledge, 2003).

Jones, D. G. 'The biomedical technologies: prospects and challenges', in Jones, D. G. and Elford, R. J. (eds), *A Glass Darkly: Medicine and Theology in Further Dialogue* (Bern: Peter Lang, 2010).

Jones, D. G. *Designers of the Future* (Oxford: Monarch, 2005).

Kant, I. *Critique of Judgment* (Indianapolis, IN: Hackett, 1987).

—. *The Critique of Judgement* (Oxford, Oxford University Press, 2007).

Kellogg, W. N. and Kellogg, L. A. *The Ape and the Child: A Study of Environmental Influence Upon Early Behaviour* (New York and London: McGraw-Hill Book Company Inc., 1933).

Latour, B. *Politics of Nature*, trans. C. Porter (Cambridge: Harvard University Press, 2004).

Le Guin, U. K. *Buffalo Gals: And Other Animal Presences* (Santa Barbara, CA: Capra Press, 1987).

Levinas, E. *Totality and Infinity* (The Hague: Martinus Nijhoff, 1969).

—. *Of God Who Comes to Mind* (Stanford, CA: Stanford University Press, 1998).

Lewis-Williams, D. *The Mind in the Cave: Consciousness and the Origins of Art* (London: Thames and Hudson, 2004).

McFarland, S. and Hediger, R. *Animals and Agency: An Interdisciplinary Exploration* (Leiden and Boston: Brill, 2009).

Molloy, C. *Popular Media and Animals* (London: Palgrave Macmillan, 2011).

Nabokov, V. *Lolita* (New York: Vintage International, 1997).

Nagel, T. 'What is it like to be a bat?', in *Philosophical Review* 83, October 1974, p. 323.

Nancy, J.-L. *Birth to Presence* (Stanford: CA, Stanford University Press, 1994).

Noske, B. *Beyond Boundaries: Humans and Animals* (Montreal/London/New York: Black Rose, 1997).

Peterson, D. and Goodall, J. *Visions of Calaban: On Chimpanzees and People* (Athens and London: The University of Georgia Press, 1993).

Philo, C. and Wilbert, C. (eds). *Animal Spaces, Beastly Places: New Geographies of Human – Animal Relations* (London and New York: Routledge, 2000).

Pick, A. *Creaturely Poetics: Animality, Vulnerability, and the Identity of Species* (New York: Columbia University Press, 2011).

Probyn, E. *Outside Belongings* (New York: Routledge, 1996).

Prosser, J. *Second Skins: The Body Narratives of Transsexuality* (New York: Columbia University Press, 1998).

Regan, T. and Singer, P. (ed.). *Animal Rights and Human Obligations* (Englewood Cliffs, NJ: Prentice Hall, 1989).

Rothfels, N. (ed.). *Representing Animals* (Bloomington, IN: Indiana University Press, 2002).

Satya, L. D. *Ecology, Colonialism and Cattle: Central India in the Nineteenth Century* (Oxford: Oxford University Press, 2004).

Savage-Rumbaugh, S. *Apes, Language and the Human Mind* (New York: Oxford University Press, 2001).

Schelling, F. W. J. *System of Transcendental Idealism (1800)* (Charlottesville, VA: University Press of Virginia, 1978).

Singer, P. (ed.). *In Defense of Animals* (New York: Basil Blackwell, 1985).

Stiegler, B. *Technics and Time 1: The Fault of Epimetheus*, trans. R. Beardsworth and G. Collins (Stanford, CA: Stanford University Press, 1998).

Tyler, T. and Rossini, M. (eds). *Animal Encounters* (Leiden: Brill, 2009).

de Waal, F. *Good Natured: The Origins of Right and Wrong in Humans and Other Animals* (Cambridge: Harvard University Press, 1996).

Wolfe, C. *Animal Rites. American Culture, the Discourse of Species, and Posthuman Theory* (Chicago, IL: University of Chicago Press, 2003).

Index